REVISED AND UPDATED

RIDING THE WAVES OF CULTURE

UNDERSTANDING DIVERSITY IN GLOBAL BUSINESS

Fons Trompenaars and
Charles Hampden-Turner

nb

NICHOLAS BREALEY
PUBLISHING

...ton

This third edition
first published in the UK by
Nicholas Brealey Publishing in 2012

3–5 Spafield Street
Clerkenwell, London
EC1R 4QB
Tel: +44 (0)20 7239 0360
Fax: +44 (0)20 7239 0370

20 Park Plaza, Suite 1115A
Boston
MA 02110, USA
Tel: 888 BREALEY
Fax: (617) 523 3708

www.nicholasbrealey.com
www.ridingthewavesofculture.com

ISBN 978-1-90483-838-8
eISBN 978-1-90483-840-1

British Library Cataloguing in Publication Data
A catalogue record for this book is available from the British Library.

Figures 14.1, 14.2, 14.3, 14.4, 14.5, 14.6, 15.1, 15.2, 15.3, 15.4, 16.1, 16.2, A.1, A.2,
A.3, A.4, and B.1 by Cenveo.

FSC
Mixed Sources
Product group from well-managed
forests, controlled sources and
recycled wood or fibre

Cert no. DNV-COC-000213
www.fsc.org
©1996 Forest Stewardship Council

Printed in Finland by Bookwell.

Contents

Foreword

SINCE THE first edition of this book in 1993, the authors have maintained the same basic message that to be effective in leading and doing business in an international context, leaders and managers will have to recognize and respect cultural differences.

In the second edition, the authors extended their support of the core constructs by providing a number of country-specific examples. They also paid particular attention to the statistical significance and reliability of their cultural database. In addition, they described a framework to reconcile the dilemmas that arise from cultural diversity. In a three-step structure, they gave exhaustive treatment to the three Rs of Recognition, Respect, and Reconciliation.

The world of business continues to move ever rapidly to the global village, accelerated by changing political, social, and economic forces enabled by air travel and communications technology, including the Internet. While cultural factors have long been recognized as critical in modern business, the earlier more anthropological ideas that emphasized differences need to be supplemented and extended by a new body of knowledge that is more relevant to today's world. The focus and need is shifting from simply understanding cultural differences and how to prevent embarrassments and resolve communication issues to how to leverage difference for competitive advantage. And this is in a world where even local business may involve leading a diverse workforce. Furthermore, studies of cultures are now clouded by the consequences of migrations, immigration and acculturation, and cultural differences across generations, along with new players such as India and South America as well as China in the center stage.

In the first half of this third edition, the authors have retained (although updated) their detailed description of their underlying cultural frameworks from earlier editions.

The second half has undergone a major revision and upgrade to reflect the changing needs of the business community readership.

Following their continuing academic and applied research, the authors have added the fourth step to build on the first three given in earlier editions. This fourth R, for Realization, is introduced in this new edition, so that culture is ever more linked explicitly to the bottom line.

There is new content on realizing the business benefits of international and transnational operations. Added to that, special treatment is given to cultural differences in alliances, mergers, and acquisitions. The authors illustrate the power of their ideas in this new edition by showing how these ideas can be applied in the cultural integration of organizations to significant advantage over conventional (financial) due diligence.

Formerly a singular cultural database, the cultural databases that now underpin this book have been extended to include not only more cases and more country data from more respondents but also a whole wealth of cultural measurements of competences, dilemmas and their reconciliations, servant leadership across cultures, innovation paradigms across cultures, and multicultural and remote team effectiveness.

The authors have mined these large databases to provide further deductive and inductive analysis to support the new content in this third edition. Also included is an analysis of some of the changes that can be identified over the last 25 years in response to the frequently asked question "Are cultures converging?" as the world becomes even more of a global village.

None of the value of the earlier editions has been lost, and this new edition provides an evidence-driven framework essential for all business leaders and managers, whether they serve as CEO of a major global corporation or play an important middle-management role in a section of their smaller local company. The latter more than ever need to interact with a workforce that is diverse, as well as with a customer and supplier base that is diverse, and, therefore, require a certain level of cultural competence.

The book will also be of value to students of business and management to help prepare them for the new world of business, which is so different from only a few years ago.

Professor Peter Woolliams, Ph.D.
Emeritus Professor, Anglia Ruskin University, UK

Acknowledgments

S INCE THE first edition of this book in 1993, many people have contributed to its further development. We wish to thank all the colleagues of our consulting firm Trompenaars Hampden-Turner Consultancy B.V. They all have contributed in many ways to the fine-tuning of the data and development of the conceptual models.

We owe a very special thank you to the everlasting support and critical analysis of Professor Peter Woolliams. He has contributed much to the body of the book and has also been central in updating and analyzing new versions of our questionnaire tools and their results. The quantitative and methodological support has been an important aspect of the success in our consulting practice. Peter, thank you so much.

And Annemieke Lof, our project support manager, has been editing much of the existing and new text contributions. The precision and diligence with which she has done this is admirable. We also thank her for the suggestions she made to improve the text. Thanks Annemieke.

We have always subscribed to Lewin's maxim that "there is nothing so practical as a good theory" but also recognize the corollary that "there is nothing like good professional practice to develop good theory." So we should also thank the myriad of participants of our presentations and workshops from our client organizations who took the time to complete our online diagnostic questionnaires and interactive tools. Their input has been of enormous value and has helped in both the development of the new constructs and their validation.

1

An Introduction to Culture

THIS BOOK is about cultural differences and how they affect the process of doing business and managing. It is not about how to understand the people of different nationalities. It is our belief that you can never understand other cultures. Those who are married know that it is impossible to ever completely understand even people of your own culture. The Dutch author became interested in this subject before it grew popular, because his father is Dutch and his mother is French. This background gave him an understanding of the fact that if something works in one culture, there is little chance that it will work in another. No Dutch "management" technique his father tried to use ever worked very effectively in his French family.

This is the context in which we started wondering if any of the American management techniques and philosophy with which we were brainwashed in many years of the best business education money could buy would apply in the Netherlands or the UK, where we came from, or indeed in the rest of the world.

Both authors have been studying the effect of culture on management for decades. This book describes much of what we have discovered. The different cultural orientations elucidated result from 25 years of academic and field research. Many of the anecdotes and cases used in the text have come up in the course of more than 1,500 cross-cultural training programs we have given in more than 25 countries. The names of the companies used in most of the cases are disguised.

Apart from the training program material, a diverse range of companies including most of the global corporates and other major players, with departments spanning more than 60 countries, have contributed to the research. To gather comparable samples, a minimum of 100 people with similar backgrounds and occupations were originally identified in each of the countries in which the companies operated to provide basic reference cultural norms. Approximately 75 percent of these participants belonged to management (managers in operations, marketing, sales, and so forth), while the remaining 25 percent were general support staff (operators, personal assistants, etc.). Our original cultural database comprised some 55,000 of these respondents and has been extended in several ways. We have added more responses from managers and business leaders across the world, which has resulted in much more than just an increase in sample sizes. This database now extends to some 80,000 participants. An additional 20,000 have completed partial responses to this basic cultural diagnostic in combination with other surveys.

With the continuing growth and pervasion of the Internet, we have continued to add many other cultural measurement instruments and have developed associated ancillary databases. These include another 20,000 responses to our deductive assessments of intercultural competence and transcultural leadership, corporate effectiveness and sustainability, cultural aspects of personality and team development, and innovation. In a separate, text-oriented database, we have collected and coded data comprising nearly 10,000 dilemmas and associated reconciliations.

In response to demand, we increasingly make adapted versions of our online tools available to other respondents, such as students of business and management and spouses of expats. These are flagged appropriately as different respondents.

With much more data to draw on, we are able to reaffirm the constructs presented in earlier editions but also to extend debate to issues of longitudinal studies of cultural shifts. Further, we are able to drill down to age and generation differences as well as functional areas and discuss issues of cultural convergence and acculturation.

The empirical results are, however, just an illustration of what we are trying to say.

This book attempts to do three things: (1) dispel the notion that there is "one best way" of managing and organizing; (2) give readers a better understanding of their own culture and cultural differences in general, by learning how to recognize and cope with these differences in a business context; and (3) provide some cultural insights into the "global"-versus-"local" dilemma facing international organizations. Possibly the most important aspect of the book is the second of these. We believe understanding our own culture and our own assumptions and expectations about how people "should" think and act is the basis for success.

The Impact of Culture on Business

Take a look at the new breed of international managers, educated according to the most modern management philosophies. They all know that in the strategic business unit (SBU), total quality management (TQM) should reign, with products delivered just in time (JIT), where customer first teams (CFTs) distribute products while subject to management-by-objectives (MBO). If this is not done appropriately, we need to business process reengineer (BPR).

But just how universal are these management solutions? Are these "truths" about what effective management really is: truths that can be applied anywhere, under any circumstances?

Even with experienced international companies, many well-intended "universal" applications of management theory have turned out badly. For example, pay-for-performance has in many instances been a failure on the African continent, because there are particular, though unspoken, rules about the sequence and timing of reward and promotions. Similarly, management-by-objectives schemes have generally failed within subsidiaries of multinationals in southern Europe, because managers have not wanted to conform to the abstract nature of preconceived policy guidelines.

Even the notion of human-resource management is difficult to translate to other cultures, coming as it does from a typically Anglo-Saxon doctrine. It borrows from economics the idea that human beings are "resources" like physical and monetary resources. It tends to assume almost unlimited capacities for individual development. In countries without these beliefs, this concept is hard to grasp and is unpopular once it is understood.

International managers have it tough. They must operate on several different premises at any one time. These premises arise from their culture of origin, the culture in which they are working, and the culture of the organization that employs them.

In every culture in the world such phenomena as authority, bureaucracy, creativity, good fellowship, verification, and accountability are experienced in different ways. That we use the same words to describe them tends to make us unaware that our cultural biases and our accustomed conduct may not be appropriate, or shared.

There is a presumption that internationalization will create, or at least lead to, a common culture worldwide. This commonality would make the life of international managers much simpler. People point to McDonald's and Coca-Cola as examples of tastes, markets, and hence cultures becoming similar everywhere. There are, indeed, many products and services becoming common to world markets. What is important to consider, however, is not what they are and where they are found physically, but *what they mean to the people in each culture.* As we will describe later, the essence of culture is not what is visible on the surface. It is the shared ways groups of people understand and interpret the world. So the fact that we can all listen to iPods and MP3 players and eat hamburgers tells us that there are some novel products that can be sold on a universal message, but it does not tell us what eating hamburgers or listening to iPods and MP3 players means in different cultures. Dining at McDonald's was at one time a show of status in Moscow, whereas it is a fast meal for a fast buck in New York. If business people want to gain understanding of and allegiance to their corporate goals, policies, products, or services, wherever they are doing business, they must understand what those and other aspects of management mean in different cultures.

In addition to exploring why universal applications of Western management theory may not work, we will try to deal with the growing dilemma facing international managers that is known as "glocalization."

As markets globalize, the need for standardization in organizational design, systems, and procedures increases. Yet managers are also under pressure to adapt their organizations to the local characteristics of the market, the legislation, the fiscal regime, the sociopolitical system, and the cultural system. This balance between consistency and adaptation is essential for corporate success.

Paralysis Through Analysis: The Elixir of the Management Profession

Peters and Waterman in *In Search of Excellence* hit the nail on the head with their critique of "the rational model" and "paralysis through analysis." Western analytical thinking (analyzing a phenomenon to death and rationally reckoning the consequences before you act) has led to many international successes in fields of technology. Indeed, technologies do work by the same universal rules everywhere, even on the moon. Yet the very success of the universalistic philosophy now threatens to become a handicap when applied to interactions between human beings from different cultures.

The human being is a special piece of technology, and the results of our studies, extensively discussed in this book, indicate that the social world of the international organization has many more dimensions to deal with.

Some managers, especially in Japan, recognize the multidimensional character of their companies. They seem able to use a logic appropriate to machines (analytic-rational) *and* a logic more appropriate to social relations (synthetic-intuitive), switching between the two as needed.

In the process of internationalization the Japanese increasingly take the functioning of local society seriously. They were not the first to observe, "Si fueris Romae, Romano vivito more" (When in Rome . . .), but they seem to act on this precept more than Westerners do. The Japanese have, moreover, added another dimension: "When in Rome, understand the behavior of the Romans, and thus become an even more complete Japanese."

In opposition we have our Western approach, based on American business education, which treats management as a profession and regards emotionally detached rationality as "scientifically" necessary. This numerical, cerebral approach dominates not only American business schools but also other economic and business faculties. Such schools educate their students by giving them the right answers to the wrong questions. Statistical analysis, forecasting techniques, and operational studies are not "wrong." These endeavors comprise important technical skills. The mistake is to assume that technical rationality should characterize the human element in the organization. No one is denying the existence of universally applicable scientific laws with objective consequences. These laws are, doubtless, culture free. However, the belief that human cultures in the workplace should resemble the laws of physics and engineering is a *cultural*, not a scientific, belief. It is a universal assumption that does not win universal agreement, or even come close to doing so.

The internationalization of business life requires more knowledge of cultural patterns. Pay-for-performance, for example, can work out well in the cultures where we have had most of our training: the US, the Netherlands, and the UK. In more communitarian cultures such as France, Germany, and large parts of Asia it may not be so successful, at least not the Anglo-Saxon version of pay-for-performance. Employees may not accept the notion that individual members of the group should excel in a way that reveals the shortcomings of other members. Their definition of an "outstanding individual" is one who benefits those closest to him or her. Customers in more communitarian cultures also take offense at the "quick buck" mentality of the best salespeople; they prefer to build up relationships carefully, and maintain them.

How Proven Formulas Can Lead to Wrong Results

Why is it that many management processes lose effectiveness when cultural borders are crossed?

Many multinational companies apply formulas in overseas areas that are derived from, and are successful in, their own culture. International management consulting firms of Anglo-Saxon origin are still using similar methods to the neglect of cultural differences.

An Italian computer company received advice from a prominent international management consulting firm to restructure to a matrix organization. It did so and failed; the task-oriented approach of the matrix structure challenged loyalty to the functional boss. In Italy bosses are like fathers, and you cannot have two fathers.

Culture is like gravity: you do not experience it until you jump six feet into the air. Local managers may not openly criticize a centrally developed appraisal system or reject the matrix organization, especially if confrontation or defiance is not culturally acceptable to them. In practice, though, beneath the surface, the silent forces of culture operate a destructive process, biting at the roots of centrally developed methods that do not "fit" locally.

The flat hierarchy, SBUs, MBO, matrix organizations, assessment centers, TQM, BPR, and pay-for-performance are subjects of discussion in nearly every bestseller about management, and not only in the Western world. Reading these books (for which managers happily do not have much time any more) creates a feeling of euphoria. "If I follow these Ten Commandments, I'll be the *modern leader*, the *change master*, the *champion*." A participant from Korea told us in quite a cynical tone that he admired the US for solving one of the last major problems in business: how to get rid of people in the process of reengineering. The fallacy of the "one best way" is a management fallacy that is dying a slow death.

Although the organizational theory developed in the 1970s introduced the environment as an important consideration, it was unable to kill the dream of the one best way of organizing. It did not measure the effects of national culture, but systematically pointed to the importance of the market, the technology, and the product for determining the most effective methods of management and organization.

If you study similar organizations in different cultural environments, you find that they often turn out to be remarkably uniform by major criteria: number of functions, levels of hierarchy, degree of specialization, and so on. Instead of proving anything, this finding may mean little more than that uniformity has been imposed on global operations, or that leading company practices have been carefully imitated, or even that technologies have their own imperatives. Research of this kind has often claimed that this "proves" that the organization is culture free. But the wrong questions have been asked. The issue is not whether a hierarchy in the Netherlands has six levels, as does a similar company in Singapore, but what the hierarchy and those levels mean to the Dutch and Singaporeans. Where the meaning is totally different—for example, a "chain of command" versus a "family"—then human-resource policies developed to implement the first will seriously miscommunicate in the latter context.

In this book we examine the visible and invisible ways in which culture impacts on organizations. The more fundamental differences in culture and their effects may not be directly measurable by objective criteria, but they will certainly play an important role in the success of an international organization.

Culture Is the Way in Which People Solve Problems

A useful way of thinking about where culture comes from is the following: *culture is the way in which a group of people solves problems and reconciles dilemmas.*[1] The particular problems and dilemmas each culture must resolve will be outlined later in this chapter. If we focus first on what culture is, perhaps it is easiest to start with an example.

Imagine you are on a flight to South Africa and the pilot says, "We have some problems with the engine, so we will land temporarily in Burundi." (For those who do not know Burundi, it is next to Rwanda.) What is your first impression of Burundi culture once you enter the airport building? It is not, "What a nice set of values these people have," or even, "Don't they have an interesting shared system of meaning." It is the concrete, observable things such as language, food, and dress. Culture comes in layers, like an onion. To understand it, you have to unpeel it layer by layer.

On the outer layer are the products of culture, such as the soaring skyscrapers of Manhattan, pillars of private power, with congested public streets between them. These products are expressions of deeper values and norms in a society that are not directly visible (values such as upward mobility, "the more, the better," status, and material success). The layers of values and norms are deeper within the "onion" and are more difficult to identify.

But why do values and norms sink down into semiawareness and unexamined beliefs? Why are they so different in different parts of the world?

A problem that is regularly solved disappears from consciousness and becomes a basic assumption, an underlying premise. It is not until you are trying to get rid of the hiccups and hold your breath for as long as you possibly can that you think about your need for oxygen. These basic assumptions define the meaning that a group shares. They are implicit.

Take the following discussion between a medical doctor and a patient. The patient asks the doctor, "What's the matter with me?" The doctor answers, "Pneumonia." "What causes pneumonia?" "It is caused by a virus." "Interesting," says the patient, "and what causes a virus?" The doctor shows signs of severe irritation, and the discussion dies. Very often that is a signal that the questioner has hit a basic assumption, or, in the words of Collingwood, an absolute presupposition about life.[2] What is taken for granted, unquestioned reality: this is the core of the onion.

National, Corporate, and Professional Culture

Culture also presents itself on different levels. At the highest level is the culture of a *national* or regional society, such as the French or west European versus the Singaporean or Asian. The way in which attitudes are expressed within a specific organization is described as a *corporate* or organizational culture. Finally, we can even talk about the culture of particular functions within organizations: marketing, research and development, personnel. People within certain functions will tend to share certain *professional* and ethical orientations. This book will focus on the first level, the differences in culture at a national level.

Cultural differences do not exist only with regard to faraway, exotic countries. In the course of our research it has become increasingly clear that there are at several levels as many differences between the cultures of West Coast and East Coast America as there are between different nations (although for the purposes of this book most American references are averaged). All the examples show that there is a clear-cut cultural border between the northwest European (analysis, logic, systems, and rationality) and the Euro-Latin (more person-related, more use of intuition and sensitivity). There are even significant differences between the neighboring Dutch and Belgians.

The average Belgian manager has a family idea of the organization. He or she experiences the organization as paternalistic and hierarchical, and, as in many Latin cultures, father decides how it should be done. The Belgian sees the Dutch manager as overly democratic: what nonsense that everybody consults everybody. The Dutch manager thinks in a way more consistent with the Protestant ethic than the Belgian, who thinks and acts in a more Catholic way. Most Dutch managers distrust authority, while Belgian managers tend to respect it.

Nearly all discussions about the unification of Europe deal with techno-legal matters. But when these problems are solved, the real problem emerges. Nowhere do cultures differ so much as inside Europe. If you are going to do business with the French, you will first have to learn how to lunch extensively. The founder of the European Community, Jean Monnet, once declared, "If I were again facing the challenge to integrate Europe, I would probably start with culture."[3] Culture is the context in which things happen; out of context, even legal matters lack significance.

The Basis of Cultural Differences

Every culture distinguishes itself from others by the specific solutions it chooses to certain problems that reveal themselves as dilemmas. It is convenient to look at these problems under three headings: those that arise from our relationships with other people; those that come from the passage of time; and those that relate to the environment. Our research, to be described in the following chapters, examines culture within these three categories. From the solutions that different cultures have chosen to these universal problems, we can further identify seven fundamental dimensions of culture. Five of these come from the first category, relationships with people, the other two from dealing with time and the environment.

Relationships with People

There are five orientations covering the ways in which human beings deal with each other. We have taken Parsons's five relational orientations as a starting point.[4]

1.   **Universalism versus particularism.** The universalist approach is roughly: "What is good and right can be defined and always applies." In particularist cultures far greater attention is given to the obligations of relationships and unique circumstances. For example, instead of assuming that the one good way must always be followed, the particularist reasoning is that friendship has special obligations and hence may come first. Less attention is given to abstract societal codes.

2.   **Individualism versus communitarianism.** Do people regard themselves primarily as individuals or primarily as part of a group? Furthermore, is it more important to focus on individuals so that they can contribute to the community as and if they wish, or is it more important to consider the community first, since that is shared by many individuals?

3.   **Neutral versus affective.** Should the nature of our interactions be objective and detached, or is expressing emotion acceptable? In North America and northwest Europe business relationships are typically instrumental and all about achieving objectives. The brain checks emotions because these are believed to confuse the issues. The

assumption is that we should resemble our machines in order to operate them more efficiently. But farther south and in many other cultures, business is a human affair, and the whole gamut of emotions is deemed appropriate. Loud laughter, banging your fist on the table, or leaving a conference room in anger during a negotiation is all part of business.

4.   **Specific versus diffuse.** When the whole person is involved in a business relationship, there is a real and personal contact, instead of the specific relationship prescribed by a contract. In many countries a diffuse relationship is not only preferred but also necessary before business can proceed.

In the case of one American company trying to win a contract with an Argentinean customer, disregard for the importance of the relationship lost the deal. The American company made a slick, well-thought-out presentation that it thought clearly demonstrated its superior product and lower price. Its Swedish competitor took a week to get to know the customer. For five days the Swedes spoke about everything except the product. On the last day, the product was introduced. Though the product was somewhat less attractive and slightly higher priced than the American version, the diffuse involvement of the Swedish company got the order. The Swedish company had learned that doing business in particular countries involves more than overwhelming the customer with technical details and fancy slides. (See Chapter 7 for further discussion of this case.)

5.   **Achievement versus ascription.** Achievement means that you are judged on what you have recently accomplished and on your record. Ascription means that status is attributed to you by birth, kinship, gender, or age, but also by your connections (the people you know) and your educational record (e.g., a graduate of Tokyo University or Haute Ecole Polytechnique).

In an achievement culture, the first question is likely to be *"What* did you study?" In a more ascriptive culture the question will more likely be *"Where* did you study?" Only if it was a lousy university or one they do not recognize will ascriptive people ask what you studied; and that will be to enable you to save face.

Attitudes with Regard to Time

The way in which societies look at *time* also differs. In some societies what somebody has achieved in the past is not that important. It is more important to know what plan the person has developed for the future. In other societies you can make more of an impression with your past accomplishments than those of today. These are cultural differences that greatly influence corporate activities.

With respect to time, the American Dream is the French Nightmare. Americans generally start from zero, and what matters is their present performance and their plan to "make it" in the future. This is *nouveau riche* for the French, who prefer the opposite—the *ancien pauvre*; they have an enormous sense of the past and relatively less focus on the present and future than Americans.

In certain cultures such as the American, Swedish, and Dutch, time is perceived as passing in a straight line, a sequence of disparate events. Other cultures think of time more as moving in a circle, the past and present together with future possibilities. This distinction makes for considerable differences to planning, strategy, investment, and views on home-growing your talent as opposed to buying it in. For more information on the time dimension-horizon, please refer to the Web support pages (page 16).

Attitudes with Regard to the Environment

An important cultural difference can also be found in the attitude toward the *environment*. Some cultures see the major focus affecting their lives and the origins of vice and virtue as residing within the person. Here, motivations and values are derived from within. Other cultures see the world as more powerful than individuals. They see nature as something to be feared or emulated.

The then chairman of Sony, Akio Morita, explained how he came to conceive of the Walkman. A lover of classical music, he wanted to have a way of listening to recordings on his way to work without bothering any fellow commuters. The Walkman was a way of not imposing on the outside world, but of being in harmony with it. Contrast that to the way most Westerners think about using the device and later versions like iPod and MP3. "I can listen to music without being disturbed by other people."

Another obvious example is the use of face masks that are worn over the nose and mouth. In Tokyo you see many people wearing them, especially in winter. When you inquire why, you are told that when people have colds or a virus, they wear them so they will not "pollute" or infect other people by breathing on them. In London they are worn by cyclists and other amateur athletes who do not want to be "polluted" by the environment.

Structure of the Book

This book will describe why there is no "one best way of managing" and how some of the difficult dilemmas of international management can be mediated. Throughout, it will attempt to give readers more insight into their own culture and how it differs from others.

Chapters 2 through 8 will initiate the reader into the world of cultural diversity in relations with other people. How do cultures differ in this respect? In what ways do these differences impact on organizations and the conduct of international business? How are the relationships between employees affected? In what different ways do people learn and solve conflicts?

Chapters 9 and 10 discuss variations in cultural attitudes to time and the environment, respectively, which have very similar consequences for organizations.

Chapter 11 discusses how general cultural assumptions about human beings, time, and the environment affect the culture of organizations. It identifies the four broad types of organization that have resulted, including their hierarchies, relationships, goals, and structures.

Chapter 12 considers how managers can prepare the organization for the process of internationalization through some specific points of intervention. This chapter is intended to deal in a creative way with the dilemmas of internationalization, as well as to reinforce the message that an international future depends on achieving a balance between any two extremes.

What will emerge is that the whole centralization-versus-decentralization debate is really a false dichotomy. What is needed is the skill, sensitivity, and experience to draw on all the decentralized capacities of the international organization.

Chapter 13 analyzes the different steps that people need to take to reconcile cultural dilemmas. This is done through a case study that elicits the various problems that occur when professional people from different cultures meet.

Chapter 14 offers our structure for dealing with cultural differences in mergers and acquisitions, which centers on a stepwise framework for securing the business case and associated mission or vision, leading to the elicitation of the key dilemmas that need to be reconciled.

Chapter 15 illustrates some ethnic differences and the effect on culture of gender, age, functional background, and type of industry. We will conclude that the cultures of nations are an important factor in defining the meaning that people assign to their environment, but that other factors should not be ignored.

Chapter 16 reflects on the components of the whole book to offer an integrative model for the future success of organizations in the effort to secure a sustainable future, based on the reconciliation of the sectional interests of stakeholders, and provides a vehicle for finally linking culture to the bottom line.

What this book attempts to make possible is the genuinely international organization, sometimes called the transnational, in which each national culture contributes its own particular insights and strengths to the solution of worldwide issues and the company is able to draw on whatever it is that nations do best.

CULTURAL DATA

Throughout the book, we give examples of "stereotypical" responses from representative samples in major countries to our basic cultural instruments to illustrate the concepts being discussed based on our earlier cultural data. These responses serve to illustrate what we might describe as the underlying cultural norms of that country relevant to the development of business and management styles prior to the boom in globalization over the last 20 years. They are intended to help the reader reflect on the origins of cultural differences relevant to business, rather than for modern-day tourists.

The effects of globalization, immigration, and other socioeconomic shifts (e.g., European convergence) based on our more recent cultural data are given special consideration in Chapter 15. It is now too simplistic to try to describe the (single) culture of country X without taking into consideration the effects of immigration, the development of multicultural societies, age and generation differences, and where corporate culture is a major variable.

Readers who would like access to our ongoing and continually updated data and data from other countries not dealt with in this book are referred to our website: www.ridingthewavesofculture.com.

Notes

1. E. Schein, *Organizational Culture and Leadership* (San Francisco: Jossey-Bass, 1985).
2. R. G. Collingwood, *Essay on Metaphysics* (Chicago: Gateway, 1974).
3. See for example: www.cerium.ca/l-europe-et-la-culture?lang=fr.
4. T. Parsons, *The Social System* (New York: Free Press, 1951).

The One Best Way of Organizing
Does Not Exist

However objective and uniform one may try to make organizations, they will not have the same meaning for individuals from different cultures. The meanings perceived depend on certain cultural preferences, which we shall describe. Likewise, the meaning that people give to the organization, including their concept of its structure, practices, and policies, is culturally defined.

Culture is a shared system of meanings. It dictates what we pay attention to, how we act, and what we value. Culture organizes such values into what Geert Hofstede calls "mental programs."[1] The behavior of people within organizations is an enactment of such programs.

Each of us carries within us the ways we have learned about organizing our experience to mean something. This approach is described as phenomenological, meaning that the way people perceive phenomena around them is coherent, orderly, and sensible.

A fellow employee from a different culture makes one interpretation of the meaning of an organization while we make our own. Why? What can we learn from this alternative way of seeing things? Can we let that employee contribute in his or her own way?

This approach to understanding an international organization is in strong contrast to the traditional approach, in which managers or researchers decide unilaterally how the organization should be defined. Traditional studies have been based on the physical, verifiable characteristics of organizations, which are assumed to have a common definition for all people, everywhere, at all times. Instead of this approach, which looks for laws and common properties among "things" observed, we shall look for consistent ways in which cultures structure the perceptions of what they experience.

Our more recent research confirms that different cultures share similar business problems but that how they (initially) approach these problems is culturally determined. The significance of these different points of view has practical implications for doing business and managing in today's world, and we will discuss how these differences can be accommodated through reconciliation.

What the Gurus Tell Us

Management gurus such as Frederick Taylor, Henri Fayol, Peter Drucker, Mike Hammer, James Champy, and Tom Peters have one thing in common: they all gave the impression, consciously or unconsciously, that there was one best way to manage and to organize. We shall be showing how very American and, in the case of Fayol, how French these assumptions were. Not much has changed in this respect since they wrote their seminal books. Is it not desirable to be able to give management a box of tools that will reduce the complexities of managing? Of course it is. We see the manager reach for the tools to limit complexity, but unfortunately the approach tends to limit innovation and intercultural success as well.

Yet studies in the 1970s already showed that the effectiveness of certain methods does depend on the environment in which we operate.

Since then, most so-called contingency studies have asked how the major structures of the organization vary in accordance with major variables in the environment. They have tended to show that if the environment is essentially simple and stable, then steep hierarchies survive, but if it is complex and turbulent, flatter hierarchies engage it more profitably. Such studies have mainly been confined to one country, usually the US. Both structure and environment are measured, and the results explain that X amount of environmental turbulence evokes Y amount of hierarchical levels, leading to Z amount of performance. The fact that Japanese corporations operated in particularly turbulent environments with much steeper hierarchies has not as a rule been addressed.

We should note that these contingency studies are still searching for one best way in specified circumstances. They still believe that their universalism is scientific, when in fact it is a cultural preference. "One best way" is a yearning, not a fact. Michel Crozier, the French sociologist, working in 1964, could find no studies that related organizations to their sociocultural environments.[2] Of course, those who search for sameness will usually find it, and if you stick to examining common objects and processes, like refining oil according to chemical science, then pipes will be found to have the same function the world over. If the principles of chemical engineering are the same, why not all principles? It seems a plausible equation.

Talcott Parsons, an American sociologist, already mid-20th century, suggested that organizations have to adapt not simply to the environment but also to the views of participating employees.[3] It has been only in recent years that this consideration of employee perceptions, and differing cultures, has surfaced in management literature.

Neglect of Culture in Action

Take the following meeting of a management team trying to internationalize a company's activities. This case is a summary of an interview with a North American human-resource manager, a case history that will be referred to throughout the book. Although the case is real, the names of the company and the participants are fictitious.

THE MISSOURI COMPUTATIONAL COMPANY (MCC)

MCC, founded in 1952, is a very successful American company. It develops, produces, and sells medium-sized and large computers. The company currently operates as a multinational in North and South America, Europe,

Southeast Asia, Australia, and the Middle East. Sales activities are regionally structured. The factories are in St. Louis and Newark (New Jersey); the most important research activities take place in St. Louis.

Production, R&D, personnel, and finance are coordinated at the American head office. Business units handle the regional sales responsibilities. This decentralized structure does have to observe certain centralized limitations regarding logos, letter formats, types of products, and financial criteria. Standardization of labor conditions, function classification, and personnel planning are coordinated centrally, whereas hiring is done by the regional branches. Each regional branch has its own personnel and finance departments. The management meets every two weeks, and this week's meeting is focusing on globalization issues.

INTERNATIONALIZATION

Mr. Johnson paid extra attention in the management meeting. As vice president of human resources worldwide, he could be facing serious problems. Management recognizes that the spirit of globalization is becoming more active every day. Not only do the clients have more international demands, but also production facilities need to be set up in more and more countries.

This morning a new logo was introduced to symbolize the worldwide image of the company. The next item on the agenda was a worldwide marketing plan.

Mr. Smith, the CEO, saw a chance to bring forward what his M.B.A. taught him to be universally applicable management tools. In addition to global images and marketing, he saw global production, finance, and human-resource management as supporting the international breakthrough.

Johnson's hair started to rise as he listened to his colleague's presentation. "The organization worldwide should be flatter. An excellent technique for this would be to follow the project approach that has been so successful in the US." Johnson's follow-up question about the acceptance of this approach in southern Europe and South America was brushed aside with a short reply regarding the extra time that would be allotted to introduce it in these cultures. The generous allocation of six months would be provided to make even the most unwilling culture understand and appreciate the beauty of shorter lines of communication.

Finally, all of this would be supported by a strong pay-for-performance system so that, in addition to having more effective structures, the employees would be directed toward the right goals.

Johnson's last try to introduce a more "human" side to the discussion concerning the implementation of the techniques and policy instruments was useless. The finance manager, Mr. Finley, expressed the opinion of the entire management team: "We all know that cultural differences are decreasing with the increasing reach of the media. We should be world leaders and create a future environment that is a microcosm of Missouri."

Mr. Johnson frowned at the prospect of next week's international meeting in Europe.

Mr. Johnson knew from experience there would be trouble in communicating this stance to European human-resource managers. He could empathize with the Europeans, while knowing that central management did not really intend to be arrogant in extending a central policy worldwide. What could he do to get the best outcome from his next meeting? We shall follow this through in Chapter 4.

Culture as a Side Dish?

Culture still seems like a luxury item to most managers, a dish on the side. In actuality, culture pervades and radiates meanings into every aspect of the enterprise. Culture patterns the whole field of business relationships. The Dutch author remembers a conversation he had with a Dutch expatriate in Singapore. The latter registered surprise when questioned about the ways in which he accommodated the local culture when implementing management and organization techniques. Before answering, he tried to find out why he should have been asked such a stupid question. "Do you work for personnel, by any chance?" Then he took the author on a tour through the impressive refinery. "Do you really think the products we have and the technology we use allow us to take local culture into consideration?"

Granted, it would be difficult for a continuous-process company to accommodate the wishes of most Singaporeans to be home at night. In other words, reality seems to show us that variables such as product, technology, and markets are much more of a determinant than culture is. In one sense this conclusion is correct. Integrated technologies have a logic of their own that operates regardless of where the plant is located. Cultures do not compete with or repeal these laws. They simply supply the social context in which the technology operates. A refinery is always a refinery, but the culture in which it is located may see it as an imperialist plot, a precious lifeline, the last chance for an economic takeoff, a prop for a medieval potentate, or a weapon against the West. It all depends on the cultural context.

It is entirely possible for organizations to be the same in such objective dimensions as physical plant, layout, or product, yet totally different in the meanings that the surrounding human cultures read into them. We once interviewed a Venezuelan process operator, showing him the company organization chart and asking him to indicate how many layers he had above and below him. To our surprise he indicated more levels than there were on the chart. We asked him how he could see these. "This person next to me," he explained, "is above me, because he is older."

One of the exercises we conduct in our workshops is to have participants choose between the following two extreme ways to conceive of a company, asking them which they think is usually true, as well as which most people in their country would opt for.

A. One way is to see a company as a system designed to perform functions and tasks in an efficient way. People are hired to perform these functions with the help of machines and other equipment. They are paid for the tasks they perform.

B. A second way is to see a company as a group of people working together. They have social relations with other people and with the organization. The functioning is dependent on these relations.

Figure 2.1 shows the wide range of national responses. Only a little more than a third of French, Korean, or Japanese managers see a com-

Percentage of respondents opting for a system rather than a social group

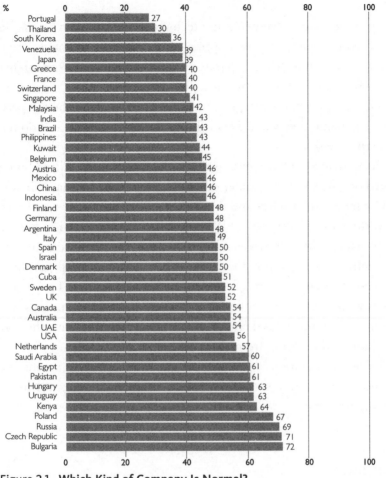

Figure 2.1. Which Kind of Company Is Normal?

pany as a system rather than a social group, whereas the British and Americans are fairly evenly divided, and there is a large majority in favor of the system in Russia and several countries of eastern Europe.

These differing interpretations are important influences on the interactions between individuals and groups. Formal structures and management techniques may appear uniform. Indeed, they imitate hard technologies in order to achieve this effect, but just as plant and equipment have different cultural meanings, so do social technologies.

An Alternative Approach

All organizational instruments and techniques are based on *paradigms* (sets of assumptions). An assumption often taken for granted is that social reality is "out there," separated from the manager or researcher in the same way as the matter of a physics experiment is "out there." The physics researchers can give the physical elements in their experiments any name they want. Dead things do not talk back and do not define themselves.

The human world, however, is markedly different. As Alfred Shutz pointed out, when we encounter other social systems, they have already given names to themselves and decided how they want to live and how the world is to be interpreted.[4] We may label them if we wish, but we cannot expect them to understand or accept our definitions, unless these definitions correspond to their own. We cannot strip people of their commonsense constructs or routine ways of seeing. They come to us as whole systems of patterned meanings and understandings. We can only try to understand, and to do so means starting with the way they think and building from there.

Hence, organizations do not simply react to their environment as a ship might to waves. They actively select, interpret, choose, and create their environments.

Summary

In spite of globalization and many merger failures, individuals and organizations continue to act as they do without considering the *meanings* they attribute to their environment. "A complex market" is not an objective description so much as a cultural perception. Complex to whom? To an Ethiopian or to an American? Feedback sessions in which people explore their mistakes can produce "useful feedback" according to American management culture and "enforced admissions of failure" in a German management culture. One culture may be inspired by the very thing that depresses another.

The organization and its structures are thus more than objective reality; they comprise fulfillments or frustrations of the mental models held by real people.

Rather than there being "one best way of organizing," there are several ways, some much more culturally appropriate and effective than others, but all of them giving international managers additional strings to their bow if they are willing and able to clarify the reactions of foreign cultures.

Notes

1. G. Hofstede, *Culture's Consequences* (London: Sage, 1980).
2. M. Crozier, *The Bureaucratic Phenomenon* (Chicago: University of Chicago Press, 1964).
3. T. Parsons, *The Social System* (New York: Free Press, 1951).
4. A. Schutz, *On Phenomenology and Social Relations* (Chicago: University of Chicago Press, 1970).

The Meaning of Culture

A FISH DISCOVERS its need for water only when it is no longer in it. Our own culture is like water to a fish. It sustains us. We live and breathe through it. What one culture may regard as essential—a certain level of material wealth, for example—may not be so vital to other cultures.

The Concept of Culture

Social interaction, or meaningful communication, presupposes common ways of processing information among the people interacting. These presuppositions have consequences for doing business as well as managing across cultural boundaries. Even "at home," managers are faced with an increasingly diverse and multicultural workforce. The mutual dependence of the actors is due to the fact that together they constitute a connected system of meanings: a shared definition of a situation by a group.

How do these shared beliefs come about, and what is their influence on the interactions between members of an organization? An absolute condition for meaningful interaction in business and management is the existence of mutual expectations.

On a cold winter night in Amsterdam I (the Dutch author) see someone enter a cigar shop. His Burberry coat and horn spectacles reveal him to be well off. He buys a pack of cigarettes and takes a box of matches. He then visits the newspaper stand, purchases a Dutch newspaper, and quickly walks to a wind-free corner near the shopping gallery. I approach him and ask if I can smoke a cigarette with him and whether he would mind if I read the second section of his paper. He looks at me unbelievingly and says, "I need this corner to light my paper." He throws me the pack of cigarettes, because he does not smoke. When I stand back, I see that he lights the newspaper and holds his hands above the flames. He turns out to be homeless, searching for warmth and too shy to purchase a single box of matches without the cigarettes.

In this situation my expectations are not met by the individual observed. My expectations about the behavior of the man say more about myself than about him. What I expect depends on where I come from and the meanings I give to what I experience. Expectations occur on many different levels, from concrete, explicit levels to implicit and subconscious ones. I am misled not only by the "meaning" of the man's clothing and appearance, but also on the simple level of the newspaper and cigarettes. When we observe such symbols, they trigger certain expectations. When the expectations of the person with whom we are communicating meet our own, there is mutuality of meaning.

The existence of mutual beliefs is not the first thing that comes to mind when you think about culture. In cultural training workshops, we often start by asking participants, "What does the concept of culture mean to you? Can you differentiate a number of components?" In 25 years we have seldom encountered two or more groups or individuals with identical suggestions regarding the concept of culture. This variety among responses shows the inclusiveness of the concept. The more difficult question is, perhaps, "Can you name anything that is *not* encompassed by the concept of culture?"

The Layers of Culture

Figure 3.1 is a graphic representation of culture as a series of nested spheres.

old culture model

Figure 3.1. A Model of Culture

The Outer Layer: Explicit Products

Go back to the temporary flight detour to Burundi from Chapter 1. What are the first things you encounter on a cultural level? Most likely it is not the strange combination of norms and values. Nor is it the sharing of meanings and value orientations. An individual's first experience of a new culture is the less esoteric, more concrete factors. This level consists of *explicit* culture.

Explicit culture is the observable reality of the language, food, buildings, houses, monuments, agriculture, shrines, markets, fashions, and art. They are the symbols of a deeper level of culture. Prejudices mostly start on this symbolic and observable level. We should never forget that, as in the Burberry coat example, each opinion we form regarding explicit culture usually says more about where *we* come from than about the community we are judging.

If we see a group of Japanese managers bowing, we are obviously observing explicit culture as the sheer act of bending. However, if we ask the Japanese, "Why do you bow?"—a question they may not welcome—we penetrate the next layer of culture.

The Middle Layer: Norms and Values

Explicit culture reflects deeper layers of culture, the norms and values of an individual group. *Norms* are the mutual sense a group has of what is "right" and "wrong." Norms can develop on a formal level as written laws, and on an informal level as social control. *Values*, on the other hand, determine the definition of "good" and "bad" and are therefore closely related to the ideals shared by a group.

A culture is relatively stable when the norms reflect the values of the group. When this is not the case, there will most likely be a destabilizing tension. In eastern Europe we have seen for years how the norms of Communism failed to match the values of society. Disintegration is a logical result.

While the norms, consciously or subconsciously, give us a feeling of "this is how I normally *should* behave," values give us a feeling of "this is how I *aspire* or *desire* to behave." A value serves as a criterion to determine a choice from existing alternatives. It is the concept an individual or group has regarding the desirable. For instance, in one culture people might agree with the value: "Hard work is essential to a prosperous society." Yet the behavioral norm sanctioned by the group may be: "Do not work harder than the other members of the group, because then we would all be expected to do more and would end up worse off." Here the norm differs from the value. If you attend a job interview, do you wear a smart business suit (because that is the expected "norm") or do you select your attire on the basis of what you believe in (your own "values")? If the decision outcomes are the same, then there is no tension, but if you prefer to dress casually but are expected to dress more formally, then there is a conflict.

Some Japanese might say that they bow because they like to greet people: that is a value. Others might say they don't know why except that they do it because the others do it. Then we are talking about a norm.

It takes shared meanings of norms and values that are stable and salient for a group's cultural tradition to be developed and elaborated.

Why have different groups of people, consciously or subconsciously, chosen different definitions of good or bad, right or wrong?

The Core: Assumptions About Existence

To answer questions about basic differences in values between cultures, it is necessary to go back to the core of human existence.

The most basic value for which people strive is survival. Historically, and presently, we have witnessed civilizations fighting daily with nature: the Dutch with rising water; the Swiss with mountains and avalanches; the Central Americans and Africans with droughts; and the Siberians with bitter cold.

Members of each civilization have organized themselves to find the ways to deal most effectively with their environments, given their available resources. Such continuous problems are eventually solved automatically. The word *culture* comes from the same root as the verb *cultivate*, meaning "to till the soil": the way people act on nature. The problems of daily life are solved in such obvious ways that the solutions disappear from our consciousness. If they did not, we would go crazy. Imagine having to concentrate on your need for oxygen every 30 seconds. The solutions disappear from our awareness and become part of our system of absolute assumptions.

The best way to test if something is a basic assumption is to note if the question provokes confusion or irritation. You might, for example, observe that some Japanese bow more deeply than others. Again, if you ask why they do it, the answer might be that they don't know but that the other person does it too (norm), or it might be that they want to show respect for authority (value). A typical Dutch question that might follow is: "Why do you respect authority?" The most likely Japanese reaction would be either puzzlement or a smile (which might be hiding irritation). When you question basic assumptions, you are asking questions that have never been asked before. It might lead to deeper insights, but it also might provoke annoyance. Try in the US or the Netherlands to raise the question of why people are equal and you will see what we mean.

Groups of people organize themselves in such a way that they increase the effectiveness of their problem-solving processes. Because different groups of people have developed in different geographic regions, they have also formed different sets of logical assumptions.

We see that a specific organizational culture or functional culture is nothing more than the way in which groups have organized themselves over the years to solve the problems and challenges presented to them. Changes in a culture happen because people realize that certain old ways of doing things do not work anymore. It is not difficult to change culture when people are aware that the survival of the community is at stake, where survival is considered desirable.

From this fundamental relationship with the (natural) environment people, and after people the community, take the core meaning of life. This deepest meaning has escaped from conscious questioning and has become self-evident, because it is a result of routine responses to the environment. In this sense culture is anything but nature.

Culture Directs Our Actions

Culture is beneath awareness in the sense that no one bothers to verbalize it, yet it forms the roots of action. This aspect made one anthropologist liken it to an iceberg, with its largest implicit part beneath the water.

Culture is made by humans, confirmed by others, conventionalized, and passed on for younger people or newcomers to learn. It provides people with a meaningful context in which to meet, to think about themselves, and to face the outer world.

In the language of Clifford Geertz, culture is the means by which people "communicate, perpetuate, and develop their knowledge about attitudes toward life. Culture is the fabric of meaning in terms of which human beings interpret their experience and guide their action."[1]

Over time, the habitual interactions within communities take on familiar forms and structures, which we will call the *organization of meaning*. These structures are imposed on the situations that people confront and are not determined by the situation itself. For example, the wink of an eye: is it a physical reflex from dust in the eye or an invitation to a prospective date? Or could it be someone making fun of you to others? Perhaps a nervous tic? The wink itself is real, but its meaning is attributed to it by observers. The attributed meaning may or may not coincide with the intended meaning of the wink. Effective social interaction, though, requires that the attributed meaning and intended meaning coincide.

Cultures can be distinguished from each other by the differences in shared meanings that they expect and attribute to their environment. Culture is not a "thing," a substance with a physical reality of its own. Rather, it is made by people interacting and, at the same time, determining further interaction.

Culture as a "Normal Distribution"

People within a culture do not all have identical sets of artifacts, norms, values, and assumptions. Within each culture there is a wide spread of these elements. This spread does have a pattern around an average. So, in a sense, the variation around the norm can be seen as a normal distribution. Distinguishing one culture from another depends on the limits we want to impose on each side of the distribution.

In principle, each culture shows the total variation of its human components. So while the US and France have many variations, there are also many similarities. The "average" or "most predictable" behavior, as depicted by Figure 3.2, will be different for these two countries.

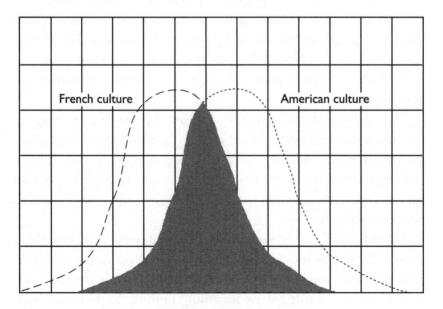

Norms and values

Figure 3.2. Culture as Normal Distribution

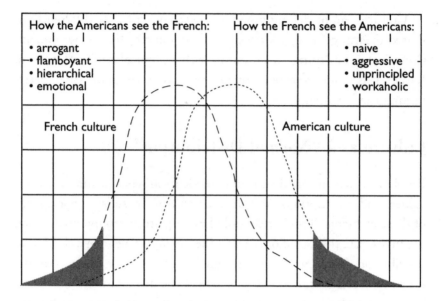

Norms and values

Figure 3.3. **Culture and Stereotyping**

Cultures whose norms differ significantly tend to speak about each other in terms of extremes (Figure 3.3). Americans might describe the French as having the behavioral characteristics shown on the left hand side of the graph, or the tail of the normal distribution. The French will use a similar caricature for the Americans, as you can see on the right hand side. This is because it is differences rather than sameness that we generally notice.

This use of extreme, exaggerated forms of behavior is *stereotyping*. It is, understandably, the result of registering what surprises us, rather than what is familiar. But there are dangers in doing this. First, a stereotype is a very limited view of the average behavior in a certain environment. It exaggerates and caricatures the culture observed and, unintentionally, the observer.

Second, people often equate something different with something wrong. "Their way is clearly different from ours, so it cannot be right." Finally, stereotyping ignores the fact that individuals in the same culture do not necessarily behave according to the cultural norm. Individual personality mediates in each cultural system.

It's true that business leaders have always been concerned with changing demographics in order to profile customers and subgroups of customers. Business leaders are discovering how rapidly they need to rethink and reassess such groupings. They have to be concerned with multiple phenomena:

- Structural changes (in population, age distributions, fecundity/ birthrates of different cultures)
- Migrations—net of immigration and emigration (acculturation, ethnicity, diversity, the development of multicultural societies)
- Changes in beliefs and values held by different people (shifts, divergences, convergence of cultural norms and values)

The total potential market is growing as the world population expands at an increasing rate, although it should be noted that this growth is not uniform and that in some areas—including Europe— the population is actually declining.

The main growth continues to occur in the Far East, especially China, India, and Korea, and in accelerating developments in South America. It stands to reason that population growth does not imply a direct growth in market opportunity, especially because countries with larger growth rates also tend to be those with lower GNP per capita. More important, population growth in these regions results in a larger low-cost labor force, which is why many US and European organizations operate in these countries.

However, even more dramatic are the changes in the structure of the population due to birthrates and life expectancy. These changes result because of differences in fecundity (fertility, health of mothers, and survival rates) and other changes in society (women in more developed societies restricting pregnancies and/or choosing to delay the onset of childbearing) combined with longer life expectancy. In some countries, such as Bangladesh, Pakistan, and India, life expectancy will double over the course of less than a century.

While migration has little effect on overall population levels, it does contribute to changes in the population structure. Immigrants usually come from different cultural backgrounds and offer and create different opportunities as well as challenges for business. Entirely new markets have been identified and satisfied (such as one for black adhesive plasters) for these immigrants as new customers. In addition, immigrants often become a new source of suppliers as they offer new, culturally led products and services to the host community—such as ethnic food shops and restaurants.

So we have to be careful when describing what we mean by the typical "French," for example, given demographic changes in the population. Do we mean today, or 20 years ago, or even before the French Revolution? Throughout this book and in explaining the fundamental ideas of culture, we will use the notion of "traditional" stereotypes to assist the reader in understanding the more important constructs. Later, we will address what real population changes mean and where and how we will need to consider acculturation and issues of cultural convergence and changes arising from aging populations and generation differences. (See Chapter 15.)

Cultures Vary in Solutions to Common Problems and Dilemmas

To explain variations in the meaning organizations have for people working in them, we need to consider variations in meanings for different cultures. If we can identify and compare categories of culture that affect organizations, this will help us understand the cultural differences that must be managed in international business.

In every culture a limited number of general, universally shared human problems need to be solved. One culture can be distinguished from another by the specific solution it chooses for those problems. The anthropologists F. Kluckhohn and F. L. Strodtbeck identify five categories of problems, arguing that all societies are aware of all possible kinds of solution but prefer them in different orders.[2] Hence, in any culture there is a set of "dominant," or preferred, value orientations. The five basic problems that humans face, according to this scheme, are as follows:

1. What is the relationship of the individual to others? (relational orientation)
2. What is the temporal focus of human life? (time orientation)
3. What is the modality of human activity? (activity orientation)
4. What is a human being's relation to nature? (person-nature orientation)
5. What is the character of innate human nature? (human nature orientation)

In short, Kluckhohn and Strodtbeck argue that people are confronted with universally shared problems emerging from relationships with fellow beings, time, activities, and (human) nature. One culture can be distinguished from another by the arrangement of the specific solutions it selects for each set of problem situations. The solutions depend on the meaning given by people to life in general and to their fellows, time, and nature in particular.

In our research we have distinguished seven dimensions of culture (Chapter 1), also based on societies' differing solutions to relationships with other people, time, and nature. The following chapters will explain these dimensions and how they affect the process of managing across cultures.

As opposed to running the risk of getting stuck by perceiving cultures as static points on a dual-axis map, we believe that cultures *dance* from one preferred end to the opposite and back. This approach means that we do not risk having one cultural category exclude its opposite, as has happened in so many similar studies, of which Hofstede's five mutually exclusive categories are the best known. Rather, we believe that one cultural category seeks to "manage" its opposite and that value dimensions self-organize in systems to generate new meanings. Cultures are circles with preferred arcs joined together. In this revised edition we have therefore introduced new questions that measure the extent to which managers seek to *integrate and reconcile* values. Further, we are testing the hypothesis that cultures that have a natural tendency to reconcile seemingly opposing values have a better chance of being successful economically than cultures that lack that inclination.

All cultures are similar in the dilemmas they confront, yet different in the solutions they find, which creatively transcend the opposites.

Summary

This chapter delineated how common meanings arise and how they are reflected through explicit symbols. We saw that culture presents itself to us in layers. The outer layers are the products and artifacts that symbolize the deeper, more basic values and assumptions about life. The different layers are not independent from one another, but are complementary.

The shared meanings that are the core of culture are made by people and are incorporated into people within a culture, yet they transcend the people in the culture. In other words, the shared meanings of a group are within the members of the group and cause them to interpret things in particular ways, but the meanings are also open to be changed if more effective "solutions" to problems of survival are desired by the group.

The solutions to three universal problems faced by humans distinguish one culture from another. The problems—people's relationship to time, nature, and other human beings—are shared by people; their solutions are not. The latter depend on the cultural background of the group concerned. The categories of culture that emerge from the solutions that cultures choose will be the subject of the next seven chapters. Their significance to work-related relationships, management instruments, and organizational structures will also be explored.

Notes

1. C. Geertz, *The Interpretation of Cultures* (New York: Basic Books, 1973).
2. F. Kluckhohn and F. L. Strodtbeck, *Variations in Value Orientations* (Westport, CT: Greenwood Press, 1961).

Relationships and Rules

P EOPLE EVERYWHERE are confronted with three sources of challenge. They have relationships with other people, such as friends, employees, customers, and bosses. They must manage time and aging. And they must somehow come to terms with the external nature of the world, be it benign or threatening.

We have already identified the five dimensions of human relationships. It has been easiest to summarize them in abstract terms that may seem rather abstruse. We list them again with some translations in parentheses.

1. Universalism versus particularism (rules versus relationships)
2. Individualism versus communitarianism (the individual versus the group)
3. Neutral versus affective (the degree to which feelings are expressed)
4. Diffuse versus specific (the degree of involvement)
5. Achievement versus ascription (how status is accorded)

These five value orientations greatly influence people's ways of doing business and managing as well as their responses in the face of moral dilemmas. A person's relative position along these dimensions guides the person's beliefs and actions through life. For example, we all confront situations in which the established rules do not quite fit a particular circumstance. Do we do what is deemed "right," or do we adapt to the circumstances of the situation? If we are in a difficult meeting, do we show how strongly we feel and risk the consequences, or do we show "admirable restraint"? When we encounter a difficult problem, do we break it apart into pieces to understand it, or do we see everything as related to everything else? On what grounds do we show respect for someone's status and power: because that person has achieved it, or because other circumstances (such as age, education, or lineage) define it? These are all dilemmas to which cultures have differing answers. Part of the purpose of culture is to provide answers and guide behavior in otherwise vexatious situations.

Before discussing the first dimension—universal versus particular forms of relating to people—let us rejoin the perplexed Mr. Johnson of the Missouri Computational Company (MCC) from Chapter 2. He is due to preside over an international human-resources meeting in which 15 national representatives are expected to agree on the uniform implementation of a pay-for-performance system. Here is some background on MCC and a summary of its main policy directives.

Since the late 1970s MCC has been operating in more than 20 countries. As its foreign sales have grown, top management has become increasingly concerned about international coordination. Overseas growth, while robust, has been unpredictable. The company has therefore decided to coordinate the processes of measuring and rewarding achievement worldwide. Greater consistency in managing country operations is also on the agenda. There is not a complete disregard for national differences; the general manager worked in Germany for five years, and the marketing manager spent seven years in the Singapore operation.

It has been agreed to introduce a number of policy principles that will permeate MCC plants worldwide. Management envisages a shareable definition of "how we do things in MCC" to let everyone in MCC, wherever the location in the world, know what the company stands for. Within this framework, there will be centrally coordinated policies for human resources, sales, and marketing.

This approach would benefit customers, since they, too, are internationalizing in many cases. They need to know that MCC could provide high levels of service and effectiveness to their businesses, which increasingly cross borders. MCC needs to achieve consistent, recognizable standards regardless of the country in which it is operating. There is already a history of standardizing policies.

THE REWARD SYSTEM

Two years ago, confronted with heavy competition, the company decided to use a more differentiated reward system for the personnel who sold and serviced midsize computers. One of the reasons was to see whether the motivation of the American sales force could be increased. In addition, the company became aware that the best salespeople often left the firm for better-paying competitors. It decided on a two-year trial with the 15 active salespeople in the St. Louis area.

Experiment with Pay-for-Performance

The experiment consisted of the following elements:

- A bonus was introduced that depended on the turnover figures each quarter for each salesperson: 100 percent over salary for the top salesperson; 60 percent for the second best; 30 percent for numbers three and four; and no bonus for the remainder.
- The base salary of all salespeople of midsize computers was decreased by 10 percent.

During the first year of the trial period there were continuous discussions among the affected employees. Five salespeople left the company, because they were convinced the system treated them unjustly. Total sales did not increase as a result of all this. Despite this disaster, management continued the experiment, based on the belief that this kind of change was necessary and would take time to be accepted.

The Universal Versus the Particular

MCC in the US is of course operating in a universalist culture. But even here a universalist solution has run into particularist problems. This first dimension defines how we judge other people's behavior. There are two "pure" yet alternative types of judgment. At one extreme we encounter an obligation to adhere to standards that are universally agreed to by the culture in which we live. "Do not lie. Do not steal. Do unto others as you would have them do unto you" (the Golden Rule), and so on. At the other extreme we encounter particular obligations to people we know. "X is my dear friend, so obviously I would not lie to him or steal from him. It would hurt us both to show less than kindness to one another."

Universalist, or rule-based, behavior tends to be abstract. Try crossing the street when the light is red in a predominantly rule-based society such as Switzerland or Germany. Even if there is no traffic, you will still be frowned at. It also tends to imply equality in the sense that all persons falling under the rule should be treated the same. Then again, situations are ordered by categories. For example, if "others" to whom you "do unto" are not categorized as human, the rules may not apply. Finally, rule-based conduct has a tendency to resist exceptions that might weaken that rule. There is a fear that once you start to make exceptions for illegal conduct, the system will collapse.

Particularist judgments focus on the exceptional nature of present circumstances. This person is not "a citizen" but is my friend, my brother, my husband, my child, or a person of unique importance to me, with special claims on my love or my hatred. I must therefore sustain, protect, or discount this person *no matter what the rules say.*

Businesspeople from both societies will tend to think each other corrupt. A universalist will say of particularists, "They cannot be trusted, because they will always help their friends," and a particularist, conversely, will say of universalists, "You cannot trust them; they would not even help a friend."

In practice we all use both kinds of judgment, and in most situations we encounter they reinforce each other. If an employee is harassed in the workplace, we would disapprove of this action, because "harassment is immoral and against company rules" and/or because "it was a terrible experience for Jennifer and really upset her." The universalist's chief objection, though, will be the breach of rules: "Employees should not have to deal with harassment in the workplace; it is wrong." The particularist is likely to be more disapproving of the fact that it caused distress to poor Jennifer.

Problems are not always so easily agreed on as this one. Sometimes rules of supposed universal application do not cover a case of particular concern very well. There are circumstances much more complex than the rules appear to have envisaged. Consider the further adventures of the Missouri Computational Company, with its head office in St. Louis intent on imposing general policy guidelines on employees of many nations.

MCC has recently acquired a small but successful Swedish software company. Its head founded it three years ago with his son Carl and was joined by his newly graduated daughter, Clara, and his youngest son, Peter, 12 months ago. Since the acquisition MCC has injected considerable capital in the company and also given the company its own computer distribution and servicing in Sweden. This has been a real boost to the business.

MCC is now convinced that rewards for salespeople must reflect the increasing competition in the market. It has decreed that at least 30 percent of remuneration must depend on individual performance. At the beginning of this year Carl married a very rich woman. The marriage is happy, and this state of affairs has had a positive effect on his sales record. He will easily earn the 30 percent bonus, though this amount will be small in relation to his total income, supplemented by his wife's and by his share of the acquisition payment.

Peter has a less happy marriage and much less money. His only-average sales figures will mean that his income will be reduced when he can ill afford it. Clara, who married while still in school, has two children and this year lost her husband in an air crash. This tragic event caused her to have a weak sales year.

At the international sales conference national MCC managers present their salary and bonus ranges. The head of the Swedish company believes that performance should be rewarded and that favoritism should be avoided; he has many employees who are not family members. At the same time, he knows that unusual circumstances in the lives of his children have made this contest anything but fair. The rewards withheld will hurt more deeply than the rewards bestowed will motivate. He tries to explain the situation to Mr. Johnson, the American HR chief, and the British representative, who both look skeptical and talk about excuses. He does not pursue the issue.

His colleagues from France, Italy, Spain, and the Middle East, who all know the situation, stare in disbelief. They would have backed him on the issue. His family later says they feel let down. This was not what they joined the company for.

This episode from our ongoing MCC case shows that universalist and particularist points of view are not always easy to reconcile. The culture you come from, your personality, your religion, and the bonds with those concerned lead you to favor one approach over another.

Universalist Versus Particularist Orientations in Different Countries

Much of the early research into this cultural dimension has come from the US and is influenced by American cultural preferences. The emerging consensus among these researchers, though, is that universalism is a feature of modernization per se, of more complex and developed societies. Particularism, they argue, is a feature of smaller, largely rural communities in which everyone knows everyone personally. The implication is that universalism and sophisticated business practice go together and that all nations might be better off for more nearly resembling the US.

We do not accept this conclusion. Instead, we believe that cultural dilemmas need to be reconciled in a process of understanding the advantages of each cultural preference. The creation of wealth and the development of industry should be an evolving process of discovering more and better universals covering and sustaining more particular cases and circumstances.

The story that follows, created by Americans Stouffer and Toby, is another exercise used in our workshops.[1] It takes the form of a dilemma that measures universal and particularist responses.

You are riding in a car driven by a close friend. He hits a pedestrian. You know he was going at least 35 miles per hour in an area of the city where the maximum allowed speed is 20 miles per hour. There are no witnesses. His lawyer says that if you testify under oath that he was driving only 20 miles per hour, it may save him from serious consequences.

What right has your friend to expect you to protect him?

- **A.** My friend has a definite right as a friend to expect me to testify to the lower figure.
- **B** He has some right as a friend to expect me to testify to the lower figure.
- **C.** He has no right as a friend to expect me to testify to the lower figure.

What do you think you would do in view of the obligations of a sworn witness and the obligation to your friend?

- **D.** Testify that he was going 20 miles an hour.
- **E.** Not testify that he was going 20 miles an hour.

Figure 4.1 shows the result of putting these questions to a variety of nationalities.[2] The percentage represents those who answered that the friend had no right or some right and would then not testify (C or B + E). North Americans and most north Europeans emerge as almost totally universalist in their approach to the problem. The proportion falls to less than 75 percent for the French and Japanese, while in Venezuela two-thirds of respondents would lie to the police to protect their friend.

Time and again in our workshops, the universalists' response is that as the seriousness of the accident increases, the obligation to help their friend decreases. They seem to be saying to themselves, "The law was broken, and the serious condition of the pedestrian underlines the importance of upholding the law." This attitude suggests that universalism is rarely used to the exclusion of particularism, rather that it forms the first principle in the process of moral reasoning. Particular consequences remind us of the need for universal laws.

Percentage of respondents opting for a universalist system rather than a particular social group
(answers C or B+E)

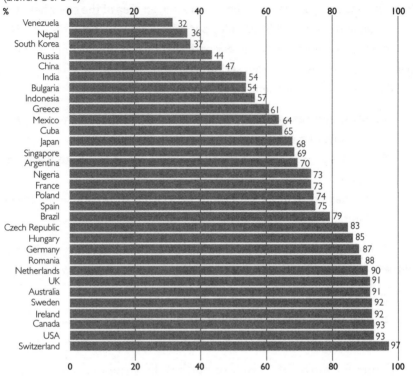

Figure 4.1. **The Car and the Pedestrian**

Particularist cultures, however, are rather more likely to support their friend as the pedestrian's injuries increase. They seem to reason, "My friend needs my help more than ever now that he is in serious trouble with the law." Universalists would regard such an attitude as corrupt. What if we all started to lie on behalf of those close to us? Society would fall apart. There is merit to this argument, but particularism, which is based on a logic of the heart and human friendship, may also be the chief reason that citizens would not break laws in the first place. Do you love your children or present them with a copy of the civil code? And what if the law becomes a weapon in the hands of a corrupt elite? You can choose what you call corruption.

In a workshop we were giving some time ago, we presented this dilemma. There was one British woman, Fiona, among the group of

French participants. Fiona started the discussion of the dilemma by asking about the condition of the pedestrian. Without that information, she said, it would be impossible to answer the question. When the group asked her why this information was so indispensable, Dominique, an employee of a French airline, interjected: "Naturally, it is because if the pedestrian is very seriously injured or even dead, then my friend has the absolute right to expect my support. Otherwise, I would not be so sure." Fiona, slightly irritated but laughing, said, "That's amazing. For me it is absolutely the other way around."

This illustration shows that we "anchor" our response in one of the two principles. All nations might agree that universals and particulars should ideally be resolved—that is, that all exceptional cases be judged by more humane rules. What differs is their starting points.

As Figure 4.1 shows, universalists are more common in Protestant cultures, where the congregation relates to God by obedience to his written laws. There are no human intermediaries between God and his adherents, no one with the discretion to hear particular confessions, forgive sins, or make special allowances. Predominantly Catholic cultures retained these features of religion, which are more relational and particularist. People can break commandments and still find compassion for their unique circumstances. God for the Catholics is like them, moreover: God will probably understand that you were lying for your friend, particularly one who had the bad luck to have the stupid pedestrian crossing in front of his car.

Countries with strongly universalist cultures try to use the courts to mediate conflicts. An American book on automobile insurance is called *Hit Me, I Need the Money*. Indeed, the US, credited with being the most litigious society on earth, has considerably more lawyers per capita than relatively particularist Japan. The more universal the country, the greater the need for an institution to protect the truth. (Incidentally, there is a strong correlation between universalism and expenditure per capita on pet food. This is not the same as pet ownership; particularist France has more dogs than universalist Germany, but French dogs are integrated into the family and eat leftovers.)

However, countries may be more or less universalist depending on what the rules are *about*. French and Italian managers, who were particularist on the traffic accident, believe that when writing on a subject as important as food, you have a universal obligation to adhere to the truth. Consider the following scenario, also described by Stouffer and Toby.

You are a newspaper journalist who writes a weekly review of new restaurants. A close friend of yours has sunk all her savings in a new restaurant. You have eaten there, and you really think the restaurant is no good.

What right does your friend have to expect you to go easy on her restaurant in your review?

- **A.** She has a definite right as a friend to expect me to go easy on her restaurant in my review.
- **B.** She has some right as a friend to expect me to do this for her.
- **C.** She has no right as a friend to expect me to do this for her.

Would you go easy on her restaurant in your review given your obligations to your readers and your obligation to your friend?

- **D.** Yes.
- **E.** No.

In this second example, a universalist's view is that as a journalist, you are writing for everyone, the universe of readers, not for your friend. Your obligation is to be "truthful and unbiased." In some cultures, then, it seems more important to universalize good taste than legal procedure. For them it is easier to leave the pedestrian in trouble than to judge the quality of food wrongly. (See Figure 4.2.)

A third dilemma we use to explore this dimension has to do with the rule of confidentiality concerning the secret deliberations of a business. (See Figure 4.3.)

You are a doctor for an insurance company. You examine a close friend who needs more insurance. You find he is in pretty good shape, but you are doubtful on one or two minor points that are difficult to diagnose.

Percentage of respondents who would not write a false review or who give no right to the friend to expect to be helped (answers C or B+E)

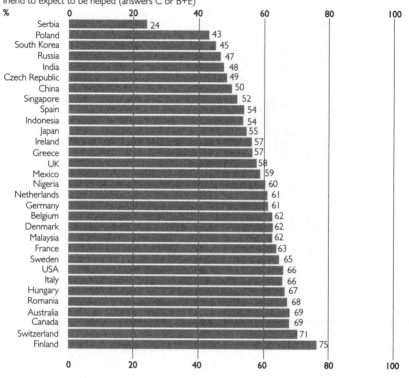

Figure 4.2. **The Bad Restaurant**

What right does your friend have to expect you to tone down your doubts in his favor?

- **A.** My friend has a definite right as a friend to expect me to tone down my doubts in his favor.
- **B.** He has some right as a friend to expect me to tone down my doubts in his favor.
- **C.** He has no right as a friend to expect me to tone down my doubts in his favor.

Would you help your friend in view of the obligations you feel toward your insurance company and your friend?

- **D.** Yes.
- **E.** No.

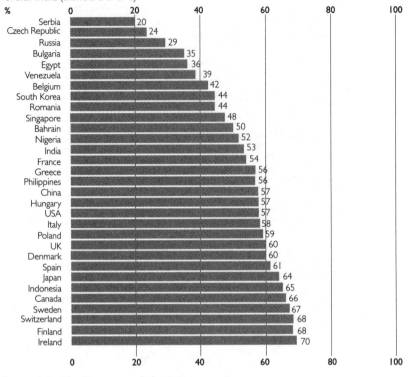

Figure 4.3. **The Doctor and the Insurance Company**

There are some differences that merit attention here between the scores on this dilemma and the previous two. The Japanese and Indonesians, especially, jump from the situational ethics they showed previously to a strongly universalistic stance on corporate confidentiality. It's altogether possible that this occurs because the situation is broader than a particular friend; at stake here is loyalty to a group or corporation versus loyalty to an individual outside that group.

This dilemma may also be presenting issues of communitarianism versus individualism, to be considered in Chapter 5. Because these dimensions are related as well as relational, we must be careful in interpreting the meaning that different national groups give them.

Universalism Versus Particularism in International Business

When companies go global, there is an almost inevitable move toward universalist ways of thinking. After all, products and services are being offered to a wider and wider universe of people. Their willingness to buy is "proof" of a universal appeal. It follows that the ways of producing the product, managing those who make it, and distributing it to customers should also be universalized. Let us consider the following examples of areas where the universalist-versus-particularist dilemma shows up:

- The contract
- Timing a business trip
- The role of the head office
- Job evaluations and rewards

The Contract

Weighty contracts are a way of life in universalist cultures. A contract serves to record an agreement on principle and codifies what the respective parties have promised to do. It also implies consent to the agreement and provides recourse if either party does not keep to its side of the deal. Introducing lawyers into the process of negotiation puts the parties on notice that any breach could be costly and that promises made initially must be kept, even if they prove inconvenient.

How might a legal contract be perceived by a more particularist business partner? There is another reason why people tend to keep their promises: they have a personal relationship with their customers, whom they hold in particular regard. If you introduce contracts with strict requirements and penalty clauses, the implied message is that one party would cheat the other if not legally restrained from doing so. Those who feel they are not trusted may accordingly behave in untrustworthy ways. Alternatively they may terminate their relationship with a universalist business partner because that partner's precautions offend them and the contract terms are too rigid to allow a good working relationship to evolve.

One serious pitfall for universalist cultures in doing business with more particularist ones is that the importance of the relationship is often ignored. The contract will be seen as definitive by the universalist, but only as a rough guideline or approximation by the particularist. The latter will want to make the contract as vague as possible and may object to clauses that are restrictive. This stance is not necessarily a sign of impending subterfuge; it may well be a preference for mutual accommodation. Given the rise of Chinese, Japanese, and Indian economic power, the automatic superiority of the universalist position can no longer be assumed. Good customer relationships and good employee relationships may involve doing *more* than the contract requires. Moreover, relationships have a flexibility and durability that contracts often lack. Asian, Arab, and Latin businesspeople may expect contracts to be qualified where circumstances have changed.

In a 10-year contract between a Canadian producer of ball bearings and an Arabic machine manufacturer, a minimum annual quantity of ball bearings was agreed on. After about six years the orders from the Middle East stopped coming in. The Canadians' first reaction was, "This is illegal."

A visit to the customer only increased their confusion. The contract had apparently been canceled unilaterally by the Arabs, because the Canadian contract-signer had left the company. The so-called universally applicable law was not considered relevant anymore in the eyes of the Arabs. What could the Canadians say against this logic, especially when they discovered that the ball bearings were never even used? It turned out that the product was purchased solely out of the particular loyalty to the Canadian contract-signer, not because of a felt legal obligation.

Timing a Business Trip

A universalist businessperson—a North American, British, Dutch, German, or Scandinavian—is wise to take much longer than usual when visiting a particularist culture. Particularists get suspicious when hurried. At least twice the time normally necessary to establish a contractual agreement is necessary to forge what has to be a closer relationship. It is important to create a sound relational and trustworthy basis that equates the quality of the product with the quality of the personal relationship. Rolls-Royce gave Toyota a deadline to make an acquisition offer, and Toyota promptly withdrew. Something similar happened in negotiations between Samsung and Fokker, when after a Dutch deadline Samsung pulled out.

This process takes a considerable amount of time, but for particularists, the time taken to grow close to your partner is saved in the avoidance of trouble in the future. If you are not willing to take time now, the relationship is unlikely to survive vicissitudes.

The Role of the Head Office

In Western countries that are high in universalism, the head office tends to hold the keys to global marketing, global production, and global human-resource management. Our own experience, though, is that, within more particularist national cultures, the writ of the head office fails to shape local ways of operating. Different groups develop their own local standards, which become the basis of their solidarity and resistance to centralized edicts. Stratified boundaries are created by the national subsidiary between itself and the head office, and differentiation is deliberately sought.

Particularist groups seek gratification through relationships, especially relationships to the leader. Generally, the more particularist, the greater the commitment between employer and employee. The employer in these cultures strives to provide a broad array of satisfactions to employees: security, money, social standing, goodwill, and socioemotional support. Relationships are typically close and long lasting. Job turnover is low, and commitments to the labor force are long term. The local chief wishes all this to redound to his or her own credit, not that of the foreign owner. Research done in an American bank with branches in Mexico found Mexican staff to be far more particularist, with a tendency to distance themselves as far as possible from the head office in the US in order to minimize universalist pressures.[3]

What frequently occurs is that foreign-based subsidiaries will *pretend* to comply with head office directives, which leads to a kind of ritualistic "corporate rain dance." They will go through the motions so long as they are under scrutiny, but they do not believe that rain will result. As soon as the attention of the head office is diverted to other matters, normal life proceeds.

Job Evaluations and Rewards

Head office policies in the human-resource area often lay down systems that all expatriate managers are required to apply locally. The logic of this universal system—that all jobs should be described, all candidates should have their qualifications compared with these descriptions, and all job occupants should have their performance evaluated against what their contracts specified they would do—is surely "beyond culture." It seems a demonstrably fair and universal way of managing. This general system sprang up in the postwar years when companies, especially American multinationals, saw rapid growth. Thousands of employees within the US needed fair methods of appraisal and promotion, and before long this situation spread to the rest of the developed world. Labor unions often gave their support to these methods, seeing them as protection from arbitrary discipline or antiunion activity. A worker could be fired only for demonstrable failure to do a defined piece of work. In such regulations there was, beyond doubt, protection for many employees. Managers had to behave consistently. They could not take harsh steps in one instance and be lenient in another.

A system designed by Colonel Hay of the American army, called the Hay job evaluation system, is now widely used in businesses to evaluate what base salaries should be for the performance of various functions. Each function and job within it is scored with the help of the employee, his or her direct superior, and a panel that includes people doing similar jobs elsewhere. This process helps to maintain internal consistency and facilitates transfers between subsidiaries throughout a company's network without changes in salary or training. Minor concessions are usually made to local conditions by way of a cost-of-living allowance, but otherwise uniformity is maintained. All this sounds highly plausible. All such procedures may appear to be working with the paperwork duly completed. But what in fact happens in more particularist societies?

The following incident occurred in a multinational oil company. During a presentation to a group of Venezuelan managers, representatives from the head office were explaining new developments in the Hay function assessment system for R&D functions. They pointed out that the function would be less clearly separated from the function holder and that there would now be "benchmarks" determining the level of the function. The Venezuelans showed the pro forma response by concluding the presentation with a loud round of applause.

After a satisfying lunch and a third glass of wine, a few of the Venezuelan managers became more talkative. They asked whether the visiting group would be interested in hearing about the Venezuelan way of assessing functions in the laboratory. "Would you like to hear what we say we do or what we really do?" they asked. Already aware of what their "party line" was, the head office representatives asked to hear what really went on.

Reality turned out to be much simpler than the complex system. Each year, the Venezuelans explained, the six-person management team got together after the assessment round. In the meeting this group decided on the most appropriate candidates for promotion. The employees selected were then rushed to the HR department in order to set up the function description required by the head office. HR had already been informed of what the score was to be for the particular functions.

This is a notable example of reverse causality. Instead of the job description and evaluation "choosing" the person that best filled the position, the person was first informally and intuitively chosen and then wrote his or her own description and evaluation.

This scenario raises the question of whether a process in which universals guide particulars is necessarily better than a process in which particular people guide and choose their universals. As the local Venezuelan boss put it, "Who decides on the promotion of *my* subordinates,

Colonel Hay or me?" The same kind of question and circularity will arise when we consider performance and achievement in Chapter 8.

Reconciling Universalism and Particularism

In all the seven cultural dichotomies we have identified, of which universalism versus particularism is the first, the two extremes can always in a sense be found in the same person. The two horns of the dilemma are very close to each other, as is easy to realize if, as a universalist, you substitute your father or daughter for the friend who is driving the car. In fruitful cross-cultural encounters both sides avoid pathological excesses. Figure 4.4, whose methodology is explained in Chapter 13, illustrates this concept.

This figure shows the beginnings of a *vicious* circle. If you follow the logic of the flow, you see that the universalist approach at best helps us to avoid the pathologies of particularism taken too far; the particularist position needs to be adopted to avoid the pathologies of

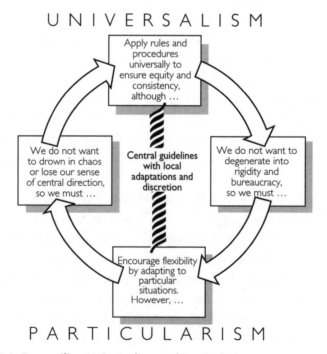

Figure 4.4. **Reconciling Universalism and Particularism**

universalism taken too far. In fact, the universalist position is encouraging opposition from the particularist position.

When the two are working effectively together, we talk about a *virtuous* circle. Here cross-cultural encounters can synergize and come out on a level much higher than what any of the cultures could achieve independently.

In one case the resolution brought a company to a higher level. A group of European microprocessor salespeople were complaining that they lost a large part of their potential market because American headquarters could not produce the adaptations that various European clients were requesting. When we conducted interviews prior to a workshop at the headquarters in California, the Americans said that they couldn't understand why their European colleagues could not grasp the loss of economies of scale and the gross undercapacity that their chips facilities experienced. It is obviously not enough simply to map the problematic nature of a dilemma as two horns, one opposing the other, as in Figure 4.5.

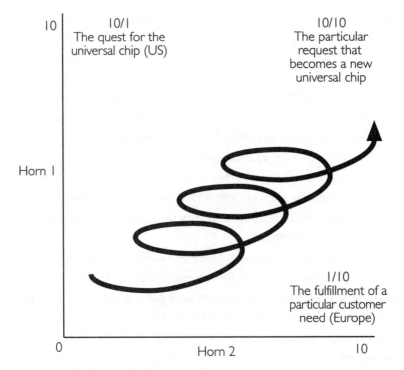

Figure 4.5. **A Virtuous Circle**

When approaching this dilemma between the two extremes, we may seek a compromise. However, a compromise is frequently worse than just choosing between one of the two horns. It could mean, for example, going for two chips instead of one universal chip. By doing this, you would lose both economies of scale and most of your clients. The best approach is to frame the dilemmas as two axes, X and Y, and then try to find a 10/10 solution. This means that the drive for the universal chip needs to be connected in some way to the process of fulfilling the particular need in Europe.

In one of our workshops the Americans proposed to invite the R&D people from some of their clients to codevelop the next (universal) chip. The Europeans, in turn, thought it would be preferable to get American R&D people over to work with local R&D people in Europe. The principle was the same, but the starting point was different. The Americans preferred to start from a universal position and have some input from the particular needs of the client. The Europeans felt more at home with first testing the value of their particular need by some universal Californian rules. Nevertheless, both were aiming for the creation of a unique, particular, customized microprocessor that might lead to a renewed spate of "universal sales."

THE CASE OF THE PHARMACEUTICAL JOINT VENTURE

Mr. Geddy Teok, an American-Chinese (second generation) employee of a large New Jersey pharmaceutical firm, was based in Tokyo. His main aim was to get a major joint venture going with one of the largest Japanese pharmaceutical manufacturers. After four years of negotiating, the supreme moment had come for signing contracts. Obviously the lawyers from HQ in New Jersey were well prepared, and they sent the contract to Geddy one week before the "ceremony."

After four years of Japanese experience, Geddy was dumbfounded when he received the document from the US. He told us at the time, "I could not even count the number of pages. There were just too many. But I remember the number of inches it measured when I laid it on the table. I would guess that with every inch, one of the Japanese would leave the room in despair. I hope they will come with a group of ten; then at least I will keep one person to talk to. The Japanese will sign contracts, but you should not take it too far."

Geddy Teok decided to call HQ and ask for some help. The legal department said that the relationship was so complex that the contract needed to cover many possible instances. Moreover, a consultancy firm that regularly advised the department said that Asians in general and Japanese in particular had a reputation of being loose in defining what was developed by them and what came from the US: "It's better to have some pain now and be clear in the terms of our relationship, than to run into problems later because of miscommunication. If they sign it, at least they show they are serious."

Geddy was in despair, but he had only a day to decide what to do. The meeting was tomorrow. Should he perhaps call the Japanese CEO, with whom he had built a solid relationship? Or should he just go for it? Geddy framed his dilemma clearly to us: "Whatever I do, it would hurt my career. If I insist on the Japanese partners signing the contract, they will see it as proof of how little trust has been developed over the years of negotiation. This might mean a postponement of the discussions and, in the worst case, the end of the deal. If I reduce the contract to a couple of pages and present it as a 'letter of intent,' HQ in general and, even worse, the whole legal department will jump on me, jeopardizing my career."

If you were Geddy, what would you do?

Being aware of the cultural dynamics does not really help you (bear in mind that if you were not aware of the cultural differences between the Japanese and the Americans, your situation would be even worse). It is not enough to say that the Americans tend to be universalist, so they believe the Japanese should sign the contract. Nor does it suffice to say that the Japanese tend to be particularist in their approach. Transcultural effectiveness is not measured only by the degree to which you are able to grasp the opposite value. It is measured by your competence in reconciling the dilemmas—that is, the degree to which you are able to make both values work together, as in the microprocessor case.

It might be advisable for Geddy to ask what the logic of the typical universalist would be in wanting to have the contract signed. In actuality, the Americans' position is: "Our trust in the other party is not sufficient, so we need the backing of a binding contract." For the Japanese, who do frequently sign contracts, the logic would be: "I'll sign the contract only if I have trust in the other party and that party sees this as a sign of respect for our relationship. Where the relationship is good enough, we can easily change the details of the contract later—for example, if the particular circumstances have changed."

We would advise Geddy to do the following. From the outset, make culture a point of discussion and tell the Japanese counterpart what kind of problem you are facing: "Our American headquarters have sent me a 1,100-page contract. Obviously this is normal practice in the US, but it was not meant to insult you." By doing this, you are sharing the dilemma. Try to establish and respect the Japanese logic by asking, "What would you do in my case?"

The actual Japanese response was another question: "How long would you stay here, Mr. Teok?" Geddy's answer was honest and brilliant at the same time: "Until the job is done, Mr. Samamoto." "In that case I'll sign the contract," replied the Japanese.

Test Yourself

In order to measure the degree to which individuals and cultures tend to reconcile, we have developed a series of questions that measure not only the degree to which respondents identify with one of the opposing values but also their tendency toward reconciliation. We are currently testing the hypothesis that the creation of wealth is highly correlated with people's capacity to reconcile. In the first dimension the issues would be the following:

Six months after the ABC mining company had signed a long-term contract with a foreign buyer to buy bauxite in 10 annual installments, the world price of bauxite collapsed. Instead of paying $4 a ton below world market price, the buyer now faced the prospect of paying $3 above.

The buyer faxed ABC to say it wished to renegotiate the contract. The final words of the fax read: "You cannot expect us as your new partner to carry alone the now ruinous expense of these contract terms."

ABC negotiators had a heated discussion about this situation. Several views were offered:

1. A contract is a contract. It means precisely what its terms say. If the world price had risen, we would not be crying; nor should they. What partnership are they talking about? We had a deal. We bargained. We won. End of story.
2. A contract symbolizes the underlying relationship. It is an honest statement of original intent. Where circumstances transform the mutual spirit of that contract, terms must be renegotiated to preserve the relationship.
3. A contract symbolizes the underlying relationship. It is an honest statement of original intent. But such rigid terms are too brittle to withstand turbulent environments. Only tacit forms of mutuality have the flexibility to survive.
4. A contract is a contract. It means precisely what its terms say. If the world price had risen, we would not be crying; nor should they. We would, however, consider a second contract whose terms would help offset their losses.

Allocate 1 to the approach you prefer and 2 to your second choice. Then, indicate similarly (with another 1 and 2) what you believe would be favored by your closest colleagues at work.

The problem that this simple case study illustrates is common to all cultures. All cultures recognize the tension from this and similar scenarios that we have expressed as a dilemma. Where cultures differ is in how they interpret (i.e., give meaning to) this problem and the direction from which they would approach a reconciled solution. Universalists will view the problem from option 1 if they reject the opportunity to connect their viewpoint with the particularist. Particularists will view the problem from option 2 if they reject the opportunity to connect their viewpoint with the universalist.

On the other hand, if universalists opt for 4, they start to view the problem from their own perspective of a universalist but seek to accommodate the opposite viewpoint of the particularist, leading to a reconciliation between the cultural differences. And similarly for the particularists who approach a reconciliation from their own perspective with option 3.

Our research has generated evidence (through triangulation) that leaders and managers who choose 3 and 4 sustain improved bottom-line business performance. (See Appendix A.)

Finally we should return to Mr. Johnson of MCC.

- What do you think will happen when he tries to introduce pay-for-performance worldwide, especially in particularistic cultures?
- Do you believe that bonuses of 30 percent, 60 percent, and 100 percent over salary, taken from the salaries of other employees, will be deemed fair?
- Will high performers be encouraged or discouraged in their work by those whose salaries have been cut in order to pay them?
- Will local management cooperate wholeheartedly in this change or find ways of getting around it?
- Does local management have it in its power to organize sales territories so that it can choose who performs well for particular areas?

The following tables show practical tips for doing business in universalist and particularist cultures.

RECOGNIZING THE DIFFERENCES

UNIVERSALIST	PARTICULARIST
Focus is more on rules than on relationships.	Focus is more on relationships than on rules.
Legal contracts are readily drawn up.	Legal contracts are readily modified.
A trustworthy person is one who honors his or her word or contract.	A trustworthy person is one who honors changing mutualities.
There is only one truth or reality, that which has been agreed to.	There are several perspectives on reality relative to each participant.
A deal is a deal.	Relationships evolve.

TIPS FOR DOING BUSINESS WITH . . .

UNIVERSALISTS *(FOR PARTICULARISTS)*	PARTICULARISTS *(FOR UNIVERSALISTS)*
Be prepared for "rational," "professional" arguments and presentations that push for your acquiescence.	Be prepared for personal "meandering" or "irrelevancies" that do not seem to be going anywhere.
Do not take impersonal, "get down to business" attitudes as rude.	Do not take personal, "get to know you" attitudes as small talk.
Carefully prepare the legal ground with a lawyer if in doubt.	Carefully consider the personal implications of your legal "safeguards."

WHEN MANAGING AND BEING MANAGED

UNIVERSALISTS	PARTICULARISTS
Strive for consistency and uniform procedures.	Build informal networks and create private understandings.
Institute formal ways of changing the way business is conducted.	Try to alter informally accustomed patterns of activity.
Modify the system so that the system will modify you.	Modify relations with you so that you will modify the system.
Signal changes publicly.	Pull levers privately.
Seek fairness by treating all like cases in the same way.	Seek fairness by treating all cases on their special merits.

Notes

1. S. A. Stouffer and J. Toby, "Role Conflict and Personality," *American Journal of Sociology*, LUI-5 (1951): 395–406.
2. As explained in Chapter 1, charts such as this one reflect responses from representative samples in major countries to our basic cultural instruments and are presented to illustrate the concepts being discussed based on our earlier cultural data. They serve to illustrate what we might describe as the underlying cultural norms of a country relevant to the development of business and management styles prior to the boom in globalization over the last 20 years. It is the rank order, rather than absolute scores, that

is relevant at this stage of discussion. For details of more recent data, cultural changes, and other countries see www.ridingthe wavesofculture.com.

3. L. A. Zurcher, A. Meadows, and S. L. Zurcher, "Value Orientations, Role Conflict, and Alienation from Work: A Cross-Cultural Study," *American Sociological Review*, no. 30 (1965): 539–48.

5

The Group and the Individual

THE CONFLICT between what each of us wants as an individual and the interests of the group to which we belong is the second of the five dimensions covering how people relate to other people. Do we relate to others by discovering what each one of us individually wants and then trying to negotiate the differences, or do we place ahead of this some shared concept of the public and collective good?

Individualism has been described by Parsons and Shils as "a prime orientation to the self," and communitarianism as "a prime orientation to common goals and objectives."[1] Just as with our first dimension, cultures do typically vary in putting one or the other of these approaches first in their thinking processes, although both may be included in their reasoning. The 80,000 managers who have answered the following question show this to be so, although the division here is not quite so sharp as for the universal-versus-particular example.[2]

Two people were discussing ways in which individuals could improve the quality of life.

   A. One said: "It is obvious that if individuals have as much freedom as possible and the maximum opportunity to develop themselves, the quality of their life will improve as a result."

B. The other said: "If individuals are continuously taking care of their fellow human beings, the quality of life will improve for everyone, even if it obstructs individual freedom and individual development."

Which of the two ways of reasoning do you think is usually best, A or B?

As Figure 5.1 shows, the highest-scoring individualists are the Israelis, Romanians, Nigerians, and Canadians, closely followed by the Americans, Czechs, and Danish, all more than 65 percent in favor of A. Some of the lowest-scoring Europeans are the French, at 41 percent. This low score may come as a surprise, but remember that the French all take vacations in August, on the same date. They join the

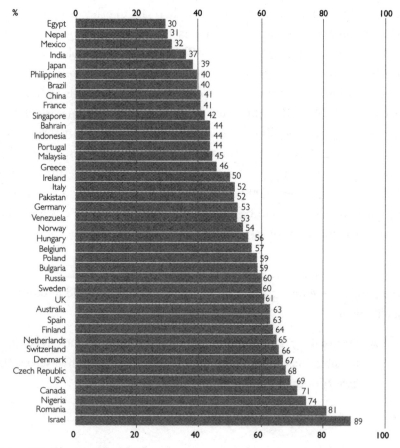

Figure 5.1. **The Quality of Life**

Club Méditerranée in order to be together. For the French, the community is France and the family. They become individualists in other social encounters. That the Japanese are not significantly more group oriented in their answers to this question than the French is particularly arresting; note also that the Chinese score as more individualist, though only slightly, than the Indians.

Concepts of Individualism and Communitarianism

Individualism is often regarded as characteristic of a modernizing society, while communitarianism calls to mind both more traditional societies and the failure of the Communist experiment. We shall see, though, that the success of growth in Asia (especially China, Hong Kong, Singapore, South Korea, and Taiwan) raises serious questions about both the success and the inevitability of individualism.

As in the case of universalism and particularism, it is probably more accurate to say that these dimensions are complementary, not opposing, preferences. They can be effectively reconciled by an integrative process—a universalism that learns its limitations from particular instances, for example—and by the individual's voluntarily addressing the needs of the larger group.

International management is seriously affected by individualist-versus-communitarian preferences within various countries. Negotiations, decision making, and motivation are the most crucial areas. Practices such as promotion for recognized achievements and pay-for-performance, for example, assume that individuals seek to be distinguished within the group and that their colleagues approve of this happening. They also rest on the assumption that the contribution of any one member to a common task is easily distinguishable and that no serious problems arise from singling him or her out for praise. None of this may, in fact, be true in more communitarian cultures.

Most of our received wisdom on this subject derives from the individualistic West, especially from theorists writing in English. The capital letter *I* is one of the most frequently used capitals in the English language. So the idea that rising individualism is part of the rise of civilization itself needs to be treated as a cultural belief rather than a fact beyond dispute. Clearly, however, it took many centuries for the individual to emerge from the surrounding community. It is generally believed that the essence of the relationship between the individual and society, at least in the West, has changed considerably since the Renaissance. In earlier societies individuals were defined primarily in terms of their surrounding community: the family, the clan, the tribe, the city-state, or the feudal group.

Individualism was much in the fore during the periods of intense innovation such as the Renaissance, the Age of Exploration, the Netherlands' Golden Age, the French Enlightenment, and the industrial revolutions of Britain and the US. A whole range of causes and effects has been offered to explain this association. Nowadays, access to the Internet offers both individual control and communities through social networking.

Individualism and Religion

There is considerable evidence that the divide between individualism and communitarianism follows the Protestant-Catholic religious divide. Calvinists had contracts or covenants with God and with one another, for which they were personally responsible. Each Puritan worshipper approached God as a separate being, seeking justification through works. Roman Catholics, for their part, have always approached God as a community of the faithful. On this point, research has found that Catholics score higher on group choices and Protestants significantly lower. Geert Hofstede's research confirms this tendency[3]—as do our own findings that Latin Catholic cultures, along with Asian cultures of the Pacific Rim, score lower on individualism than the Protestant West: for instance, the UK, Scandinavia (as a rule), the Netherlands, Germany, the US, and Canada.

Individualism and Politics

Individualism has been adopted or opposed by different political factions in the history of countries, and the strength of that ethic today depends to a large extent on the fortunes of its advocates. It triumphed in the US but is still adamantly opposed by the French Catholic tradition. Eighteenth-century France, though, was exposed to the pleasures of individualism by Voltaire and Rousseau. Later, in the 19th century, the French socialists pointed to the positive effects of individualism while outlining a new independence from traditional structures and rejecting the authority of religious, economic, and intellectual hierarchies. French business may have been affected forever by the fact that the pro-business French liberal party was in power when France fell suddenly to the Nazis in 1940. The fortunes of British individualism, at least in commerce, have been affected by Prime Minister Thatcher and her revolution.

Does Modernization Imply Individualism?

That individualism, or self-orientation, is a crucial element of modern society has been argued by Ferdinand Tönnies.[4] He suggested that in modernizing we emerge from *Gemeinschaft,* a family-based, intimate social context in which the person is not sharply differentiated, into *Gesellschaft*, a workplace of individual tasks and separated responsibilities. Adam Smith, too, saw the division of labor as individualizing.[5] Max Weber saw many meanings in individualism: dignity, autonomy (meaning "self-rule"), privacy, and the opportunity for the person to develop.[6]

We take it for granted in many Western countries that individual geniuses create businesses, invent new products, deserve high salaries, and shape our futures. But do they? How much credit is due to them and how much due to the patterns of organized employees? Why is the awarding of Nobel Prizes for science to single individuals becoming the exception? If a creative genius combines ideas, where did such ideas come from if not the community? Are we really self-made, or did our parents, teachers, families, and friends have a hand in it?

The following dilemma, which explores this dimension, shows that people from different cultures make different choices about appropriate ways of working.

Which kind of job is found more frequently in your organization?

A. Everybody works together and you do not get individual credit.
B. Everybody is allowed to work individually and individual credit can be received.

Figure 5.2 shows the results of these answers. It differs from the previous illustrations of responses to dilemmas in that nationals are much more divided in their approach. However, the range between countries remains great. Only 43 percent of the Japanese believe that a job is where one is allowed to work individually, whereas at the

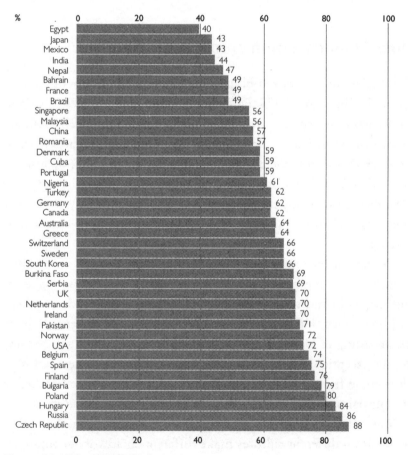

Figure 5.2. **What Kind of Job**

other extreme this is the experience of approximately 80 to 90 percent of Czechs, Poles, Bulgarians, Hungarians, and Russians. This rate of course has a strong relationship with recent political organization in the latter countries. Again we would emphasize the rank order of country samples rather than absolute percentages.

Which Community?

Individuals are either self-oriented or community oriented, though we must be careful in generalizing about which "community" a particular culture identifies with. The high internal variation of scores in our research, we believe, has to do with the numerous communities with which different cultures choose to identify. Take, for example, the following question.

A defect is discovered in an installation. It was caused by negligence of one of the members of a team. Responsibility for this mistake can be carried in various ways.

- **A.** The person causing the defect by negligence is the one responsible.
- **B.** Because he or she happens to work in a team, the responsibility should be carried by the group.

Which one of these two ways of taking responsibility do you think is usually the case in your society, A or B?

This question triggers a number of scores that are consistent with the previous question, but we can also identify a number of shifts. This variance has to do with the heterogeneity of the concept of "community" or "group." For each single society, it is necessary to determine the group with which individuals have the closest identification. They could be keen to identify with their trade union, their family, their corporation, their religion, their profession, their nation, or the state apparatus. The French tend to identify with *la France, la famille, le cadre*; the Japanese with the corporation; the former eastern bloc with the Communist Party; and Ireland with the Roman Catholic Church. Communitarian goals may be good or bad for industry depending on the community concerned, its attitude, and its relevance to business development.

Figure 5.3 shows that the impact of Communist organization on Russian and eastern European managers has been extremely limited. They, along with Cuba, score highest on the individual responsibility assumption. Americans are just above the middle of the range at 54 percent, slightly below several European countries. Japan scores at 32 percent individualist, while Indonesia takes the communitarian crown with 16 percent. The approach to the situation will of course differ in

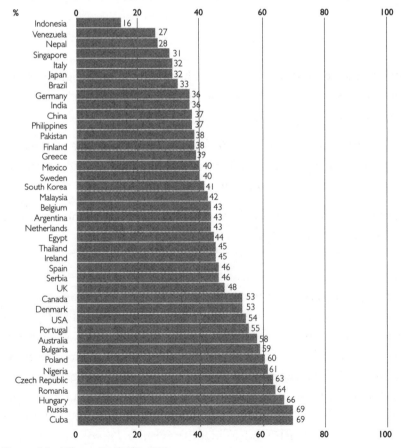

Figure 5.3. Whose Fault Was It?

relation to these groups they identify with; if Americans are criticized, there is a good chance that Jack will put an elbow into Pete's stomach, while asking whose rotten idea it was, whereas the Italians will walk out as having suffered a group insult, regardless of the fact that it was Giorgio who did it.

Is Individualism a Corporate Requirement?

While the French experience individualism more negatively, the more optimistic philosophy of Germany sees, in the words of Simmel, "an organic unity of individual and society."[7] The US, with its vast acreage available to migrating individuals, is often seen as the world's major exponent of individualism and correspondingly scores highest, or nearly so, on most of our research instruments. Tocqueville, the 19th-century French aristocrat, described Americans as exhibiting "a strong confidence in self, or reliance upon one's own exertion and resources." The "Commission of National Goals" reporting to President Eisenhower claimed that the possibility of individual self-realization was the central goal of American civilization.

Yet there were and are dissenting voices on the usefulness of individualism even in the US. The Harvard sociologist Daniel Bell accused consumerist-type individualism, what he terms modernism, of weakening America's industrial infrastructure.[8] As the information society develops, those with a communitarian ethos disseminate information faster. Information is shareable in a way physical products are not. Bell and Nelson saw a shift from "tribal brotherhood," which excludes individuality, to "universal otherhood," which includes it while still focusing on superordinate group goals.[9]

A visionary call for the integration of individualism and communitarianism came from Émile Durkheim, the 19th-century French sociologist. He saw communitarianism taking both primitive and more modern forms. In its primitive form the society has a communitarian conscience from which none dare deviate. The individual is dominated by the community. Durkheim called this mechanical solidarity, and he saw it as losing ground because industry requires a division of labor, which mechanical solidarity is slow to accommodate. This view would help explain the early economic success of individualist (and Protestant) nations.

But Durkheim also saw a later, more sophisticated form of voluntary integration among sovereign beings, which he called organic solidarity. The extension of the division of labor would cause the individual to share fewer and fewer characteristics with other individuals in the same society and would call for a new form of social integration. This new form involved biological-type integration as found in developing organisms, which are both differentiated and integrated. In 1965 Paul Lawrence and Jay Lorsch found that highly creative plastics companies prospering in turbulent environments were both more highly differentiated and more highly integrated.[10] It was a vindication of the model of organic growth, and it pointed to an increasingly necessary synthesis of individualism and communitarianism in increasingly complex, differentiated, and interdependent societies. We see the issue as essentially circular, with two "starting points." (See Figure 5.4.) It is a complex of events that reinforces itself through a feedback loop. A

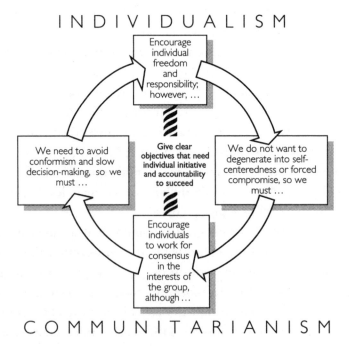

Figure 5.4. Reconciling Individualism and Communitarianism

virtuous circle has favorable results, and a vicious circle has detrimental results. A virtuous circle can transform into a vicious circle if eventual negative feedback is ignored.

We all go through these cycles, but we start from different points and conceive of the points as either means or ends, depending on the situation. The individualist culture sees the individual as "the end" and improvements to communal arrangements as the means to achieve it. The communitarian culture sees the group as its end and improvements to individual capacities as a means to that end. Yet if the relationship is truly circular, the decision to label one element as an end and another as a means is arbitrary. By definition, circles never end. Every "end" is also the means to another goal.

This is closer to our own conviction that individualism finds its fulfillment in service to the group, while group goals are of demonstrable value to individuals only if those individuals are consulted and participate in the process of developing them. The reconciliation is not easy, but it's possible.

Every parent knows this intuitively. Are you raising your child to become independent at the age of 18, or do you try to develop the child to become a good family member? We all know that the answer to both is "yes." Parents around the world try to develop a child into a self-supporting person who will choose to become a good family member. Here again we find the essence of reconciliation. One value increases the quality of the seemingly opposing one.

Individualism Versus Communitarianism in International Business

What are the practical issues raised by differences in degrees of individualism or communitarianism? Consider our ongoing case of MCC and the luckless Mr. Johnson.

During a meeting in Milan, Mr. Johnson presented ideas for the payment scheme to motivate the sales force. He became annoyed at the way these meetings were always run and decided to introduce guidelines on how all future meetings should be conducted. He did not like the Singaporean and African representatives always turning up in groups. They should, he said, confine themselves to one representative only, please. And could Mr. Sin from Singapore make sure that his boss was always represented by the same person and not different people on each occasion?

These suggestions were not very popular among some of the managers. Mr. Sin, Mr. Nuere from Nigeria, and Mr. Calamier from France wanted to know the reasons for these comments. Mr. Sin asked why, since different issues were on the agenda, they should not have different representatives who were knowledgeable about the various items. The discussion was going nowhere, and after an hour had passed, Mr. Johnson suggested that the issue be put to a vote, confident that most of his European managers would back him.

Unfortunately, this suggestion, too, proved controversial. Mr. Calamier threw up his hands and said he was "shocked that on such a sensitive and important issue" Mr. Johnson would "seek to impose this decision on a minority." He said there really should be a consensus on this matter even if it took another hour. Mr. Sin agreed that "voting should be saved for trivial questions." Johnson looked to the German and Scandinavian representatives for support, but to his consternation they agreed that consensus should be given more of a chance. He was too frustrated to respond to the Dutch manager's suggestion that they vote on whether to vote. Finally, the Nigerians recommended that at the very least a discussion and/or voting should be postponed until the next meeting. How else were those present supposed to solicit the views of their colleagues in their home offices? Wearily, Mr. Johnson agreed. Further discussions about the reward system would have to wait too.

Representation

It should be evident from the preceding passage that communitarian cultures prefer plural representation. The Singaporeans, Nigerians, and French seek negotiating groups, which are microcosms of the interests of their entire national subsidiaries. In the face of unexpected demands, communitarians will wish to confer with those back home. Rarely does a single Japanese go to an important negotiation. Meanwhile, to Anglo-Saxons a single representative voting his or her private conscience on behalf of constituents is the foundation stone of parliamentary democracy. To more communitarian cultures, those at the meeting are delegates, bound by the wishes of those who sent them.

Status

Unaccompanied people in communitarian cultures are assumed to lack status. If there is no one to take notes for you or help you carry bags, you cannot be very important. If you arrive unaccompanied in Thailand, for example, people may seriously underestimate your status and power at home.

Translators

In Anglo-Saxon negotiations the translator is supposed to be neutral, like a black box through which words in one language enter and words in another language exit. The translator in more communitarian cultures will usually serve the national group, engaging members in lengthy asides and attempting to mediate misunderstandings arising from culture as well as language. Often he or she may be the top negotiator in the group and is an interpreter rather than a translator.

Decision Making

Communitarian decision making typically takes much longer and involves sustained efforts to win over everyone to achieve consensus. Voting down the dissenters, as often happens in English-speaking Western democracies, is not acceptable. There will usually be detailed consultations with all those concerned, and because of pressures to agree on collective goals, consensus will usually be achieved. If the group or home office is not consulted first, an initial "yes" can easily become a "no" later. The many minor objections that tend to be raised are typically practical rather than personal or principled, and the consensus may be modified in many respects. Since those consulted will usually have to implement the consensus, this latter phase of implementation typically proceeds smoothly and easily. The time "wasted" (from an individualist's perspective) is saved when the new procedures operate as envisioned. The Japanese *ringi* process, in which proposals circulate and are initialed by agreeing participants, is the most famous example of communitarian decision making, but it can lead to lengthy delays.

A Japanese company had a factory built in the south of the Netherlands. As is usual, the project was carried out with acute attention to detail. In the designing phase, though, the company discovered that it had not considered one restriction. The legal minimum height for workshops was four centimeters higher than the design. A new design, which needed extensive consultation with many people at the head office in Tokyo, took one full month per centimeter for approval.

It is far too easy for North Americans and northwest Europeans, used to individualism, to jeer at such delays. Our own procedures can err in the opposite direction. The decision-making process in individualistic cultures is usually comparatively short, with a "lonely individualist" making decisions in a few fateful seconds. While this approach may make for quicker deliberations, "one-minute managers," and so on, it will often be discovered months later that the organization has conspired to defeat decisions that the managers never liked or agreed to. Saving time in decision making is often followed by significant delays due to implementation problems.

The individualist society, with its respect for individual opinions, will frequently ask for a vote to get all noses pointing in the same direction. The drawback is that within a short time they are likely to have reverted to their original orientation. The communitarian society will intuitively refrain from voting, because the vote will not show respect to the individuals who are against the majority decision. It prefers to deliberate until consensus is reached. The final result takes longer to achieve, but it will be much more stable. In individualistic societies there is frequently disparity between decision and implementation.

Individualism, Communitarianism, and Motivation

The relationship between individual and group also plays a central role in what motivates people. Mr. Johnson believed that he and MCC knew what motivated people: extra salary rewards paid to high-performing individuals. It had seemed so obvious in the meetings back in Missouri, but now he was having doubts. After the earlier discussion, could he be sure of anything?

Mr. Johnson finally managed to compromise on the representation issue by allowing each national office to send up to three people, if desired, but no more. This decision had not been voted on. Everyone had agreed. Now he could start to tackle the introduction of pay-for-performance, bonuses, and merit pay for next year.

He started, as usual, with an overview of the situation in the US. It had been three years since the system was first introduced. In general, he explained, they could detect a link between the use of this system and computer sales, although it had to be mentioned that a similar system had failed miserably in the manufacturing department. A different type of achievement-based reward system was currently being tested. No problems were anticipated with this revised system. "In summary," Johnson said, "we are strongly convinced that we need to introduce this system worldwide."

The northwest European representatives voiced their carefully considered but positive comments. Then the Italian representative, Mr. Gialli, began describing his experience with the system. In his country, the pay-for-performance experiment did much better than he had expected during the first three months, but the following three months were disastrous. Sales were dramatically lower for the salesperson who had performed the best during the previous period. "After many discussions," he continued, "I finally discovered what was happening. The salesperson who received the bonus for the previous period felt guilty in front of the others and tried extremely hard the next quarter not to earn a bonus."

The Italian manager concluded that for the next year of this experiment, the Italian market should be divided into nine regions. All sales representatives within one region should be allowed to either allocate the bonus earned in their region to individual performers or share it equally. The blunt Dutch manager's reaction was, "I have never heard such a crazy idea."

This incident shows that there are at least two sources of motivation. People work for extrinsic money rewards or for the positive regard and support of their colleagues. In more communitarian cultures, this second source of motivation may be so strong that high performers would rather share the fruits of their efforts with colleagues than take extra money for themselves as individuals.

Western theories of motivation have individuals growing out of early, and hence primitive, social needs into an individually resplendent self-actualization at the summit of the hierarchy. Needless to say, this line of thought does not achieve resonance the world over, however sound a theory it may be for the US and northwest Europe. The Japanese notion of the highest good is harmonious relationships within and with the patterns of nature; the primary orientation is to other people and to the natural world.

Differences in Organizational Structure

In individualistic cultures organizations (from the Greek *organon*) are essentially instruments. They have been deliberately assembled and contrived in order to serve individual owners, employees, and customers. Members of organizations enter relationships because it is in their individual interests to do so. Their ties are abstract, legal ones, regulated by contract. The organization is a means to achieving what its actors want for themselves. In so far as they cooperate, it is because they have particular interests at stake. Each performs a differentiated and specialized function and receives an extrinsic reward for doing so. Authority originates in an individual's skill at performing tasks, and an individual's knowledge is used to make the organizational instrument work effectively.

In communitarian cultures the organization is not the creation or instrument of its founders so much as a social context that all members share and that gives them meaning and purpose. Organizations are often likened to a large family, community, or clan that develops and nurtures its members and may live longer than they do. The growth and prosperity of organizations are not considered bonanzas for individual shareholders or gravy trains for top managers, but are valuable ends in themselves. These considerations will be discussed in depth in Chapter 11.

Reconciling Individualism and Communitarianism

Again, Figure 5.4 represents essentially a *vicious* circle, since one value is tied to the seemingly opposing value in such a way that they avoid each other's pathologies. It is a mistake to believe that individualists do not care for communities. Individualistic Americans are joiners par excellence and have probably formed more voluntary associations than any other culture. From Mothers Against Drunk Driving to the Michigan Militia and beyond, Americans form groups readily. But here "voluntary associations" is a giveaway, because the term conveys that in the beginning was the voluntary individual and then the group was formed from such people. In communitarian Japan, by contrast, the individual alone is not regarded as a mature state. The word for a mature individual translates as "person-among-others." In the beginning is the group: how can I as an individual serve the group better? From that competence I derive my status.

It is evident that putting either the individual or the community first does not preclude a country from encompassing both values. Consider the following crucial incident.

WHO MADE A SERIOUS MISTAKE?

Jean Safari was investigating a serious error made by a Japanese worker at the Japanese subsidiary of a US multinational. A component had been inserted upside down, and the entire batch had been pulled out of production to be reworked. The cost of this event was high.

Jean asked the Japanese plant director for information about the employee who had made the error. Had she been identified? What action was being taken against her? She was amazed when the director claimed not to know. "The whole work group has accepted responsibility," he told her. "As to the specific woman responsible, they have not told me, nor did I ask. Even the floor supervisor does not know, and if he did, he would not tell me either."

But if everyone is responsible, then in effect no one is, Jean argued. They are simply protecting each other's bad work.

"This is not how we see it," she was told. The plant manager was polite but firm. "I understand that the woman concerned was so upset that she went home. She tried to resign. Two of her coworkers had to coax her back again. The group knows she was responsible, and she feels ashamed. The group is also aware that she is new and that they did not help her enough, or look out for her, or see to it that she was properly trained. This is why the whole group has apologized. I have their letter here. They are willing to apologize to you publicly."

"No, no. I don't want that," said Jean. "I want to stop it from happening again." She wondered what she should do.

Should Jean insist on knowing who the culprit was? Should the culprit be punished?

It is a fallacy to believe that because the group will not reveal who made the error, the perpetrator of that error escapes without sanction. The sanction depends on whether the group supports or opposes high quality and high productivity. If the group supports management objectives so that the community is united, those "letting the group down" will experience shame in a shame culture. There is abundant evidence that the perpetrator of this error has already experienced shame. She went home rather than face her coworkers. The issue of the extent to which other team members should have helped her learn is also something on which the team has the best information. In a Japanese context, it is best left to them.

Reconciliation has occurred. While the individualist assumption is that individuals who make a mistake should be punished for it and thereafter become better team members, communitarian logic is the reverse: through team membership we support individuals so that they become better individual workers. If a mistake is made, only the immediate group needs to know. As well as avoidance of shame, the reconciliation lies in the fact that the group has taken care of the individual's mistake, and no extra punishment is required.

Test Yourself

In order to measure the degree to which the individual and the group are reconciled, we have asked several thousand participants to answer a series of questions that have been captured in our separate dilemma database. Again, two choices represent the either-or type of answer, while two alternatives are reconciled answers. One starts with the individual and includes the group, while the other starts with the group and then reconciles the individual. What would be your choice?

Several managers were discussing whether close cooperation or fierce competition was the most salient mark of the successful enterprise. Here are four statements:

1. Competition is the supreme value of any successful economy or company. Attempts by major parties to cooperate usually end in collusion against one or more of them.
2. Competition is the supreme value of any successful economy or company because this involves serving customers better than our rivals, thereby assuring the public interest.
3. Cooperation among stakeholders is the supreme value because this shared aim makes companies fiercely competitive toward outsiders, thereby fulfilling personal interests.
4. Cooperation among stakeholders is the supreme value. Personal rivalry and competing for self-advancement are seriously disruptive of effective operations.

Allocate 1 to the approach you prefer and 2 to your second choice. Then, indicate similarly what you believe would be favored by your closest colleagues at work.

Answer 1 affirms competitive individualism and rejects communitarian cooperation, while answer 4 is the exact opposite. Answer 2 starts by affirming competitive individualism, but by connecting it to communitarian cooperation, it reconciles it into an integrity that we might call "co-opetition." Answer 3 suggests the same end result, but the spiral is now counterclockwise, from the cooperating group to the competing individual.

In Figure 5.5 the results of earlier competitions are cooperatively integrated, before a new phase of competition begins.

The following tables show practical tips for doing business in individual and communitarian cultures.

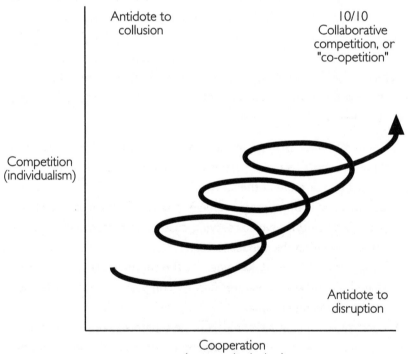

Figure 5.5. **Competition or Cooperation?**

Recognizing the Differences

INDIVIDUALISM	COMMUNITARIANISM
More frequent use of the "I" form.	More frequent use of the "we" form.
Decisions are made on the spot by representatives.	Decisions are referred back by delegate to the organization.
People ideally achieve alone and assume personal responsibility.	People ideally achieve in groups, which assume joint responsibility.
Vacations are taken in pairs, even alone.	Vacations are taken in organized groups or with the extended family.

Tips for Doing Business with . . .

INDIVIDUALISTS *(FOR COMMUNITARIANS)*	COMMUNITARIANS *(FOR INDIVIDUALISTS)*
Prepare for quick decisions and sudden offers not referred to HQ.	Show patience for time taken to consent and to consult.
A negotiator can commit those who sent him or her and is reluctant to go back on an undertaking.	A negotiator can agree only tentatively and may withdraw an undertaking after consulting with superiors.
The toughest negotiations were probably already done within the organization while preparing for the meeting. You have a tough job selling them the solution to this meeting.	The toughest negotiations are with the communitarians you face. You must somehow persuade them to cede to you points that the multiple interests in your company demand.
Conducting business alone means that this person is respected by his or her company and has its esteem.	Conducting business when surrounded by helpers means that this person has high status in his or her company.
The aim is to make a quick deal.	The aim is to build lasting relationships.

WHEN MANAGING AND BEING MANAGED

INDIVIDUALISTS	COMMUNITARIANS
Try to adjust individual needs to organizational needs.	Seek to integrate personality with authority within the group.
Introduce methods of individual incentives such as pay-for-performance, individual assessment, and managing by objectives.	Give attention to esprit de corps, morale, and cohesiveness.
Expect job turnover and mobility to be high.	Have low job turnover and mobility.
Seek out high performers, heroes, and champions for special praise.	Extol the whole group and avoid showing favoritism.
Give people the freedom to take initiative.	Hold up superordinate goals for all to meet.

Notes

1. T. Parsons and E. A. Shils, *Towards a General Theory of Action* (Cambridge, MA: Harvard University Press, 1951).
2. However, combining these responses with other questions based on similar constructs that differentiate orientation to individuals or groups does provide a reliable and statistically significant index along this cultural dimension.
3. G. Hofstede, *Culture's Consequences* (London: Sage, 1980).
4. F. Tönnies, *Community and Society*, trans. C. P. Loomis (New York: Harper & Row, 1957).
5. A. Smith, *The Wealth of Nations*. (Buffalo, NY: Prometheus Books, 1991 edition). (Originally published in 1776.)
6. M. Weber, *The Theory of Social and Economic Organization* (New York: Free Press, 1947).
7. G. Simmel, *The Sociology of Simmel*, trans. K. H. Wolff (Glencoe, IL: Free Press 1950).
8. D. Bell, *The Cultural Contradictions of Capitalism* (New York: Basic Books, 1976).
9. D. Bell and B. Nelson, *The Idea of Usury* (Chicago: University of Chicago Press, enlarged 2nd edition, 1969).
10. P. R. Lawrence and J. W. Lorsch, *Organization and Environment: Managing Differentiation and Integration* (Homewood, IL: Irwin, 1967).

6

Feelings and Relationships

IN RELATIONSHIPS between people, reason and emotion both play a role. Which of these dominates will depend on whether we are *affective*, meaning that we show our emotions, in which case we probably get an emotional response in return, or are emotionally *neutral* in our approach.

Affective Versus Neutral Cultures

Members of cultures that are affectively neutral do not telegraph their feelings but instead keep them carefully controlled and subdued. In contrast, in cultures high in affectivity people show their feelings plainly by laughing, smiling, grimacing, scowling, and gesturing; they attempt to find immediate outlets for their feelings. We should be cautious in not overinterpreting such differences. Neutral cultures are not necessarily cold or unfeeling, nor are they emotionally constipated or repressed. The amount of emotion people show is often the result of convention. In a culture in which feelings are controlled, irrepressible joy or grief will still signal loudly. In a culture where feelings are amplified, they will have to be signaled more loudly still in order to register at all. In cultures where everyone emotes, people may not find words or expressions adequate for their strongest feelings, since the words and expressions have all been used up.

A workshop exercise under this heading asks participants how they would behave if they felt upset about something at work. Would they express their feelings openly? Figure 6.1 presents the relative positions of a representative sample of countries on the extent to which exhibiting emotion is acceptable. It is least acceptable in Ethiopia and Japan, where our database shows a score of close to 80 percent

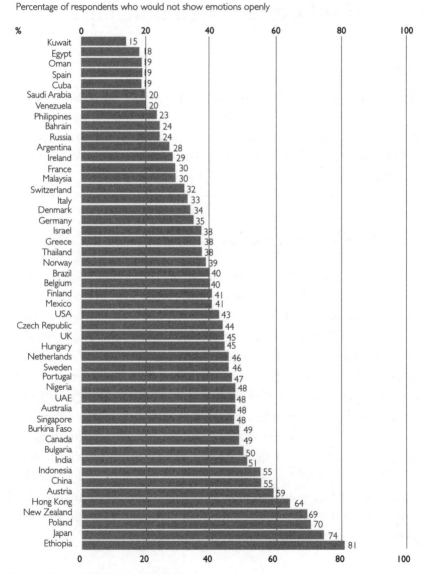

Percentage of respondents who would not show emotions openly

Country	%
Kuwait	15
Egypt	18
Oman	19
Spain	19
Cuba	19
Saudi Arabia	20
Venezuela	20
Philippines	23
Bahrain	24
Russia	24
Argentina	28
Ireland	29
France	30
Malaysia	30
Switzerland	32
Italy	33
Denmark	34
Germany	35
Israel	38
Greece	38
Thailand	38
Norway	39
Brazil	40
Belgium	40
Finland	41
Mexico	41
USA	43
Czech Republic	44
UK	45
Hungary	45
Netherlands	46
Sweden	46
Portugal	47
Nigeria	48
UAE	48
Australia	48
Singapore	48
Burkina Faso	49
Canada	49
Bulgaria	50
India	51
Indonesia	55
China	55
Austria	59
Hong Kong	64
New Zealand	69
Poland	70
Japan	74
Ethiopia	81

Figure 6.1. **Feeling Upset at Work**

on the neutral orientation. There are considerable variances among European countries, with Austria the most neutral (59 percent) and Spain, Italy, and France the least (19 percent, 33 percent, and 30 percent, respectively). You can see that Hong Kong and Japan both score much lower than Singapore or Indonesia; there is no general pattern by continent.

Typically, reason and emotion are of course combined. In expressing ourselves, we try to find confirmation of our thoughts and feelings in the response of our audience. When our own approach is highly emotional, we are seeking a *direct* emotional response: "I have the same feelings as you on this subject." When our own approach is highly neutral, we are seeking an *indirect* response: "Because I agree with your reasoning or proposition, I give you my support." On both occasions approval is being sought, but different paths are being used to this end. The indirect path gives us emotional support contingent on the success of an effort of intellect. The direct path allows our feelings about a factual proposition to show through, thereby "joining" feelings with thoughts in a different way.

Consider a scene in which the Italian office of MCC has made a proposal to allow the sales personnel to decide as a group whether they wish to have individual incentives or to share bonus payments among the whole team, while identifying the persons responsible for winning the bonus. You will recall that this was the idea the Dutch representative called "crazy" in Chapter 5.

Raising his voice, Mr. Pauli, Gialli's colleague, responded, "What do you mean, a crazy idea? We have carefully considered the pros and cons and believe that it would greatly benefit the buyer."

"Please, don't get overexcited," implored Mr. Johnson. "We need to provide solid arguments and should not get sidetracked by emotional irrelevancies."

Before the Dutch representative, Mr. Bergman, had a chance to explain why he thought it was a crazy idea, the two Italian colleagues left the room for a time-out. "This is what I call a typical Italian reaction," Mr. Bergman remarked to his colleagues. "Before I even had a chance to give my arguments as to why I think the idea is crazy, they walk out."

The other managers were squirming uncomfortably in their chairs. They did not know what to think. Mr. Johnson got up and left the room to talk to the Italians.

It is easy for Britons, North Americans, or northwest Europeans to sympathize with Johnson or Bergman about "excitable" Italians. After all, either the incentive system works or it does not. This fact will not change, however strongly we feel. It is a matter of trial and observation. According to this approach, neutrality is a means to an end. The time to get emotional is when the incentives work or fail to work, at which point either pleasure or disappointment is appropriate. In the big picture, control of our feelings is a sign of civilization, is it not?

Such explanations show that we can offer good reasons for any cultural norm. The Italians were angry because they identified emotionally with their sales team and knew intuitively that working hard for each other as well as for customers was the motivation of an excellent salesperson. They felt the same way they knew their sales force would feel about the emotional rewards for hard work. Mr. Bergman's "reasonable judgment" was not relevant to Italians. Since when is the intrinsic pleasure found in work a matter of "fact," anyway? It is deeply personal and cultural. As Pascal wrote, "The heart has its reasons which reason knows nothing of." But then, he was a Frenchman.

And what about the verdict of the Prime Court in Italy in 1996, which indicates that husbands are allowed to beat their wives if they are in a passionate mood and as long as it is done infrequently? The Italian judge did find compelling evidence that the husband had hit his wife so hard that she had to be hospitalized; however there was no "systematic and conscious brutality." The victim, Anna Mannino, was reportedly pleased with the final verdict, since she found her partner a "model husband." In fact, she had never accused him. The hospital did!

Degrees of Affectivity in Different Cultures

The amount of visible "emoting" is a major difference among cultures. We may think that a Frenchman who curses us in a traffic accident is truly enraged, close to committing violence. In reality, he may simply be getting his view of the facts in first and may expect an equal stream of vituperation from us in return. He may well be even further from violence as a result of this expression. There are norms about acceptable levels of vehemence, and these levels can be much higher in some countries than in others.

Americans, for example, tend to be on the expressive side. Perhaps this is because with so many immigrants and such a large country, they have had to break down social barriers again and again. The habit of using diminutives ("Chuck" instead of Charles, "Bob" instead of Robert), as well as "smile" buttons, welcome wagons, and the speed with which cordial and informal relationships are made, all testify to the need to resocialize in new neighborhoods several times in a lifetime.

This is a markedly different experience from life in smaller countries such as Sweden, the Netherlands, Denmark, and Norway. There it may be harder to avoid than to meet those of your generation with whom you grew up. Friendships tend to start early in life and last many years, so the need to be effusive with relative strangers is much less pronounced.

There is a tendency for those with norms of emotional neutrality to dismiss anger, delight, or intensity in the workplace as "unprofessional." Mr. Pauli at MCC has obviously "lost his cool," a judgment that assumes the desirability of a cool exterior to begin with. In fact, Pauli probably regards Bergman as emotionally dead, or as hiding his true feelings behind a mask of deceit. As we shall see in Chapter 7 when we go on to discuss how specific, as opposed to diffuse, emotions can be, there are really two issues wrapped up in the question of emotional display: Should emotion be *exhibited* in business relations? Should it be *separated* from reasoning processes lest it corrupt them?

Americans tend to *exhibit emotion, yet separate it* from "objective" and "rational" decisions. Italians and south European nations in general tend to *exhibit and not separate.* Dutch and Swedes tend *not to exhibit and to separate.* Once again, there is nothing "good" or "bad" about these differences. You can argue that emotions held in check will twist your judgments despite all efforts to be "rational." Or you can argue that pouring forth emotions makes it harder for anyone present to think straight. Similarly, you can scoff at the "walls" separating reasons from emotions, or argue that because of the leakage that so often occurs, these walls should be thicker and stronger.

North Europeans watching a south European politician on television disapprove of waving hands and other gestures. So do the Japanese, whose saying "Only a dead fish has an open mouth" compares to the English "Empty vessels make the most noise."

Beware Humor, Understatement, or Irony

Cultures also vary on the permissible use of humor. In Britain or the US the authors often start workshops with a cartoon or anecdote that makes a joke about the main points to be covered. This form of icebreaker is always a success. Hence, one of the first workshops in Germany was launched, with some confidence, with a cartoon deriding European cultural differences. Nobody laughed; indeed, the audience was taking notes and looked puzzled. As the week went by, however, there was a lot of laughter in the bar and, eventually, even in the sessions. It was simply that levity was not permissible in a professional setting, between strangers.

The British use humor a lot to release emotions dammed up behind the "stiff upper lip." They also regard understatement as funny. If a Briton speaks of being "underwhelmed" by someone's presentation, or regarding it with "modified rapture," that is a way of *controlling* emotional expression while at the same time triggering emotional release in the form of laughter. The individual thereby has it both ways. A Japanese superior will similarly rebuke an incompetent subordinate by exaggerated deference: "If you could see your way to kindly troubling yourself in a matter so minor, I would be in your debt." In affective language, this translates as "Do it or else."

Unfortunately, understatements of this kind, along with throwaway lines and jokes, are almost always lost on foreigners, even if they speak the language well enough for normal discourse. Humor is language dependent and relies on a quick sense of the meaning of words. "She was a good cook, as cooks go, and as cooks go, she went." This is funny only if you are familiar with the colloquialism "as (something) goes," meaning "compared with other (somethings)," in which case "went" takes you by surprise. Not only is it hard for foreigners to release emotion in this way, but also they are unlikely to grasp the fact that understatements are actually intended ironically. They are more likely to see the English or Japanese as being opaque, as usual. Any statement that means the opposite of what it literally states may be hard on foreign managers and should be avoided. If insiders all laugh, the foreigner feels excluded, deprived of the emotional release the rest have enjoyed.

Intercultural Communication

A variety of problems of communication across cultural boundaries can arise from the differences between affective and neutral approaches. In our workshops we frequently ask the participants to describe the concept of intercultural communication. They list instruments—language, body language—and more general definitions such as the exchange of messages and ideas. Communication is of course essentially the *exchange of information*, be it words, ideas, or emotions. Information, in turn, is the *carrier of meaning*. Communication is possible only between people who to some extent share a system of meaning, so here we return to our basic definition of culture.

Verbal Communication

Western society has a predominantly verbal culture. We communicate with paper, film, and conversation. Two of the bestselling computer programs in the Western world, word processing and graphics, were developed to support verbal communication. We become nervous and uneasy once we stop talking. However, our styles of discussion differ widely. For the Anglo-Saxons, when A stops, B starts; it is not polite to interrupt. The even more verbal Latins integrate slightly more than this; B will frequently interrupt A, and vice versa, to show how interested each is in what the other is saying.

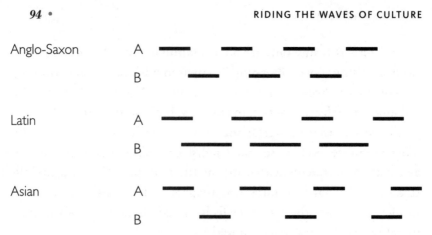

Figure 6.2. **Styles of Verbal Communication**

The pattern of silent communication depicted in Figure 6.2 for Asian languages frightens the Westerner. The moment of silence is interpreted as a failure to communicate, but this is a misunderstanding. Let us reverse the roles: how can the Westerner communicate clearly if the other person is not given time to finish his or her sentence, or to digest what the speaker has been saying? It is a sign of respect for the other person if you take time to process the information without talking yourself.

Tone of Voice. Another cross-cultural problem arises from tone of voice. Figure 6.3 shows typical patterns for Anglo-Saxon, Latin,

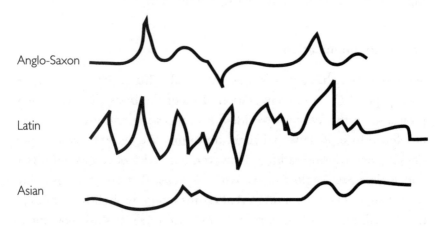

Figure 6.3. **Tone of Voice**

and Asian languages. For some neutral societies, ups and downs in speech suggest that the speaker is not serious. In most Latin societies, though, this "exaggerated" way of communicating shows that you have your heart in the matter. Asian societies tend to have a much more monotonous style; self-controlled, it shows respect. Frequently, the higher the position a person holds, the lower and flatter his or her voice.

A British manager posted to Nigeria found that it was effective to raise his voice for important issues. His Nigerian subordinates saw this unexpected explosion by a normally self-controlled manager as a sign of extra concern. After experiencing success in Nigeria, he was posted to Malaysia. Shouting there was a sign of loss of face; his colleagues did not take him seriously, and he was transferred out.

The Spoken Word. The most obvious verbal process is the spoken word, regardless of the importance of rhythm, pace, or humor. English-speaking nations have the enormous advantage of more than 300 million speakers who understand their language. However, as we all know, even the English and Americans are "separated" by a common language that is used differently in different contexts and that has some serious differences as well in the meanings of individual words. English speakers also face an enormous disadvantage, which is that it is difficult to ever speak another language; its nationals will allow you only so much accent before switching to English themselves. To express yourself in another language is a necessary, if not a sufficient, condition for understanding another culture.

Nonverbal Communication

Research has shown that at least 75 percent of all communication is nonverbal. This figure is the minimum for the most verbal cultures of all. In Western societies *eye contact* is crucial to confirm interest. However, the amount differs sharply from society to society. An Italian visiting professor at Wharton arrived on campus in Philadelphia, Pennsylvania, and was surprised to be greeted by several students. His expressive Italian nature drove him eventually to catch one of them and ask him if he knew who he was. The student said he was afraid he did not. "So why did you greet me?" "Because it seemed as if you knew me, sir." The professor realized that in the US eye contact between strangers is supposed to last only for a split second.

Leonel Brug, a colleague at the Trompenaars Hampden-Turner, was brought up in both Curaçao and Suriname. As a boy, he would try to avoid eye contact, whereupon his Curaçao grandmother would slap him (in some cultures body talk is highly effective) and say, "Look me in the face." Respecting an elder involves eye contact. Leonel learned fast, and when in Suriname he looked his other grandmother straight in the face to show respect. She slapped him too; respectful kids in Suriname do not make eye contact.

Touching other people, the *space* it is normal to keep between you, and assumptions about *privacy* are all further manifestations of the extent to which cultures are affective or neutral. Never help an Arab lady out of a bus; it might cost you your contract.

Reconciling Neutral and Affective Cultures

Highly neutral and highly affective (expressive) cultures have problems doing business with each other. The neutral person is easily accused of being ice-cold with no heart; the affective person is seen as out of control and inconsistent. When such cultures meet, the first essential is to recognize the differences and to refrain from making any judgments based on emotions or the lack of them.

The power of reconciliation can be shown if we observe what happens when seemingly opposing values are disconnected. Emotions that are expressed without any "neutral" brake easily verge on the uncontrolled "neurotic." Likewise, an overly neutral person may become an iceman who dies of a heart attack because of unexpressed emotions.

The traditional wooden roller-coaster ride has been a major attraction of amusement parks for nearly a hundred years. In recent decades promoters have tried to give even greater thrills with "white-knuckle rides." The engineering of such rides requires the design engineer to provide a series of accelerations and twists to excite with just enough respite for the rider to recover before the next thrill. Western joyriders scream and wave their arms to participate in the spirit of the experience.

Supported by modern electronics and safety features, this extreme form of entertainment is now big business, and specialist manufacturers from the US and Europe have sought to export their offerings. One Californian company installed several of its rides in Japan. In spite of a well-proven design, Japanese riders frequently received head injuries. Observation revealed that the Japanese riders were more likely to keep their heads low or forward in a semibowed posture, thereby striking the bar designed to hold them in place, rather than taking a more upright, arm-waving position. Expensive modifications to prevent head injuries were required—to the point where safety legislation in Japan requires design solutions to take regard of the citizens' relative neutrality. Their neutrality did not, of course, mean that they were not experiencing the thrill! It is just that they were trying to control it by lowering their heads.

Test Yourself

Consider the following question:

In a meeting you feel insulted because your business counterpart tells you that your proposal is insane. What is your response?

1. I will not show that this person has hurt or insulted me, because that would be seen as a sign of weakness and would make me more vulnerable in the future.
2. I will not show that I am hurt, because that would spoil our relationship. This restraint will allow me later to tell the counterpart how much I was hurt by the comment so that he or she might learn from it. I would rather show my emotions when the counterpart has more chance to improve our business relationship.

3. I will show clearly that I am insulted so that my counterpart gets the message. I believe the clarity of my message will allow me to be able to control even greater emotional upset in the future.

4. I will show clearly that I am insulted so that my counterpart gets the message. If business partners cannot behave themselves properly, they have to bear the consequences.

Indicate with 1 the approach you prefer and with 2 your second choice. Similarly, indicate (with 1) the approach you believe would be favored by your closest colleagues at work and (with 2) the approach you believe would be their second choice.

Obviously, answer 1 conveys that you prefer to be neutral and reject affectivity in response. Answer 4 clearly reflects a preference for emotional outbursts regardless of their consequences for the relationship. Answer 2 supports the neutral point of departure in order to show emotions more effectively in the future. Answer 3 takes an expressive point of departure in order to stabilize future emotional interactions.

The following tables show practical tips for doing business with neutral and affective cultures.

RECOGNIZING THE DIFFERENCES

NEUTRAL ORIENTATION	AFFECTIVE ORIENTATION
People do not reveal what they are thinking or feeling.	People reveal thoughts and feelings verbally and nonverbally.
Tension may (accidentally) be revealed in the face and posture.	Transparency and expressiveness release tension.
Emotions often dammed up will occasionally explode.	Emotions flow easily, effusively, vehemently, and without inhibition.
Cool and self-possessed conduct is admired.	Heated, vital, animated expressions are admired.

Tips for Doing Business with . . .

NEUTRALLY ORIENTED PEOPLE
(FOR AFFECTIVELY ORIENTED INDIVIDUALS)

AFFECTIVELY ORIENTED PEOPLE
(FOR NEUTRALLY ORIENTED INDIVIDUALS)

NEUTRALLY ORIENTED PEOPLE	AFFECTIVELY ORIENTED PEOPLE
Ask for time-outs from meetings and negotiations where you can patch each other up and rest between games of poker with the Impassive Ones.	Do not be put off your stride when they create scenes and get histrionic; take time-outs for sober reflection and hard assessments.
Put as much as you can on paper beforehand.	When they are expressing goodwill, respond warmly.
Their lack of emotional tone does not mean they are disinterested or bored; it means only that they do not like to show their hand.	Their enthusiasm, readiness to agree, or vehement disagreement does not mean that they have made up their minds.
The entire negotiation is typically focused on the object or proposition being discussed, not so much on you personally.	The entire negotiation is typically focused on you personally, not so much on the object or proposition being discussed.

When Managing and Being Managed

NEUTRALLY ORIENTED PEOPLE	AFFECTIVELY ORIENTED PEOPLE
Avoid warm, expressive, or enthusiastic behavior. Such behavior is interpreted as lack of control over your feelings and inconsistent with high status.	Avoid detached, ambiguous, and cool demeanors. Such demeanors will be interpreted as negative evaluation, as disdain, dislike, and social distance. You are excluding them from "the family."
If you prepare extensively beforehand, you will find it easier to "stick to the point"— that is, to the neutral topics being discussed.	If you discover whose work, energy, and enthusiasm has been invested in which projects, you are more likely to appreciate tenacious positions.
Look for subtle indications that the person is pleased or angry, and amplify their importance.	Tolerate great "surfeits" of emotionality without getting intimidated or coerced, and moderate their importance.

7

How Far We Get Involved

Closely related to whether we show emotions in dealing with other people is the degree to which we engage others in *specific* areas of life and single levels of personality, versus *diffusely* in multiple areas of our lives and at several levels of personality at the same time.

Specific Versus Diffuse Cultures

In specific-oriented cultures a manager *segregates out* the task relationship he or she has with a subordinate and insulates this relationship from other dealings. Say a manager supervises the sale of integrated circuits. Were she to meet one of her sales reps in the bar, on the golf course, during vacation, or in the local DIY superstore, almost none of her authority would diffuse itself into these relationships. Indeed, she might defer to the sales rep as a more skilled DIY practitioner, or ask advice on improving her golf game. Each area in which the two encounter one other is considered apart from the other, a *specific* case.

However, in some countries every life space and every level of personality tends to permeate all others. *Monsieur le directeur* is a formidable authority wherever you encounter him. If he runs the company, it is generally expected that his opinions on haute cuisine are better than those of his subordinates. His taste in clothes and value as a citizen are all permeated by his directorship, and he probably expects to be deferred to by those who know him, whether they are in the street, the club, or a shop. Of course, reputation always leaks to some extent into other areas of life. This extent is what we measure for specificity (small) versus diffuseness (large).

Kurt Lewin, the German-American psychologist, represented the personality as a series of concentric circles with "life spaces" or "personality levels" between.[1] The most personal and private spaces are near the center. The most shared and public spaces are at the outer peripheries. As a German-Jewish refugee in the US, Lewin was able to contrast U-type (American) life spaces with G-type (German) life spaces. These are illustrated in Figure 7.1.

Lewin's circles show Americans, in the U-type circle, as having much more public than private space, segregated into many specific sections. The American citizen can have a standing and reputation at work, in the bowling club, at the Parent-Teachers Association, among fellow computer hackers, and in the local chapter of the Veterans of Foreign Wars. Colleagues who enter any of these spaces are

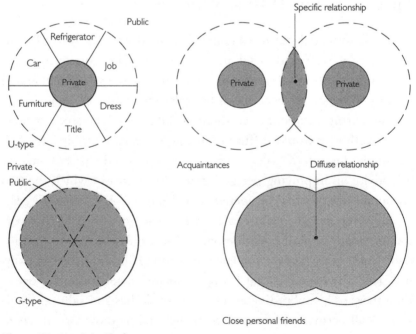

Figure 7.1. Lewin's Circles

not necessarily close or lifetime buddies. They may not feel free to call on the person if the subject is not computers or bowling. One reason why the American personality is so friendly and accessible (illustrated by the dotted lines) is that being admitted into one public layer is not a very big commitment. You "know" the other for limited purposes only.

Contrast this with the G-type circle. Here access to life spaces is guarded by a thick line. It is harder to enter, and you need the other's permission. The public space is relatively small. The private spaces are large and *diffuse*, which means that once a friend is admitted, access is gained into all, or nearly all, your private spaces. Moreover, your standing and reputation cross over these spaces. Herr Doktor Muller is Herr Doktor Muller at his university, at the butcher's shop, and at the garage; his wife is also Frau Doktor Muller in the market, at the local school, and wherever else she goes. She is not simply joined diffusely to her husband; she is also joined to his job and title. In the US, in contrast, the British author has been introduced at a reception following a graduation ceremony as Dr. Hampden-Turner, but at a party for much the same people a few hours later as Charles Hampden-Turner. He has also been introduced as "I want you all to meet my very good friend Charles . . . what's your surname?" In the US a title is a *specific* label for a *specific* job in a *specific* place.

For all these reasons Germans may be thought of by Americans as remote and hard to get to know. Americans may be thought of by Germans as cheerful and garrulous, yet superficial, people who let you into a very small corner of their public lives and regard you as peripheral.

Borders and barriers between "life spaces" have physical dimensions as well. As accompaniment to the tale of the Italian visiting professor in Chapter 6, the Dutch author recounts his own experience on arriving as a student at the Wharton School, in Philadelphia. Steve, a new American friend, rushed to help me move in. In gratitude for his hard work on the hot summer day, I asked him to stay for a while and have a beer. I went to wash up and returned to get him a beer out of the refrigerator. I did not need to; he had already opened the refrigerator and was helping himself. For him, a refrigerator was my public space into which I had invited him. To me and most of my Dutch compatriots, it was definitely private space. A few days later I was struck by a similar event. I was inquiring about transportation across town, when Denise, a fellow student, tossed me her car keys and said to call her when I was finished with my errand. I could not believe it. To me, a car was certainly private space. Have you ever tried to borrow a German acquaintance's Mercedes?

In the US, where people are relatively mobile, furniture, cars, and similar possessions can be semipublic. People will hold garage sales and yard sales: exhibiting very personal items on tables in a yard for all not only to see but also to purchase. They may be as open with intimate personal experiences. It is not rare to be regaled at a party with confessions of sexual incompatibility from a complete stranger. You even suspect he has forgotten your name by the time his story is finished. An American cartoon by Jules Feiffer has the antihero Bernard Mergendeiler explain to his audience, "I met this *marvelous* girl. I've told all my friends and colleagues at work. I go up to strangers in the street and tell them about her. I've told nearly *everyone*—except her. Why give her the advantage?"[2]

Clearly this character's public spaces overwhelm his private one. He confesses in the first to avoid communication in the second.

The situation in France or Germany is much different. You have only to note the high hedges and shuttered windows to appreciate French concern for large private spaces. If you are invited to dinner in a French home, that invitation extends to only the rooms in which that hospitality occurs. If you start wandering around the house, you may offend. If your hostess goes into her study to find a book you are discussing, and you follow her, that may be considered a trespass into her private domain.

The concentric circles are not simply in the mind, but refer as well to spaces in which we live.

The concepts of the specific and the diffuse help us to make sense of the dispute being described in the MCC head office, involving Mr. Johnson (American), Mr. Bergman (Dutch), and Messrs. Gialli and Pauli (Italian). Mr. Johnson and Mr. Bergman, while not in agreement on permissible levels of emotional expression (Mr. Johnson being more affective), *are* in agreement on the separation of reason from emotion. Americans and Dutch both believe that there are specific times, places, and spaces for being reasonable and specific times, places, and spaces for being affective. To the perplexity and dismay of both men, the Italians have "thrown a tantrum" in the middle of a meeting, on serious, professional issues.

Let us continue the story.

As the representative from head office, Mr. Johnson felt largely responsible for the developments at the meeting. The Italians' behavior seemed strange to him. Mr. Bergman had just wanted to discuss a key aspect of the consistency of the reward system, and they did not even give him a chance to explain his position. Moreover, the Italians had refused to put any solid arguments on the table themselves.

When Johnson entered Mr. Gialli's room, he said, "Paolo, what's the problem? You shouldn't take this too seriously. It's just a business discussion."

"Just a business discussion?" Gialli echoed with unconcealed rage. "This has nothing to do with a business discussion. It is typical for that Dutchman to attack us. We have our own ways of being effective, and then he calls us crazy."

"I didn't hear that," Johnson said. "He simply said that he found your group-bonus idea crazy. I know Bergman, and he didn't intend that to refer to you."

"If that's so," countered Gialli, "why is he behaving so rudely?"

Johnson realized how deeply his Italian colleagues had been offended. He went back to Bergman, took him aside, and told him about his conversation with Gialli. "Offended!" said Bergman. "Let them have the self-control to respond to professional arguments. I don't understand why they are so hotheaded, anyway. They know we have done extensive research on this. Let them listen first. You have to remember that these Latins never want to be bothered with facts."

The Italians' reaction is of course readily understandable if you grasp that their feelings about group bonuses as opposed to individual bonuses, their sympathy with their sales force and customers, and the proposal they put forward are *one diffuse whole*. To call "the idea" crazy is to call *them* crazy and to question their ability to represent the cultural views of fellow Italians. It offends them to the core. Their ideas are not separated from themselves. If they "thought of it" and if it represents "Italian thinking," then the proposition is an extension of their personal honor.

One problem with the overlap between U-types and G-types is that the U-type sees as impersonal something the G-type sees as highly personal. Italian views on the effectiveness of group bonuses are tied to their diffuse sense of private space. (See Figure 7.2.) It is not "just a business discussion" taking place in a realm apart from their private selves, but a discussion touching on what it means to be a feeling, thinking Italian. Pleasure and pain, as well as acceptance and rejection, ramify more widely in the diffuse system. You cannot criticize Italians as generators of a crazy idea without profoundly affecting their whole system. When Americans "let in" a German, French, or Italian colleague to share one compartment of their public space and show their customary openness and friendliness, that person may assume that he or she has been admitted to diffuse private space. People in such cases may expect the American to show equivalent friendship in all life spaces and may be offended if the American comes to their town without contacting them. They might also be offended by criticism-

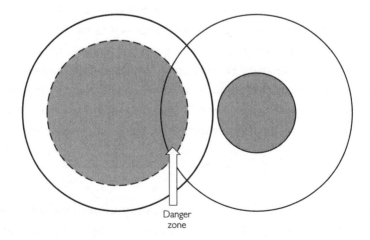

Figure 7.2. **The Danger Zone**

as-a-professional, which they take to be attack-by-a-close-friend. Or they may be offended when admiration-as-between-electronic-engineers goes no deeper than that.

Losing Face

Specific cultures, with their small areas of privacy clearly separated from public life, have considerable freedom for direct speech. "Do not take this personally" is a frequent comment. In relationships with diffuse people this approach can be an insult. American and Dutch managers find it particularly easy to inadvertently insult their opposite diffuse partners (see Mr. Johnson's problems with the Italians in the preceding section). This is because they do not understand the principle of losing face, which is what happens when something that people perceive as being private is made public. The importance of avoiding loss of face is why in diffuse cultures so much more time is taken to get to the point; it is necessary to avoid private confrontation because it is impossible for participants not to take things personally. The Dutch author always tries to avoid asking Dutch audiences for criticism after one of his workshops; the experience is much the same as being machine-gunned. Afterward, however, they tend to ask the corpse for the next date it will be available. In contrast, English and French managers will make a few mild suggestions in a context of positive congratulation, never to be heard from again.

At an international university at which I (the Dutch author) was teaching, a Ghanaian student wrote a paper for me that I was unable to grade at more than four out of ten, a fail. All scores were posted on a notice board. The student said that this act would be a public insult to him, impossible for me as a respected professor to perpetrate, although he agreed with the mark. What I should do was to mark the paper "I" (incomplete) for the board, while feeding the actual grade into the system.

National Differences

National differences are sharp under the headings of specificity and diffuseness. The range is illustrated well by responses to the following situation.

A boss asks a subordinate to help him paint his house. The subordinate, who does not feel like doing it, discusses the situation with a colleague.

A. The colleague argues: "You don't have to paint if you don't feel like it. He is your boss at work. Outside he has little authority."

B. The subordinate argues: "Despite the fact that I don't feel like it, I will paint it. He is my boss, and you can't ignore that outside of work either."

In specific societies, where work and private life are sharply separated, managers are not at all inclined to assist. As one Dutch respondent observed, "House painting is not in my collective labor agreement." Figure 7.3 shows the proportion of managers who would not paint the house, around 80 percent or higher in the UK, the US, Switzerland, and most of northern Europe. We found that 71 percent of Japanese would not either, but in the diffuse Asian societies of China and Nepal and African societies of Nigeria and Burkina Faso the majority would. (Surprised by the Japanese score, we reinterviewed some Japanese respondents. They replied that the number most probably had to do with the fact that the Japanese never paint houses, which illustrates the relativity of empirical data.) The range of differences is not so steeply graded as when we looked at the basic cultural divides of Chapters 3 and 4, but it is nevertheless clearly a source of deep potential incomprehension.

Negotiating the Specific-Diffuse Cultural Divide

Doing business with a culture more diffuse than our own feels excessively time consuming. Some nations refuse to do business in a mental subdivision called "commerce" or "work" that is kept apart from the rest of life. In diffuse cultures, everything is connected to everything. Your business partner may wish to know where you went to school, who your friends are, and what you think of life, politics, art, literature, and music. This is not "a waste of time," because such preferences reveal character and form friendships. They also make deception nearly impossible. As with the example in Chapter 1 of the Swedish

Percentage of respondents who would not paint the house

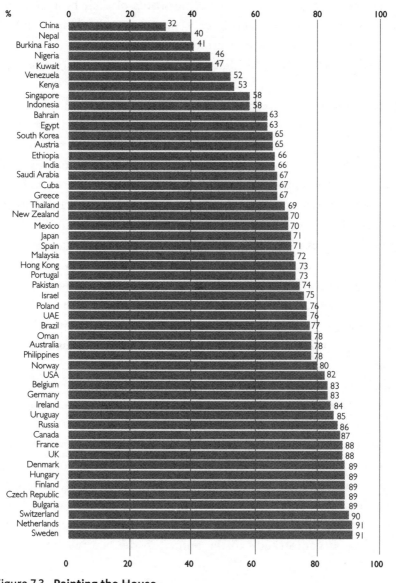

Figure 7.3. **Painting the House**

company that beat an American company having a technically superior product for a contract with a South American customer, the up-front investment in building relationships in such cultures is as important as the deal, if not more so. The Swedes invested a whole week in the selling trip, the first five days of which were not related to the business at all. They just shared the diffuse life spaces of their hosts, talking about common interests. Only *after* a "private space" relationship had been established were the Argentineans willing to talk business. And that had to include several life spaces, not just one. In contrast, the Americans invested only two days in the trip, knowing they had a superior product and presentation, and were turned down.

It is really a question of priority. Do you start with the specific and neutral proposition and later get to know those interested in that proposition? Or do you start with people you can trust because you have invited them into multiple life spaces and then move on to business? Both approaches make good sense to those living in that culture, but each plays havoc with the other. The American team members found themselves continually interrupted by "personal" questions and "social distractions," and when the corporate jet arrived on schedule to take them home, they had not adequately covered the business agenda. The Argentineans, to the Americans, seemed unable or unwilling to stick to the point. The Argentineans, for their part, found the Americans too direct, impersonal, and pushy. They were nonplussed by the Americans' apparent belief that you could use logic to force someone to agree with you.

In other words, specificity and diffuseness are about strategies for getting to know other people.

The diagram on the left in Figure 7.4 shows the typically diffuse strategy common in Japan, Mexico, France, and much of southern Europe and Asia. Here you "circle around" the stranger, getting to know the person diffusely, and come down to the specifics of the business only later when relationships of trust have been established. On the right you get "straight to the point," to the neutral, "objective"

Diffuse, high context
(from general to
specific)

Specific, low context
(from specific to
general)

Figure 7.4. **Circling Around**

aspects of the business deal, and *if* the other party remains interested, then you "circle around," getting to know the person in order to facilitate the deal.

Both approaches claim to save time. In the diffuse approach you do not get trapped in an eight-year relationship with a dishonest partner, because you detect any unsavory aspects early on. In the specific approach you do not waste time wining and dining a person who is not fully committed to the specifics of the deal.

Specific cultures and diffuse cultures are sometimes called *low context* and *high context*. Context has to do with how much you have to know before effective communication can occur, how much shared knowledge is taken for granted by those in conversation with each other, and how much reference there is to tacit common ground. Cultures with high context such as Japan and France believe that strangers must be "filled in" before business can be properly discussed. Cultures with low context such as the US and the Netherlands believe that each stranger should share in rule making, and the fewer initial structures there are, the better. Low-context cultures tend to be adaptable and flexible. High-context cultures are rich and subtle, but they carry a lot of "baggage" and may never really be comfortable for foreigners who are not fully assimilated. There is growing evidence, for example, that Westerners working for Japanese companies are never wholly "inside." It is similarly hard to feel fully accepted within the richness of French culture with its thousands of diffuse connections.

There is a tendency for specific cultures to look at objects, specifics, and things before considering how they are related. The general tendency for diffuse cultures is to look at relationships and connections before considering all the separate pieces. The configuration is circular. (See Figure 7.5.)

The Effect of Specific-Diffuse Orientation on Business

That Americans choose MBO (management by objectives) and pay-for-performance as favorite devices to motivate employees testifies in part to their specific orientation. In MBO you first agree on the "objec-

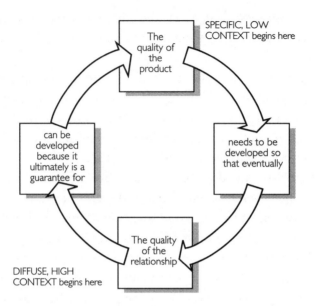

Figure 7.5. The Specific-Diffuse Circle

tives"—that is, the specifics. Supervisor A agrees with subordinate B that B will work toward agreed objectives in the coming quarter and that evaluation of his or her work will take as a benchmark the objectives agreed to. Worthy objectives satisfactorily achieved will make for a productive relationship between A and B. What could be fairer or more logical? Why would the whole world not agree to do this?

This system does not appeal to diffuse cultures because they approach the issue from the opposite direction. *It is the relationship between A and B that increases or reduces output, not the other way around.* Objectives or specifics may be out of date by the time evaluation comes around. B may not have performed as promised yet done something more valuable in altered circumstances. Only strong and lasting relationships can handle unexpected changes of this kind. Contracts and small print face backward in such cultures.

Japanese corporate cultures, for example, use terms unfamiliar to Westerners that are clearly aimed at putting the diffuse before the specific. They speak of "acceptance time," the time necessary to discuss proposed changes before they are implemented. They speak of *nemawashi*: literally, binding the roots of shrubs and trees before transplanting them. This term refers to extensive consultations before implementing changes. All these constitute the "circling around before coming to the point" that we saw in Figure 7.4.

Pay-for-performance is not very popular in diffuse cultures because it arbitrarily severs relationships. It says, "You are solely responsible for what you sold this month" when, in fact, other salespeople may have helped you, and your superiors may have inspired you or instructed you to act in more effective ways. To claim most or all of the rewards for yourself denies the importance of relationships, including feelings of affection and respect for superiors and peers with whom you have diffuse contacts and shared private life spaces.

Expressions such as "Do not mix business with pleasure" and "Don't talk shop" testify to the desire in some cultures to keep specific life spaces separate from each other. Arguably it is harder to coerce people or subordinate them if their lives are honeycombed with separate compartments. In this situation only one area of somebody's life can be dominated, and the individual can call on personal resources in other areas. Diffuse cultures have "all their eggs in one basket." Again, we are talking about *relative* and not absolute separation. There is always a kind of wall between life spaces in most cultures.

Diffuse cultures tend to have lower turnover and employee mobility, because of the importance of "loyalty" and the multiplicity of human bonds. They tend not to "headhunt" or lure away employees from other companies with high (specific) salaries. Takeovers are rarer in diffuse cultures, because of the disruption caused to relationships and because shareholders (often banks) have longer-term relationships and cross-holdings in each other's companies and are less motivated by the price of shares.

Pitfalls of Performance Evaluation

Specific cultures find it much easier to criticize people without devastating the whole life space of the target of that criticism. There are at least two tragic corporate cases in which criticism during performance evaluations by Western superiors led to their murder by outraged targets.

In one case a Dutch doctor whose job was to evaluate a Chinese subordinate working in the company clinic had a "frank discussion" of the latter's shortcomings. In his view these shortcomings could easily be remedied by the company's training courses. Yet to the Chinese doctor who had worked closely with the Dutch doctor, and whom he regarded as a "father figure," the criticism was a savage indictment, a total rejection, and a betrayal of mutual confidence. The next morning he knifed his critic to death. One can imagine the Dutch ghost protesting that he had never said his Chinese colleague was not a fine fellow; it was only his medicine he was worried about.

In a second case a British manager who fired an employee in Central Africa was later poisoned, with the seeming connivance of the other African employees. The fired man had many hungry children and had stolen meat from the company cafeteria. In a diffuse culture "stealing" is not easily separable from domestic circumstances, and the Western habit of separating an "office crime" from a "problem at home" is not accepted.

We must be careful, however, not to regard diffuse cultures as "primitive." Japanese corporations give bigger salaries to workers with larger families, help in the search for housing, and often provide recreation facilities, vacations, and consumer products at favorable prices. Another pair of options we use to test for cultural diffuseness is the following.

A. Some people think a company is usually responsible for the housing of its employees. Therefore, a company has to assist an employee in finding housing.

B. Other people think the responsibility for housing should be carried by the employee alone. It is so much to the good if the company helps.

Figure 7.6 shows the percentage of managers who do not think that housing is a company's responsibility. Only 45 percent of Japanese managers think that it is not, as opposed to 85 percent of Americans. The vast majority of all north European managers do not expect com-

Percentage of respondents who disagree

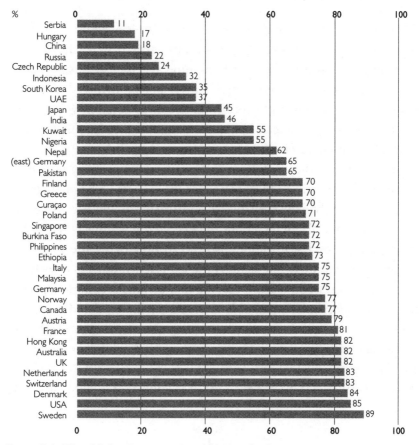

Figure 7.6. **Should the Company Provide Housing?**

pany help, whereas in most Asian countries the majority does. The exception is Singapore, where Western principles have become much more widespread. It is also instructive to note the impact of Communist regimes on the various European countries that appear at the top of the chart.

Japanese consumers may reject Western imported goods because their value is specific; Japanese corporations produce goods with benefits diffused through their society. So we buy more than a Honda motor scooter; we "buy" economic and social development for our society, a highly diffuse concept.

The Mix of Emotion and Involvement

There are naturally various combinations of levels of emotion or affectivity (high to low, or neutral) each with its particular "reach" or scope (diffusing several life spaces or remaining specific). A business partner can be emotional and expressive yet not be involved *with you*. Someone may be cool and neutral, yet deeply involved in your private spaces. Another person can be expressive and involved, or neutral and uninvolved. Four combinations are described by Talcott Parsons.[3] As Figure 7.7 shows, they yield four different sorts of primary response.

In diffuse-affective (DA) interactions the expected relational reward is *love*, a strongly expressed pleasure diffusing many life spaces. In diffuse-neutral (DN) interactions the expected reward is *esteem*, a less strongly expressed admiration also spread over many life spaces. In specific-affective (SA) interactions the expected reward is *enjoyment*, a strongly expressed pleasure specific to a certain occasion or performance. In specific-neutral (SN) interactions the expected reward is *approval*, a job, a task, or an occasion-specific expression of positive but yet neutral approbation. Certainly, these four quadrants might also contain negative evaluations: *hate* (DA), *disappointment* (DN), *rejection* (SA), and *criticism* (SN), for example. It is important to remember that

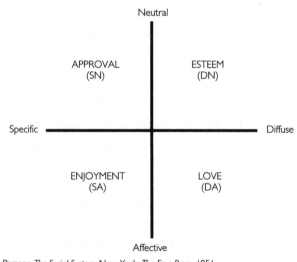

Source: Talcott Parsons, *The Social System*. New York: The Free Press, 1951.

Figure 7.7. The Emotional Quadrant

love and responsiveness have their mirrors in hate and rejection, while more neutral cultures do not risk such extreme mood swings.

We have tried to measure the relative national preferences for love, esteem, enjoyment, and approval by using the following question, which is taken from some earlier work by L. R. Dean.[4]

Which of the following four types of people do you prefer to have around you? Review these descriptions carefully, and then indicate the one that most closely relates to your preference and the one that represents your second preference.

- **A.** People who completely accept you the way you are and feel responsible for your personal problems and welfare (combines diffuse and affective: love).
- **B.** People who do their work, attend to their affairs, and leave you free to do the same (specific and neutral: approval).
- **C.** People who try to improve themselves and have definite ideals and aims in life (diffuse and neutral: esteem).
- **D.** People who are friendly and lively and enjoy getting together to talk or socialize (specific and affective: enjoyment).

Figure 7.8 shows how a number of nationalities score in this exercise. We see that Americans score high both on emotion and specificity. The Japanese and Germans are both in the Diffuse/Neutral quadrant; the Italians are situated in the Diffuse/Affective quadrant. Once again there are no firm rules by continent, although if we try to picture the most important regional cultural differences, we get the division presented in Figure 7.9.

American (West Coast) enthusiasms tend to be for specific issues and causes and belong, as it were, in separate boxes; that is, saving the redwoods, rebirthing, nanotechnology, virtual reality, and so on. DA cultures spill over between life spaces. Dishonor to a family member disgraces the family and must be avenged. You may not be able to work in the same company as a person with whom your uncle has a feud going back 10 years.

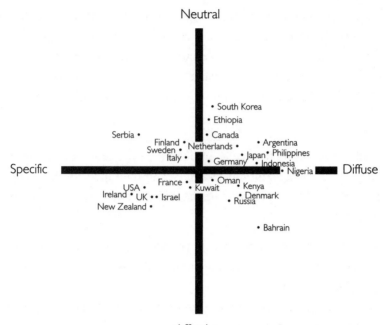

Figure 7.8. **What Type of People Do You Prefer Around You?**

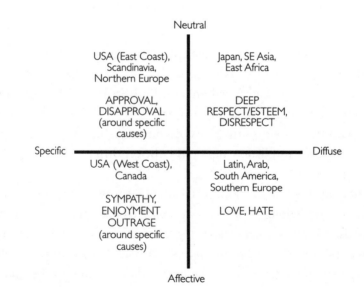

Figure 7.9. **Regional Cultural Differences**

On one occasion a Dutch and a Belgian manager disagreed on a fiscal issue in politics. The Dutch manager let the disagreement stand, in a separate compartment as he saw it, and tried to get on with other business. For the Belgian their disagreement colored everything. The Dutch manager could not be a trusted partner if his views on the fiscal issue were so mistaken. The Dutchman's desire to move on to other business was a slight to the Belgian's feeling of profound disturbance in their relationship. Their business dealings were broken off.

North Europeans, especially Scandinavians, are somewhat less specific than Americans, but they are more disapproving of overt emotion. As with the Japanese, however, they sanction alcohol to loosen inhibitions. The lack of explicit emotion does not mean that people do not feel for each other. It means that a "soft pedal" is used to communicate emotions, but these small signs can, as is evident, speak volumes to the recipient who understands how to read them.

Reconciling Specific-Diffuse Cultures

This is perhaps the area in which balance is most crucial, from both a personal and a corporate point of view. The specific extreme can lead to disruption and the diffuse extreme to a lack of perspective; a collision between them results in paralysis. It is the interplay of the two approaches that is the most fruitful, recognizing that privacy is necessary but that complete separation of private life leads to alienation and superficiality; that business is business, but stable and deep relationships mean strong affiliations.

The need for interplay is shown by the following case.

It was in the late 1980s and early 1990s that merger mania hit the airline industry. John Perrish, of British Airways (BA), was sitting at his desk wondering what to do in the latest discussions on the alliance with US Air. As a marketing manager, he was worried that the results of passenger studies would jeopardize the long-term development of an airline serving the global passenger. The studies revealed that American passengers were increasingly less willing to pay high ticket prices. Competition among American airlines was a price issue rather than a quality issue.

In Europe, business-class travel was still characterized by high prices, and competition was aimed at legroom, quality of meals, and flexibility of changing routes. It seemed that the service was seen in dramatically different ways by American and European passengers. The globalization that would result from the alliance would force both partners to rethink what a true global client expects.

Peter Butcher, John's counterpart at US Air, could not resist making cynical comparisons and often said, "John, you might say that we in the US tend to view passengers as a 'piece of meat' that needs to travel from New York to Los Angeles, and in Europe people are willing to include their stomach for an extra $300 during a one-hour flight." Indeed, at BA passengers are served a hot breakfast on a flight from London to Amsterdam that is no longer than 40 minutes. John's reply was as biting: "I remember I once had a first-class flight from Detroit to Chicago of just over an hour. It took off at 6.30 A.M., and around 7, long after our seat belts were loosened, I wondered when breakfast would be served. I couldn't smell anything. I asked the flight attendant when I could expect a breakfast. I took her by surprise with that question. Two minutes later she came back with a big smile, asking, 'Sir, we have pretzels or potato chips: which do you prefer?' I said that a cup of coffee would do."

When clients' expectations are so diverse around the world, how would you advise John and Peter to approach their global marketing campaign?

It is obvious that American passengers and the airlines serving them share a perception of a very specific relationship. You are a person who needs to go from point A to point B in a safe, reliable, and inexpensive way. Period. In Europe and Asia the involvement is perceived as going beyond safety and reliability. When flying with Singapore Airlines, for example, we can see a mutual need to involve the whole person. This diffuse relationship is expressed by excellent service, high-quality food, and a general attitude of customer focus. In much of the US and on some airlines in Europe, neither client nor airline feels the need to get involved beyond a safe and fast trip for as low a price as possible. It is up to the client to decide.

However, in the case of BA and US Air it was not as simple. To serve global clients, they first needed to decide what level of integration was necessary. KLM and Northwest Airlines, for example, have decided to integrate their schedules and parts of their financial and booking systems. But KLM's service is still different in many ways from that on Northwest Airlines.

What do you do when the alliance goes beyond the technicalities and includes the service on board? A compromise is not desirable, because not many passengers desire hot pretzels or lukewarm breakfasts. SAS tried, by introducing a business class, to leave the choice to the passenger. But what about serving the global customer? The challenging question becomes: How could the excellence of our specific services increase the quality of the holistic approach to the passenger? The reconciling graph could be as shown in Figure 7.10.

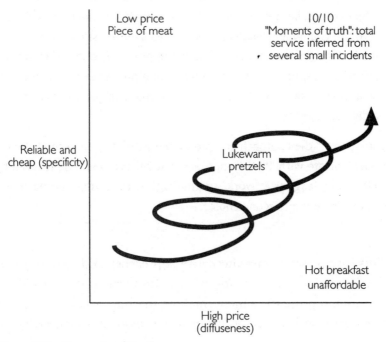

Figure 7.10. **Moments of Truth**

Test Yourself

Consider the following case:

A group of managers and financial analysts were arguing about whether profitability or ongoing stakeholder relationships, most especially between company and customers, formed the best way of monitoring organizational effectiveness. Four positions were advanced:

1. Feedback within close customer relationships represents the timeliest advice about corporate effectiveness. Its value is its inclusivity. Profits measure what is taken out of a relationship, not what is staked or contributed.
2. Feedback within close customer relationships represents the timeliest advice about corporate effectiveness. Because customers generate the funds used to pay profits, the quality of these relationships anticipates profitability.
3. Profitability or shareholder value is the prime criterion of corporate effectiveness, because it distills in one precise and unambiguous measure the vitality and value of all activities by other stakeholders.
4. Profitability or shareholder value is the prime criterion of corporate effectiveness, because it proclaims in one precise and unambiguous measure that labor works for capital and that business exists to enrich individual owners.

Indicate with "1" the approach you prefer and with "2" your second choice. Similarly, indicate with "1" the approach you believe would be favored by your closest colleagues at work, and indicate with "2" the approach you believe would be their second choice.

This case presents four alternative approaches to the criteria that need to be used to define organizational effectiveness. If you think an organization is primarily a moneymaking machine, you would opt for answer 4. Answer 1 rejects specificity, while answer 2 is a reconciliation starting from a diffuse point of departure. Answer 3 reconciles the diffuse responsibility starting from a specific standpoint of profitability or shareholder value.

The following tables show practical tips for doing business in specific and diffuse cultures.

RECOGNIZING THE DIFFERENCES

SPECIFIC ORIENTATION	DIFFUSE ORIENTATION
Relationships are direct, to the point, and purposeful.	Forms of relating are indirect, circuitous, and seemingly "aimless."
People are precise, blunt, definitive, and transparent.	People are evasive, tactful, ambiguous, and even opaque.
Principles and consistent morality stand independent of the person being addressed.	Morality is highly situational and depends on the person and context encountered.

TIPS FOR DOING BUSINESS WITH . . .

SPECIFICALLY ORIENTED PEOPLE *(FOR DIFFUSELY ORIENTED INDIVIDUALS)*	DIFFUSELY ORIENTED PEOPLE *(FOR SPECIFICALLY ORIENTED INDIVIDUALS)*
Study the objectives, principles, and numerical targets of the specific organization with which you are dealing.	Study the history, background, and future vision of the diffuse organization with which you expect to do business.
Be quick, to the point, and efficient.	Take time, and remember there is more than one way to skin a cat.
Structure the meeting with time intervals and agendas.	Let the meeting flow, occasionally nudging its process.
Do not use titles or acknowledge skills that are irrelevant to the issue being discussed.	Respect a person's title, age, and background connections, whatever issue is being discussed.
Do not be offended by confrontations; they are usually not personal.	Do not get impatient when people are indirect or circuitous.

WHEN MANAGING AND BEING MANAGED

SPECIFICALLY ORIENTED PEOPLE	DIFFUSELY ORIENTED PEOPLE
Management is the realization of objectives and standards with rewards attached.	Management is a continuously improving process by which quality improves.
Private and business agendas are kept separate from each other.	Private and business issues interpenetrate.
Conflicts of interest are frowned on.	Consider an employee's whole situation before you judge him or her.
Clear, precise, and detailed instructions are seen as assuring better compliance, or as allowing employees to dissent in clear terms.	Ambiguous and vague instructions are seen as allowing subtle and responsive interpretations through which employees can exercise personal judgment.
Begin reports with an executive summary.	End reports with a concluding overview.

Notes

1. K. Lewin, "Some Social-Psychological Differences Between the US and Germany," in *Principles of Topological Psychology*, ed. K. Lewin (New York: McGraw-Hill, 1936).
2. J. Feiffer, *Hold Me* (New York: Knopf, 1968).
3. T. Parsons and E. A. Shils, *Towards a General Theory of Action* (Cambridge, MA: Harvard University Press, 1951), 128–33.
4. L. R. Dean, "The Pattern Variables: Some Empirical Operations," *American Sociological Review*, no. 26 (1961), 80–90.

How We Accord Status

ALL SOCIETIES give certain of their members higher status than others, signaling that unusual attention should be focused on such people and their activities. While some societies accord status to people on the basis of their achievements, others ascribe it to them by virtue of age, class, gender, education, and so on. The first kind of status is called *achieved* status and the second *ascribed* status. While achieved status refers to *doing*, ascribed status refers to *being*.

When we look at a particular person, we are partly influenced by his or her track record (e.g., top Eastern Division salesperson for five consecutive years). We may also be influenced by other attributes of the person:

- Age (a more experienced salesperson)
- Gender (very masculine and aggressive)
- Social connections (friends in the highest places)
- Education (top scholar at the Ecole Polytechnique)
- Profession (electronics is the future)

While there are ascriptions that are not logically connected with business effectiveness, such as gender, skin color, or birth, some ascriptions do make good sense in predicting business performance: age and experience, education and professional qualifications. Education and professional qualifications, moreover, are related to an individual's earlier schooling and training and are therefore not unconnected with achievement. A culture may ascribe higher status to its better-educated employees in the belief that scholarly success will lead to corporate success. This is a generalized expectation and may show up as a "fast-track" or "management-trainee" program that points a recruit to the top of the organization.

With the issue of status in mind, let us get back to the trials of Mr. Johnson, who, you may recall, is struggling with a walkout by Italian managers. Mr. Gialli and Mr. Pauli left the room furious when their suggested modification to the pay-for-performance plan was called "a crazy idea" by Mr. Bergman from the Netherlands. In order to save the situation, Johnson has turned to shuttle diplomacy. Like a youthful Henry Kissinger (Johnson is only 35), he finds himself moving between the two parties to settle the dispute. He rapidly begins to feel less like Kissinger and more like Don Quixote.

The Italian managers were far from assuaged. One even referred unpleasantly to "the American cult of youth: mere boys who think they know everything." So when the Spanish HR manager, Mr. Munoz, offered to mediate, Johnson readily agreed. It occurred to him that Spanish culture might be closer to Italian culture, not to mention the fact that Munoz was some 20 years his senior and thus could hardly be accused of inexperience.

While hopeful that Munoz might succeed, Johnson was astonished to see him bring the Italians back into the conference room in minutes. Munoz was not, in Johnson's view, the most professional of HR managers, but he was clearly expert at mending fences. It was at once apparent, however, that Munoz was now backing the Italians' call for modifications to the pay-for-performance plan. The problem as he saw it, and the Italians agreed, was that under the current plan winning salespeople were going to earn more than their bosses. Subordinates, they believed, should not be allowed to undermine their superiors in this way. Mr. Munoz explained that back in Spain his sales force would probably simply refuse to embarrass a boss in this way; or perhaps one or two, lacking in loyalty to the organization, might, in which case they would humiliate the boss into resignation. Furthermore, since the sales manager was largely responsible for the above-average performance of his team, was it not odd, to say the least, that the company would be rewarding everyone except the leader? The meeting broke for lunch, for which Johnson had little appetite.

As we can see, different societies confer status on individuals in different ways. Mr. Munoz carried more clout with the Italians for the same reason that Johnson had less: they respected age and experience much more than the specific achievements that had made Johnson a fast-tracker in the company. Many Anglo-Saxons, including Mr. Johnson, believe that ascribing status for reasons other than achievement is archaic and inappropriate to business. But is achievement orientation really a necessary feature of economic success?

Status-by-Achievement and Economic Development

Most of the literature on achievement orientation sees it as part of "modernization," the key to economic and business success. The theory goes that once you start rewarding business achievement, the process is self-perpetuating. People work hard to assure themselves of the esteem of their culture, and you get "the achieving society," as David McClelland, the Harvard professor, defined his own culture in the late 1950s.[1] Only nations setting out on an empirical investigation of "what works best," and conferring status on those who apply it in business, can expect to conduct their economies successfully. This is the essence of Protestantism: the pursuit of justification through works that long ago gave achievers a religious sanction—and capitalism its moving spirit.

According to this view, societies that ascribe status are economically backward, because the reasons they have for conferring status do not facilitate commercial success. Catholic countries ascribing status to more passive ways of life, Hinduism associating practical achievements with delusion, and Buddhism teaching detachment from earthly concerns are all forms of ascribed status that are thought to impede economic development. Ascription has been seen as a feature of countries either late to develop or still underdeveloped. In fact, ascribing status has been considered "dangerous for your economic health."

To measure the extent of achieving versus ascribing orientations in different cultures, we used the following statements, inviting participants to mark them on a five-point scale (1 = strongly agree, 5 = strongly disagree).

1. The most important thing in life is to think and act in the ways that best suit the way you really are, even if you do not get things done.
2. The respect a person gets is highly dependent on the person's family background.

Figures 8.1 and 8.2 show the percentage of participants who disagree with each of these statements. The countries in Figure 8.1 where only a minority disagree with "getting things done" are, broadly speaking, ascriptive cultures—very broadly speaking, because there are in fact fewer than 10 societies, English-speaking and Scandinavian countries, where there is a majority in favor of getting things done even at the expense of personal freedom to live as you feel you should. The US is clearly a culture in which status is mainly achieved, as shown by Figure 8.2; 87 percent of Americans disagree that status depends mainly on family background. Several societies that are ascriptive in the first figure (the Czech Republic, for example) do in fact show majorities against the proposition that status is largely dependent on family; aspects of ascription vary greatly from country to country.

Both figures show that there is a correlation between Protestantism and achievement orientation, with Catholic, Buddhist, and Hindu cultures scoring considerably more ascriptively. There is, incidentally, no correlation between support for achievement or ascription and the age, sex, or education of respondents across our database as a whole, although there is for these factors in some societies.

A second glance at the scores shows that there are growing difficulties with the thesis that an achievement orientation is the key to economic success. In the first place, Protestant cultures are no longer growing faster than Catholic or Buddhist ones. Catholic Belgium, for example, has a slightly higher GDP per capita than the more Protestant Netherlands. Catholic France and Italy have been growing faster than the UK or parts of Protestant Scandinavia. Japan, South Korea, Taiwan, Singapore, and Hong Kong are influenced by Buddhism and

Percentage of respondents who disagree

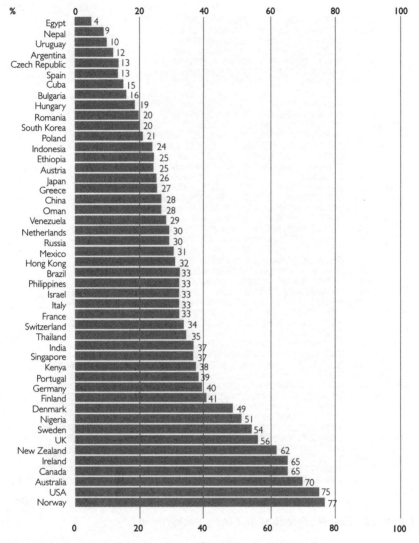

Figure 8.1. Acting as Suits You Even if Nothing Is Achieved

Confucianism. It is certainly not evident that Japan's habit of promoting by seniority has weighed its corporations down beneath piles of deadwood. In short, there is no evidence that either orientation belongs to a "higher" level of development, as modernization theorists used to claim.

Percentage of respondents who disagree

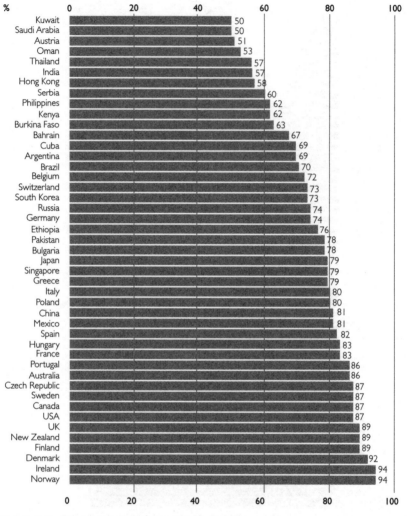

Figure 8.2. **Respect Depends on Family Background**

What appears to be happening is that some highly successful business cultures are ascribing status to people, technologies, or industries that they anticipate will be important to their future as an economy, with the result that these people and sectors receive special encouragement. In other words, ascribing *works with* achieving by generating social and economic momentum toward visualized goals.

Ascription and Performance

Andrew, a British manager and trained geologist, had been working for a French oil company for 20 years and was still confused by one aspect of his colleagues' behavior. He found that his fellow French geologists would simply not tolerate outside criticism of their profession. Initially he would get puzzled looks and frowns if he admitted he did not know the answer to some technical question in front of lay-people. Once when he said he would have to "look up" something, his French colleagues were overtly annoyed with him. He was confused because in his view geologists are frequently asked questions for which they do not have answers right at hand, or for which there is no answer. Be that as it may, his French fellows would chide him for admitting this publicly. They believed he was letting his profession down.

This experience is supported by research undertaken at INSEAD business school in France by André Laurent.[2] He found that French and Italian managers were much more emphatic about "knowing all the answers" than managers from many other cultures.

Notice, though, the effect that ascription has on performance. The French geologists are determined to live up to their ascribed status, which, in turn, can lead to higher performance. Hence, it can be a self-fulfilling prophecy: through living up to the status ascribed to them, they "deserve" the status that was given to them before they actually earn it. In practice, then, achieving status and ascribing status can be finely interwoven.

The European Community (EC) is a prime example of an ascribed self-fulfilling prophecy; its importance and power in the world was proclaimed before it had achieved anything.

The interweaving of ascribing and achieving orientations is a feature of the world's leading economies, Japan and Germany. Both cultures tend to confine achieving *as individuals* to school. Thereafter, managers are supposed to cooperate. Achievement becomes less a task for individuals jostling each other for advantage than for whole groups, led by those who excelled earlier and individually.

We must bear these distinctions in mind when we examine the data presented earlier. Ascribing and achieving can be exclusive of each other, but they are not necessarily so. Your achieving can drive your ascribing, as when you "land winners." Or ascribing can drive achieving, as when key industries are first targeted and then won by "national champions."

The belief that electronic equipment made by Olivetti, Bosch, Siemens, or Alcatel is more important to the EC than enhanced expertise in distributing hamburgers or bottling colas is not entirely mistaken. You can ascribe greater importance to supposedly "key" industries on the basis of bad judgment or of good judgment. It is at least arguable that an economy needs to master electronics if it seeks to maintain competitiveness in manufacturing, since machines are increasingly monitored, controlled, and retooled electronically. You have a choice, then, of ascribing status to electronics *before* the achievements of manufacturing lapse or *afterward*. A culture that insists on waiting for dire results before changing course may handicap itself. Intelligent anticipation requires ascribing importance to certain projects, just as joint ventures, strategic alliances, and partnerships require us to value a relationship *before* it proves successful.

Negotiations Between Achievement- and Ascription-Oriented Cultures

It can be extremely irritating to managers from achieving cultures when an ascriptive team of negotiators has some éminence grise hovering in the background to whom they have to submit any proposals or changes. It is not even clear what this person does. Such people will not say what they want, but simply expect deference not just from you but also from their own team members, who are forever watching for faint signs of assent or dissent. It is equally upsetting for ascriptive cultures when the "achieving team" wheels in its aggressive young men and women who spout knowledge as if it were a kind of ammunition before which the team opposite is expected to surrender. It is rather like having to play a game with a toddler holding a toy gun: there is a lot of noise coming from someone who is of no known authority or status.

Indeed, sending whiz kids to deal with people 10 to 20 years their senior often insults the ascriptive culture. The reaction may be: "Do these people think that they have reached our own level of experience in half the time? That a 30-year-old American is good enough to negotiate with a 50-year-old Greek or Italian?" Achievement cultures must understand that some ascriptive cultures, the Japanese especially, spend much on training and in-house education to ensure that older people actually are wiser for the years they have spent in the corporation and for the sheer number of subordinates briefing them. It insults an ascriptive culture to do anything that prevents the self-fulfilling nature of its beliefs. Older people are held to be important *so that* they will be nourished and sustained by others' respect. A stranger is expected to facilitate this process, not challenge it.

Consider a Japanese-Dutch negotiating session. When Dutch experts in finance, marketing, and human resources meet their Japanese opposite numbers, the Dutch approach is to try to clarify facts and determine who holds the decision-making power. To the Dutch, the Japanese will appear evasive and secretive, not revealing anything. For the Japanese, these matters are not "facts" so much as mutual understandings between their leaders and themselves, which the Dutch seem to be prying into. This "prying" may come across as disrespectful. Anyway, it is for the leader of the negotiating team to say what these relationships are if he or she chooses to.

At a conference on a Japanese-Dutch joint venture held in Rotterdam, a Japanese participant fell ill. A member of the Dutch delegation approached Mr. Yoshi, another Japanese delegate with fluent English and outstanding technical knowledge, and asked if he would replace the sick man in a particular forum. Mr. Yoshi demurred, and the Dutchman was annoyed at the lack of a straight response. Several minutes later the leader of the Japanese delegation, Mr. Kaminaki, announced that Mr. Yoshi would replace the sick man because Mr. Kaminaki was appointing him to the task. It was made abundantly clear whose decision that had been.

The Translator's Role

Analogous to this case, in negotiations it often emerges that the translator from an ascriptive culture behaves "unprofessionally" according to the standards of achieving cultures. According to British, German, North American, Scandinavian, and Dutch values, the translator is an achiever like any other participant, and the height of his or her achievement should be to give an accurate, unbiased account of what was said in one language to those speaking the other language. The translator is supposed to be neutral, a black box serving the interests of modern language comprehension, not the interests of either party who may seek to distort meanings for personal own ends.

In other cultures, however, the translator is doing something else. A Japanese translator, for example, will often take a minute or more to "translate" an English sentence 15 seconds long. In addition, there is often extensive colloquy between the translator and the team he or she serves about what the opposite team just said. Japanese translators are interpreters, not simply of language but also of gesture, meaning, and context. Their role is to support their own team and possibly even to protect the team from confrontational conduct by the Western negotiators. They may protect superiors from rudeness and advise the team how to counter opposition tactics. The "translator" is very much on the ascribing team's side, and if the achievement-oriented team seeks flawless, if literal, translation, it should bring its own translator. This option may not actually improve relationships, because members of Asian teams are accustomed to speaking among themselves, in the belief that foreigners do not understand. If you take along someone fluent in their tongue, they will have to withdraw in order to confer. Your "contribution" to mutual understanding may not be appreciated.

The Role of Titles

The use and mention of titles with business cards and formal introductions can be complex. Both authors carry three kinds of cards to introduce themselves. In the Middle East and southern Europe formal titles received for formal education are diffused through several contexts to elevate one's status. In Britain, however, presenting oneself as "doctor" may suggest an excessively academic bent for a business consultant. It may not be considered relevant for a consultant to have a Ph.D., and if attention is drawn to it, the status claimed is not necessarily legitimate. Achievement in a university may even disqualify a person from likely achievement in a corporation.

We might expect a similar situation in the US, another achievement-oriented, yet specific, society. However, the "inflation" of qualifications in the US makes it legitimate to draw attention to higher degrees from good universities, provided this information is relevant to the task at hand. Typically the specialty is mentioned: M.B.A., sociology, and so on.

In diffuse cultures it is important to *tie in* your status with your organization. Here your achievement as an individual will be discounted compared with the status your organization ascribes to you. It is therefore important to say not just that you are chief but also what you are chief of: marketing, finance, human resources, and so on. Many a deal has been lost because the representative was not seen to have high status back home. Ascriptive cultures must be assured that your organization has considerable respect for you and that you are at or near the top.

Relationship with the Mother Company

In the value system of individualist, achievement-oriented cultures, the specific "word" of the representative pledges the company to any commitment made. The individual has the delegated authority to use personal judgment. In ascriptive cultures, the individual, unless head of the organization, almost never has the personal discretion to commit the company without extensive consultations. Moreover, an individual from an ascriptive culture may not really believe that the achieving representative has this authority either. Hence, agreements are tentative and subject to back-home ratification. It is partly for this reason that your title and power "back home" are important to the ascriptive negotiator. How can you deliver your company if you are not high in its status hierarchy? If you send an impetuous, though clever, youth, you cannot be very serious. It is much to your benefit to send senior people if you are visiting an ascriptive culture, even if they are less knowledgeable about the product. It could also be important to ask for senior people in the ascriptive culture to attend in person and meet their opposite numbers. The closer you get to the top, the more likely it is that promises made in negotiations will be kept.

Status Symbols

We are now beginning to see more clearly why pay-for-performance and bonuses to high achievers whatever their rank can be upsetting to ascriptive cultures. The superior is *by definition* responsible for increased performance, so relative status is unaffected by higher group sales. If rewards are to be increased, this must be done proportionately to ascribed status, not directed to the person closest to the sale. If the leader does something to reduce his or her own status, *all of the leader's subordinates are downgraded as a consequence.*

On arrival in Thailand a British general manager refused to take his predecessor's car. The Thai finance manager asked the new GM what type of Mercedes he would like, then. The GM asked for a Suzuki or a Mini, anything that could be handled easily in the congested traffic in Bangkok.

Three weeks later the GM called the finance manager and asked about prospects for the delivery of his car. The Thai manager lost his reserve for a moment and exclaimed, "We can get you a new Mercedes by tomorrow, but Suzukis take much, much longer." The GM asked him to see what he could do to speed up the process. After four weeks the GM asked to see the purchase order for the car. The purchasing department replied that, because it would take so long to get a small car, the decision had been made to order a Mercedes.

The GM's patience had run out. At the first management meeting he brought the issue up and asked for an explanation. Somewhat shyly, members of the predominantly Thai management team explained that they could hardly come to work on bicycles.

In this case the status of each member was interdependent. Had the British GM ordered an even more expensive car, all the other managers might have moved up a notch. In ascriptive societies you "are" your status. It is as natural to you as your birth or formal education (rebirth), through which your innate powers were made manifest. Ascribed status simply "is" and requires no rational justification, although such justifications may exist. For example, a preference for males, for greater age, or for social connections is not usually justified or defended by the culture ascribing importance to older men from "good" families. That does not mean it is irrational or without competitive advantage, however; it simply means that justifications are not offered and not expected. It has always been so, and if this means making a major effort to educate staff as they age, that is all the better, but it is *not* the basis for preferring older people in the first place.

Achievement-oriented organizations justify their hierarchies by claiming that senior people have "achieved more" for the organization; their authority, justified by skill and knowledge, benefits the organization. Ascription-oriented organizations justify their hierarchies by "power to get things done." This may consist of power *over* people and be coercive, or power *through* people and be participative. There is high variation within ascriptive cultures, and participative power has well-known advantages. Whatever form power takes, the ascription of status to people is intended to be exercised as power, and that power is supposed to enhance the effectiveness of the organization. The sources of ascribed status may be multiple, and trying to alter it by promotion on the grounds of achievement can be hazardous.

An achievement-oriented Swedish manager was managing a project in Pakistan. A vacancy needed to be filled, and after careful assessment the Swedish manager chose one of his two most promising Pakistani employees for promotion. Both candidates were highly educated, with Ph.D.s in mechanical engineering, and in Pakistan both were known authorities in their field. Although both had excellent performance records, Mr. Kahn was selected on the basis of some recent achievements.

Mr. Saran, the candidate not chosen, was upset by the turn of events. He went to his Swedish boss for an explanation. However, even an explanation based on the specific needs of the business did not calm him. How could this loss of face be allowed?

The Swedish manager tried to make the engineer understand that only one of the two could be promoted, because there was only one vacancy. One of them was going to be hurt, even though they were both valued employees. He made no progress. The reason, as he eventually learned, was the fact that Mr. Saran received his Ph.D. two years before Mr. Khan from the same American university. Saran was expected to have more status than his colleague because of this. His family would never understand. What was this Western way of treating ascribed status so lightly? Should not more than just the achievements of the past months be considered?

It is important to see how different the logics of achievement and ascription are and not consider either as worthless. In achieving countries people are evaluated by how they performed the allocated function. Relationships are functionally specific: I relate to you as, say, a sales manager. The justification of my role lies in the sales records. Another person in that role must be expected to be compared with me and I with that person. Success is universally defined as increased sales. My relationship to manufacturing, R&D, planning, and so on, is instrumental. I either sell what they have developed, manufactured, and planned, or I do not. I *am* my functional role.

In ascribing cultures status is attributed to those who "naturally" evoke admiration from others, which means older people, highly qualified people, and/or people skilled in a technology or project deemed to be of national importance. To show respect for status is to assist the person so distinguished in fulfilling the expectations the society has of him or her. The status is generally independent of task or specific function. The individual is particular and not easily compared with others. His or her performance is partly determined by his subordinates' loyalty; which loyalty they must display. He or she *is* the organization in the sense of personifying it and wielding its power.

Achievement-oriented corporations in Western countries often send young, promising managers on challenging assignments to faraway countries without realizing that the local culture will not accept their youthfulness and/or gender however well they achieve. A young (aged 34), talented, female marketing manager had worked for an

American company in both the US and Britain. She was so success-ful in her second year there that she was named the most promis-ing female manager in Britain. This vote of confidence influenced her decision to accept an offer to transfer as director of marketing to her company's operation in Ankara, Turkey. She knew she had always been able to win the support and trust of her subordinates and colleagues.

The first few weeks in Ankara were as usual in a new job, get-ting to know the local business, the staff, and how to get things done. Luckily, she knew one of the marketing managers, Guz Akil, who had been her marketing assistant in London. They had worked well together.

Working as hard as she could over the first few months, she found her authority gradually slipping away. The most experienced Turk, Hasan (aged 63), informally but consciously took over more and more of her authority, getting things done where her own efforts were frustrated, although his marketing knowledge was only a fraction of her own. She had to watch him exercise influence, which most often led to unsatisfactory results. Through Guz she learned that the head office complied with this arrangement, communicating more and more through Hasan, not her. She also heard that 10 years earlier an American male manager the same age she was had been withdrawn because of his inability to command local managers effectively. He was now working with much success for a competitor back in the US.

When this case was presented in a workshop in San Francisco, pointing out the dangers of a universalist system for personnel plan-ning, one female manager expressed concern. "You should not linger on this issue," she stated. "You are advising us to discriminate on the basis of gender and age, or allow our overseas subsidiaries to do so. In this country you could get sued for that."

Her point was well taken in that cultural preferences often have the force of law as well as custom. Refusal to send young women managers to Turkey because they are young and female is probably illegal, yet to send them is to confront them with difficulties that they may not have the capacity to surmount, through no fault of their own.

The more they achieve, the more they seem to subvert the ascription process. A better tactic can be to make a young female an assistant or adviser to indigenous managers. She will make up for any deficits in knowledge they have, while using local seniority to get things done. Such a posting could be paid and evaluated in the same way as for a chief in an achievement-oriented culture, perhaps with a bonus for culture shock. You cannot replace Turkish cultural norms with American ones if you seek to be effective in Turkey. Doing so will not work in the long run, and in the short run it can be costly.

Toward Reconciliation

Despite far more emphasis on either ascription or achievement in certain cultures, the two orientations can be seen to develop together. Those that "start" with ascribing usually ascribe not just status but also future success or achievement and thereby help to bring it about. Those that "start" with achievement usually also start to ascribe importance and priority to the people and projects that have been successful. Hence, all societies ascribe and all achieve after a fashion. It is once again a question of where a cycle begins.

It was in 1985 that Belly Electronics (BE) started to manufacture in South Korea. The fast-changing prices in consumer electronics had forced the San Francisco–based company to decentralize its production facilities. After some serious starting losses BE began to recover, and late in 1989 it could report some promising profits. Early in 1991 margins came under pressure because of Thai and Vietnamese competition. BE decided to reengineer its business processes following its major competitors in the region.

For the first time BE flew in experienced US managers from the Bay Area. Their approach was consistent and had made them managers of the year at BE for similar turnaround projects in California and Massachusetts. On the basis of a continuous improvement program Korean managers were put under pressure to "get their act together." Something said by the first US manager is still remembered in Seoul: "Ladies and gentlemen, we are on a burning platform. Figures tell us there is not much time left. Competitors in the region are doing much better than we are; in fact, comparative research shows that our benchmark companies in California and Thailand are outperforming us by 35 percent on quality and 42 percent on quantity per worker. I therefore give you six months to get the numbers up and then to become a profit-generating company. Let us show that we are a worthwhile company in BE by achievements and not just promises."

After disappointing results a second US manager was flown in, but his similar approach made no difference. Interviews with the key Korean players were not helpful. Loss after loss was defended by the same response: "We are trying, but it is not easy in Korea. Fierce competition explains a lot, but we need to stop turnover of personnel so we can trust each other more."

Jerome Don was asked to come to the rescue of BE-Korea. He was known for turning companies around with impressive skill in both South America and Asia. He started by telling Korean managers that his predecessors were right in their approach: "We are on a burning platform, but I ask you to help us to save this facility because it is so important to BE. I'll give you three years to get your act together, and I'll help you whenever you need me."

Within six months BE-Korea was profitable. Quality went up, and improved morale resulted in 60 percent lower staff turnover. Mr. Don did not know exactly what happened, but he had done the same in South America and now in Asia.

Why was Jerome Don successful in Korea, while his predecessors had not been?

The initial actions by the American managers were counterproductive. In the great American tradition the turnaround managers started at the top of Figure 8.3 and focused on the reward that people could get for their achievements. The Koreans became even more nervous than they had been before the intervention, because basic trust seemed to be lacking. They were afraid to be judged on their past performance.

Figure 8.3. **Reconciling Achievement and Ascription**

Jerome Don gave his Korean colleagues three years to get their act together. By doing so, he intuitively ascribed status to the Korean organization. This ascription of status gave the Koreans the trust they needed in conveying that they were respected for who they were based on their years at BE. The result was that they were inspired to work even harder. From ascribed status comes achievement.

Test Yourself

Consider the following scenario:

There are different grounds for according status to employees, based either on what people have succeeded in doing or on what qualities are attributed to them by the social system.

Now consider these statements:

1. Status should lie in the permanent attributes of employees—that is, their education, seniority, age, position, and level of responsibility ascribed. Status should not change according to occasion or just because of recent successes. It reflects intrinsic worth, not the latest forays.

2. Status should lie in the permanent attributes of employees—that is, their education, seniority, age, position, and level of responsibility ascribed. Such status tends to be self-fulfilling, with achievement and leadership resulting from what the corporation values in you and expects of you.

3. Status is a matter of what the employee has actually achieved, his or her track record. Yet over time this deserved reputation becomes a permanent attribute, allowing success to be renewed and enabling even more achievement to occur.

4. Achievement or success is the only legitimate source of status in business. The more recent the achievement, the better and more relevant it is to current challenges. Achievement gets its significance from the humble nature of the individual's birth and background and from success in beating the odds.

Indicate with 1 the approach you prefer and with 2 your second choice. Similarly, indicate with 1 the approach you believe would be favored by your closest colleagues at work, and indicate with 2 the approach you believe would be their second choice.

If you chose answer 2 or 3, you have expressed a belief in reconciling achieved and ascribed status. Answer 2 affirms socially ascribed status that leads to achievement and success (the Korean case was based on a similar principle). Answer 3 affirms achieved status that is believed to lead to social ascription. In both cases the integrity lies in the self-fulfilling sense of self-worth. Answers 1 and 4, respectively, reject achieved and ascribed status.

The following tables show practical tips for doing business in ascription- and achievment-oriented cultures.

RECOGNIZING THE DIFFERENCES

ACHIEVEMENT ORIENTATION

Use of titles only when relevant to the competence the person brings to the task.

Respect for superiors in the hierarchy is based on how effectively they perform their jobs and how adequate their expertise is.

Most senior managers are of varying age and gender and have shown proficiency in specific jobs.

ASCRIPTION ORIENTATION

Extensive use of titles, especially when they clarify the person's status in the organization.

Respect for superiors in the hierarchy is seen as a measure of people's commitment to the organization and its mission.

Most senior managers are male, middle-aged, and qualified by their background.

TIPS FOR DOING BUSINESS WITH . . .

ACHIEVEMENT-ORIENTED PEOPLE
(FOR ASCRIPTION-ORIENTED INDIVIDUALS)

Make sure your negotiation team has enough data, technical advisers, and knowledgeable people to convince the other company that the project, jointly pursued, will work.

Respect the expertise and information of your counterparts even if you suspect they are short of influence back home.

Use the title that reflects how competent you are as an individual.

Do not underestimate the need of your counterparts to do better or do more than is expected. To challenge is to motivate.

ASCRIPTION-ORIENTED PEOPLE
(FOR ACHIEVEMENT-ORIENTED INDIVIDUALS)

In order to convince the other company that you consider this negotiation important, make sure your negotiation team consists of enough older, senior officials, as well as others with formal titles.

Respect the status and influence of your counterparts even if you suspect they lack experience. Do not make them feel foolish.

Use the title that reflects your degree of influence in your organization.

Do not underestimate the need of your counterparts to make their ascriptions come true. To challenge is to subvert.

WHEN MANAGING AND BEING MANAGED

ACHIEVEMENT-ORIENTED PEOPLE	ASCRIPTION-ORIENTED PEOPLE
Respect for a manager is based on knowledge and skills.	Respect for a manager is based on seniority.
Management by objectives and pay-for-performance are effective tools.	Management by objectives and pay-for-performance are less effective than direct rewards from the manager.
Decisions are challenged on technical and functional grounds.	Decisions are challenged only by people with higher authority.

Notes

1. D. McClelland, *The Achieving Society* (New York: Van Nostrand, 1950).
2. A. Laurent in G. Inzerilli and A. Laurent, "The Concept of Organizational Structure" (working paper, University of Pennsylvania and INSEAD, 1979); "Managerial Views of Organizational Structure in France and the USA," *International Studies of Management and Organizations* 13 (1983): 1–2, 97–118.

How We Manage Time

IF ONLY because managers need to coordinate their business activities, they require some kind of shared expectations about time. Just as different cultures have different assumptions about how people relate to one another, so they approach time differently. This chapter is about the relative importance cultures give to the past, present, and future. Does an achievement-oriented culture believe that the future must be better than the past or present, since it is there that aspirations are realized? Does a relationship-oriented culture, on the other hand, see the future as threatening, likely to loosen current bonds of affection? How we think of time has its own consequences.

As well as cultural differences about the past, present, and future, there are additional factors, what we might call subcomponents of the time dimension. These subcomponents include the following:

- Whether time is sequential (a series of linear passing events) or synchronic (in which we can work on tasks in parallel).
- The magnitude of time horizon—the duration of thinking time. Is a business plan for the next three months, three years, or three decades?
- Clock or event time? Do we get the job done in the scheduled time or deliver a better job a little later?

These factors are all interrelated, so that ideas about the future and memories of the past both shape present action.

The Concept of Time

Primitive societies may order themselves by simple notions of "before" and "after" moons, seasons, sunrises, and sunsets. For educated societies the concept of time is increasingly complex. Running through all our ideas of time are two contrasting notions: time as a line of discrete events, minutes, hours, days, months, and years, each passing in a never-ending succession; and time as a circle, revolving so that the minutes of the hour repeat, as do the hours of the day, the days of the week, and so on.

In the Greek myth the Sphinx, a monster with the face of a woman, the body of a lion, and the wings of a bird, asked all wayfarers on the road to Thebes, "What creature is it that walks on four legs in the morning, two legs at noonday, and three legs in the evening?" Those unable to answer she ate. Oedipus, however, answered, "Man," and the Sphinx committed suicide. He had grasped that this riddle was a metaphor for time. Four legs was a child crawling, two legs the adult, and three legs an old person leaning on a stick. By his thinking in a longer sequence about time, the riddle was solved. He had also understood that, within the riddle, time orientations had been compressed or synchronized and that language allows us to do this.

Anthropologists have long insisted that how a culture thinks of time and manages it is a clue to the meanings its members find in life and the supposed nature of human existence. Kluckhohn and Strodtbeck identified three types of culture: present-oriented, which is relatively timeless, is without tradition, and ignores the future; past-oriented, mainly concerned with maintaining and restoring traditions in the present; and future-oriented, envisioning a more desirable future and setting out to realize it.[1] It is chiefly people falling into the third category who experience economic or social development.

Time is increasingly viewed as a factor that organizations need to manage. There are time-and-motion studies, time-to-market, and just-in-time, along with ideas that products age or mature and have a life cycle similar to that of human beings. Uniquely in the animal kingdom, humans are aware of time and try to control it. Humans think almost universally in categories of past, present, and future but do not give the same importance to each. Our conception of time is strongly affected by culture, because time is an idea rather than an object. How we think of time is interwoven with how we plan, strategize, and coordinate our activities with others. It is an integral dimension of how we organize experience and activities.

When we create instruments to measure time, we shape our experience of it. We can differentiate between duration and succession and make fine distinctions within the compass of astronomical time, which is the time taken for Earth to revolve around the sun. We can think of time as fixed in this way by the motion of the planet, or we can think of time as experienced subjectively; on a jet aircraft, the position of the plane is sometimes shown on a map of the earth. We appear to be crawling very, very slowly toward our destination.

The experience of time means that we can consider a past event now (out of sequence, as it were) or envision a future event. In this way past, present, and future are all compressed. We can consider what competitive move to make today, based on past experience and with expectations of the future. This is an interpretative use of time.

Time has meaning not just to individuals but also to whole groups or cultures. Émile Durkheim, the French sociologist, saw it as a social construct enabling members of a culture to coordinate their activities.[2] This view has important implications in a business context. The time agreed for a meeting may be approximate or precise. The time allocated to complete a task may be vitally important or merely a guide. There may be an expectation of mutual accommodation as to the exact time when a machine and its microprocessor are ready to be assembled, or there may be a penalty clause of thousands of dollars a day imposed by one party on another. Intervals between inspections may be indicators of a manager's level of responsibility: is he or she left for three months or three years to get on with the job? Organizations may look ahead a long way or may get obsessed by the monthly reporting period.

Orientations to Past, Present, and Future

Saint Augustine pointed out in his *Declarations* that time as a subjective phenomenon can vary considerably from time in an abstract conception. In its abstract form we cannot know the future, because it is not yet here, and the past is also unknowable; we may have memories, partial and selective, but the past has gone. The only thing that exists is the present, which is our sole access to the past or future. Augustine wrote, "The present has, therefore, three dimensions . . . the present of past things, the present of present things, and the present of future things."

The idea that at any given moment the present is the only real thing, with the past and future ceasing to be or yet to come, must be qualified by the fact that we think *about* past and future in the present. However imperfect our ideas about past or future, they influence our thinking powerfully. These subjective times are ever present in our judgment and our decision making. Although our lives may be consciously oriented to the future success of the enterprise, past experiences have deeply affected our perceptions of that future, as does our present mood. There is a potentially productive tension among the three, along with the ever-pressing question as to whether the future can benefit from past and present experiences (although companies, it is often remarked, have no memory). All three perceptions of time unite in our actions. It is as true to say that our expectations of the future determine our present as it is to say that our present action determines the future; as true to say that our present experience determines our view of the past as to say that the past has made us what we are today. This statement is not simply juggling terms; it is describing how we think. We can make ourselves miserable in the present if a long-expected payment is delayed to the future. We can as easily discover in the present a fact that makes what we did in the past far more justifiable. In fact, an important part of creativity is to assemble past and present activities, plus conjectures about the future, in new combinations.

Different individuals and different cultures may be more or less attracted to past, present, or future orientations. Some live entirely in the present, or try to. "History is more or less bunk," as Henry Ford put it, and inquiry into things past is best forgotten. Some dream of a world that never was and seek to create it from their own imaginings and yearnings, or they may seek the return of a golden age, a Napoleonic legend reborn, a new frontier similar in its challenges to the Wild West. They believe that the future is coming to them, as a destiny, or that they alone must define it. Others live in a nostalgic past to which everything attempted in the present must appeal.

Sequentially and Synchronically Organized Activities

We have seen that at least two images can be extracted from the concept of time. Time can be legitimately conceived of as a line of sequential events passing us at regular intervals. It can also be conceived of as cyclical and repetitive, compressing past, present, and future by what they have in common: seasons and rhythms. At one extreme, then, is the person who conceives of time as a dotted line with regular spacing. Events are organized by the number of intervals before or after their occurrence. Everything has its time and place as far as the sequential thinker is concerned. Any change or turbulence in this sequence will make the sequential person more uncertain. Try jumping into a line in Britain. You will learn that orderly sequence has stern defenders. Everyone must wait his or her turn; first come, first served. It is part of "good form." In London the Dutch author once saw a long line of people waiting for a bus, when it started pouring with rain. They all stood stolidly getting soaked, even though cover was close by, lest they lose their sequential order. They preferred to do things right rather than do the right thing. In the Netherlands you could be the queen, but if you are in a butcher's shop with number 46 and you step up for service when number 12 is called, you are still in deep trouble. Nor does it matter if you have an emergency; order is order.

Going from A to B in a straight line with minimal effort and maximum effect is known as efficiency. This principle has a major influence on the conduct of business in northwestern Europe and North

152 •   RIDING THE WAVES OF CULTURE

America. The flaw in this thinking is that "straight lines" may not always be the best way of doing something; it is blind to the effectiveness of shared activities and cross-connections.

In a butcher's shop in Italy, the Dutch author once saw the butcher unwrap salami at the request of one customer and then shout, "Who else for salami?" The sequential idea is not entirely absent; people still pay in turn when they are finished, but a customer who has all he or she wants (the salami, which was at the ready) might as well pay and leave earlier than someone wanting additional cuts. The method serves more people in less time.

At a butcher's shop in Amsterdam or London, the butcher calls a number; unwraps, cuts, and rewraps each item the customer wants; and then calls the next number. Once one of us ventured the suggestion, "While you have the salami out, cut a pound for me too." Customers and staff practically went into shock. The system may be inefficient, but they were not about to let some wise guy change it.

The synchronic method, however, requires that people track various activities in parallel, rather like a juggler with six balls in the air, each being caught and tossed in rhythm. It is not easy for cultures that are not used to it. Edward T. Hall, the American anthropologist, described what we call synchronic as *polychronic*, putting emphasis on the number of activities run in parallel.[3] There is a final, established goal, but there are numerous and possibly interchangeable stepping-stones to reach it. A person can "skip between stones" on the way to the final target.

In contrast, the sequential person has a "crucial path" worked out in advance with times for the completion of each stage. The person hates to be thrown off this schedule or agenda by unanticipated events. In *The Silent Language* Hall revealed that Japanese negotiators would make their major bids for a concession *after* their American partners were confirmed on their return flights from Tokyo. Rather than risk their schedules, Americans would often concede to the Japanese demands.

Synchronic, or polychronic, styles are extraordinary for those unused to them. The Dutch author once purchased an airline ticket from a woman at a ticket counter in Argentina who, while making out the ticket (correctly), was talking on the telephone to a friend and admiring her coworker's baby. People who do more than one thing at a time can, without meaning to, insult those who are used to doing only one thing.

Likewise, people who do only one thing at a time can, without meaning to, insult those who are used to doing several things. A South Korean manager explained his shock and disappointment on returning to the Netherlands to see his boss:

"He was on the phone when I entered his office, and as I came in, he raised his left hand slightly at me. Then he rudely continued his conversation as if I were not even in the room with him. Only after he had finished his conversation five minutes later did he get up and greet me with an enthusiastic, but insincere, 'Kim, happy to see you.' I just could not believe it."

To a synchronic person, not being greeted spontaneously and immediately, even while the other person is still talking on the telephone, is a slight. The whole notion of "sequencing" your emotions and postponing them until other matters are out of the way suggests insincerity. You show how you value people by "giving them time" even if they show up unexpectedly.

Sequential people tend to schedule tightly, with thin divisions between time slots. It is rude to be even a few minutes late, because the whole day's schedule of events is affected. "I'm running late," the scheduler will complain, as if the speaker were a train or an airline. Time is viewed as a commodity to be used up, and lateness deprives the other of precious minutes in a world where "time is money."

Synchronic cultures are less insistent on punctuality, defined as a person's arriving at the agreed moment of passing time increments. It is not that the passage of time is unimportant, but that several other cultural values vie with punctuality. It is often necessary to "give time" to people with whom you have a particular relationship (see the discussion of universalism versus particularism in Chapter 4). It may be required that you show affective pleasure on meeting a friend or relation unexpectedly (see the discussion of the affective versus the neutral approach in Chapter 6). Your schedule is not an excuse for passing such people by. Your mother, fiancée, or friend could be seriously offended. Raymond Carroll, the French anthropologist, tells of an American girl who left a note for her French lover asking if he could he let her know if he wanted to see her this evening, as if not she would like to make other plans. The Frenchman was offended. Her schedule should not get in the way of their spontaneously affective and particular relationship.[4] People prominent in a hierarchy must also be "given time" if encountered (see status by achievement versus status by ascription in Chapter 8). For all such reasons, meeting times may be approximate in synchronic cultures. The range is from 15 minutes in Latin Europe to part or all of a day in the Middle East and Africa. Given the fact that most of those with appointments to meet are running other activities in parallel, any waiting involved is not onerous, and late arrival may often even be a convenience, allowing some time for unplanned activities.

Even the preparation of food is affected by time orientations. In sequential, punctual cultures, exactly the right quantity of food will usually be prepared, and in such a way that it might spoil or get cold if the guests are not on time. In synchronic cultures, there is usually more than enough food in case more guests drop by unexpectedly, and it either is not the kind that spoils or else is cooked as wanted.

Measuring Cultural Differences in Relation to Time

The methodology used in this book to measure approaches to time comes from Tom Cottle, who created the "circles test."[5] The question asked was as follows:

Think of the past, present, and future as being in the shape of circles. Please draw three circles in the space available, representing past, present, and future. Arrange these circles in any way you want that best shows how you feel about the relationship of the past, present, and future. You may use different sizes of circles. When you have finished, label each circle to show which one is the past, which one the present, and which one the future.

Cottle ended up with four possible configurations. First, he found absence of relationship. Figure 9.1 shows that on our measurements this is a typically Russian and Venezuelan approach to time; there is no connection between past, present, or future, though in the Russians' view the future is much more important than the present and more important than the past. The second Cottle configuration was temporal integration. Here we see Malaysia and Japan as good examples where past, present, and future fully overlap. The third is a partial overlap of the circles with good examples shown in Figure 9.1: this last configuration is characteristic of the Belgians and Germans, who see a smaller overlap. In this they are not dissimilar to the British, who have a rather stronger link to the past. It is the present that is less important. The Germans put the most emphasis on the present, whereas the Belgians view all three aspects of time as equally important. Both are quite different from the French, for whom all three aspects overlap considerably; they share this view with the Malaysians. In the fourth approach, we see that past, present, and future are touching but not overlapping, hence not "sharing" regions of time between them. A

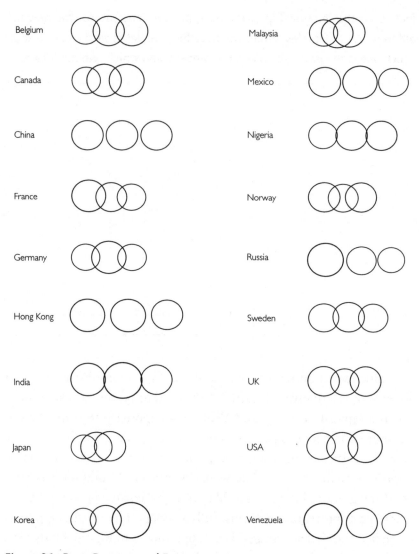

Figure 9.1. Past, Present, and Future

good example here is India and Nigeria, where they seem to have a logical flow with the time periods not affecting each other much.

The foregoing interpretations and inferences derived from these circles diagrams are facilitated by taking into account other discriminating questions from our surveys and the other aspects of the time dimension as discussed in the following sections.

Time Horizon

The circles test measured how different cultures assign different meanings to past, present, and future. We have used another test developed by Cottle to see whether people share a short-term or a long-term time horizon.[6] The "duration inventory" inquires into the manner in which people perceive the boundaries separating past, present, and future as well as the extension of each. We have paraphrased the inventory in order to make it shorter, since we are concerned with only one of the 58 items in the questionnaire.

The question is as follows:

Consider the relative significance of the past, present, and future. You will be asked to indicate your relative time horizons for the past, present, and future by giving a number:

7 = years
6 = months
5 = weeks
4 = days
3 = hours
2 = minutes
1 = seconds

My past started . . . . . . ago, and ended . . . . . . ago.
My present started . . . . . . ago, and ended . . . . . . from now.
My future started . . . . . . from now, and ended . . . . . . from now.

We have taken the average of each of the six scores and calculated an average score per country, for which significant differences can be identified. (See Figure 9.2.) The longest horizon is found in Hong Kong and the shortest in the Philippines.

Our time horizon significantly affects how we do business. It is obvious that the relatively long-term vision of the Japanese contrasts with the "quarterly thinking" of the Americans. This contrast was

7 = year   I = seconds

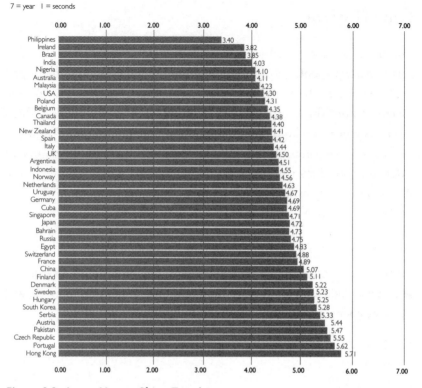

Figure 9.2. Long- Versus Short-Termism

shown in a striking way when the Japanese were trying to buy the operations of Yosemite National Park, in California. The first thing they submitted was a 250-year business plan. Imagine the reactions of the Californian authorities: "Gee, that is 1,000 quarterly reports."

The long Swedish horizon is explained by the country's long dark winters. There are only a few bright months in which you have to plan for the whole year.

However, there are some striking differences among long-term past orientation, the perceived extension of the present, and a long-term view of the future. A selection of scores is presented in Figures 9.3 and 9.4.

The duration questionnaire also allowed us to check the overlap between time horizons—that is, the degree of synchronicity. Correlations found are high and significant compared with the overlap of the circles discussed earlier.

7 = years, I = seconds

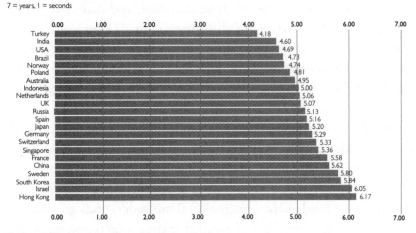

Figure 9.3. Average Time Horizon: Past

7 = years, I = seconds

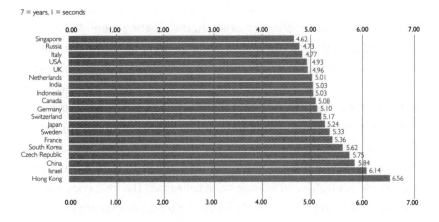

Figure 9.4. Average Time Horizon: Future

Time Orientations and Management

Business organizations are structured in accordance with how they conceive of time. Corporations have whole departments given over to planning, to scanning the environment for new trends, to getting production out faster, to shortening the time-to-market, which is defined as the time interval between a customer's demanding a product and

that product's being designed, manufactured, and delivered. Strategies, goals, and objectives are all future oriented. Joint ventures and
partnerships are agreements about how the future should jointly be
engaged. "Motivation" is about what we can give to a person now so
that he or she will work better in the future. Progress, learning, and
development all assume an augmentation of powers over time, as does
the habit of paying senior people more for the experience supposedly
accumulated over time. When orientations to time differ within corporations spanning different cultures, confusion can occur. Let us return
to the sorrows of young Mr. Johnson of MCC. A good lunch makes
even the most fundamental intercultural misunderstandings seem like
ripples on a lake. Johnson had asked that the group reconvene at 2:00
P.M. precisely, because they had a tight agenda for the afternoon.

At 1:50 P.M. most participants returned to the meeting room. At 2:05 Johnson started pacing restlessly. Munoz and Gialli were still down the hall making telephone calls. They came in at 2:20. Johnson said, "Now, gentlemen,
can we finally start the meeting?" The Singaporean and African representatives looked puzzled. They thought the meeting had already started.

The first point on the agenda was the time intervals determining bonuses
and merits. All except the American, Dutch, and other northwest European
representatives complained that these intervals were far too frequent. To
Johnson and his Dutch and Scandinavian colleagues the frequency was obviously right. "Rewards must closely follow the behavior they are intended to
reinforce; otherwise you lose the connection." The manager from Singapore
said, "Possibly, but this go-for-the-quick-buck philosophy has been losing us
customers. They don't like the pressure we put on at the end of the quarter.
They want our representatives to serve them, not to have private agendas.
We need to keep our customers long term, not push them into buying so
that one salesperson can beat a rival."

The American view of the future is that the *individual* can direct it
by personal achievement and inner-directed effort. This is why Johnson, backed by Dutch and Scandinavian managers, is keen to give
pay-for-performance at regular intervals. Yet because the individual

achiever cannot do very much about the *distant* future—there are simply too many events that could occur—the US's idea of the future is short term, something controllable from the present. Hence the accusation of "going for the quick buck" and the great importance given to the next quarterly figures. If the future is to be better, it is by steadily increasing increments of sales and profits. There is no excuse, ever, for not doing better now, since success now causes increased successes in the future.

It is insightful to compare the French respondents with the Americans. In French culture the past looms far larger and is used as a context in which to understand the present. Past, present, and future overlap synchronically, so that the past informs the present, and both inform the future. By way of example, the Dutch author describes visiting the futuristic La Défense business district in Paris around the turn of the century. My French colleague was delayed, so I picked up a brochure at the reception desk. It was about the company's achievements during the 1980s. I read it with interest, and as my colleague was further delayed, I asked the receptionist for a more recent one. She handed me a copy of the same brochure I had just read. She said it had been printed only two months ago and was the most recent available. Future opportunities for this company were very apparently connected to the success of the past.

Human Relations and Orientations to Time

Different orientations are also reflected in the quality of human bonds within an organization, as well as between the corporation and its partners. Any lasting relationship combines past, present, and future with ties of affection and memory. The relationship is its own justification and is enjoyed as a form of durable companionship extending both far back and far forward. Cultures that think synchronically about time are more "we" oriented (communitarian) and usually more particularist in valuing people known to be special.

The cultures concerned with sequential time tend to see relationships as more instrumental. The separation between time intervals seems also to separate means from ends, so that higher pay is the means toward still higher performance, and my customer's purchase is the means by which I will receive a higher bonus. The relationship is not entered into for its own sake but in order to enhance the income of each party and the profit of the organization. The future looms large because present activity is but a means for realizing it. The important result is in the (near-term) future. Gratification is postponed because it will soon be greater.

Whether relationships unmediated by calculation of future gain are not closer and more amenable to dialogue is a compelling question. Given the sheer complexity of modern business and the mounting volume of information that must be communicated, the durable, synchronic relationship in which the past, present, and future of the partners are bound together in coevolution may be becoming a more effective way to manage. Certainly the idea that synchronic cultures are somehow "primitive" because their schedules are looser is not borne out. Sequential cultures in which human resources are seen as a variation on physical plant, equipment, and cash are more likely to have we-them relationships or, to quote Martin Buber, I-it.[7]

Time Orientation and Authority

In nations in which the past looms large and time orientations overlap, status is more likely to be legitimized by ascription based on durable characteristics such as age, class, gender, ethnicity, and professional qualification. Past qualifications—for example, study at *les grandes écoles*—explain present eminence and promising futures, all of which are closely connected and synchronized.

On the other hand, when a person's career in Hollywood is "only as good as the last performance," the future is a sequence of episodes of relative success and failure. People will unburden themselves of relationships and dependencies not useful in the next stage of their careers, just as the original American immigrants cut off their roots. The authority of the individual will depend on the latest achievement; those on the top today may be gone tomorrow. It is also the case that the authority of the individual can easily be challenged and assessed. What did the person do in the most recent time interval? We find a reflection of this approach in the project-group organization pioneered by NASA and popular in North America and northwestern Europe. Different parts of the organization are identified by and rewarded according to the fortunes in the future of the project being undertaken. Successes grow incrementally; failures are pruned back. Within the group those contributing most to the project are also rewarded accordingly.

Policies of Promotion and Performance Evaluation

Sequential and synchronic cultures, and those concerned more with the past in comparison with those concerned more with the future, may assess and promote differently. In sequential cultures the supervisor is concerned with how the employee has performed over the previous interval. The more that employee can be held responsible for a rise or fall in fortune, the better, and supervisors will be tempted to minimize their own roles, or that of their relationship with the employee, so as to help the employee to see his or her own recent achievement separated out as an increment of gain or loss. In more synchronic organizations, on the other hand, the employee may be favorably assessed and promoted for the positive relationship established with the supervisor, who sees that relationship developing over time and accumulating knowledge and mutuality. Supervisors gladly acknowledge their role in advancing a subordinate's career, as in the master-apprentice system in Germany.

Managing Change in a Past-Oriented Culture

The English author was recently in Ethiopia with a Dutch manager who was frustrated by his unsuccessful efforts to organize a Management of Change seminar with Ethiopian managers. The managers all kept harking back to a distant and wealthy era in Ethiopian civilization and would not incorporate any developmental principles that were not based in this past. After a discussion with the Ethiopian colleagues, we decided to study some Ethiopian history books, reviewing them from the perspective of modern management. What had Ethiopia done right in that period to make its cities and trade flourish? The company also had a rich history within Ethiopia, and these records too were studied. The Dutch manager posed the challenge anew. The future was now seen as a way of re-creating some of the greatest glories of the past; suddenly, the Management of Change seminar had captured everyone's enthusiastic support.

This is not a remote case applicable only to Ethiopia. All change includes continuity; that is, staying the same *in some respects* so as to preserve your identity. Many cultures decline to change at the behest of Western consultants unless the ways in which they will preserve their identity are made clear to them. Synchronic cultures carry their pasts through the present into the future and will refuse to consider changing unless convinced that their heritage is safe.

A large American telecommunications company introduced a technically superior product on the world market. It planned to focus specifically on increasing sales in Latin America, where it had not been all that successful previously. The only serious competitor was a French company, which had an inferior product but whose after-sales support was reputedly superior.

The Americans went to substantial pains to prepare their first presentation in Mexico. "Judgment day" would begin with a video presentation of the company and its growth potential in the medium-long term. Afterward the vice president of the group would personally give a presentation to the Mexican minister of communications. Also meticulously planned was the two-hour lunch. Knowing Mexican culture, they believed this was where the battle would be fought. The afternoon session was reserved for questions and answers. The company jet would then be ready to leave Mexico City in the last departure slot. It was tight, efficient, and appreciated, right?

Wrong; the Mexican team threw off the schedule right away by arriving one hour late. Then, just as the Americans were introducing the agenda for the day, the minister was called out of the room for an urgent phone call. He returned a while later to find that the meeting had gone on without him. The Mexicans were upset that the presentation had proceeded, that the after-sales service contract was separate from the sales contract, and that the presentation focused only on the first two years after installation rather than the longer-term future together.

The French, meanwhile, prepared a loosely structured agenda. They determined some of the main goals to be attained by the end of the two-week visit. The timing, the where, and the how were dependent on factors beyond their control, so they left them open. A long presentation on the historical background of the French state-owned company was prepared for the minister and his team. The company had done business with Mexico's telephone system as early as 1930 and wanted to reestablish a historic partnership. As far as the French were concerned, the after-sales service, which extended indefinitely, was part of the contract. It was the French who received the order for a product known in the industry to be technologically less sophisticated.

What had gone wrong for the Americans? The main mistake was creating a tight, sequential agenda, which was almost inevitably thrown off by Mexican officials, who had deliberately built slack into their procedures and pursued agendas that were multiple and (to the Americans) distracting. The belief that the technologically superior product *should* win the contract is part of the original cultural bias in which each episode within a sequence is separated out. The Mexicans were interested in the product only as part of an ongoing relationship, an issue that the synchronic French were also careful to stress. Similarly the Americans separated the after-sales service contract from the rest, presumably because it occurred at a later period. Both French and Mexican cultures see these time intervals as joined.

The French emphasis on the historic renewal of French-Mexican bonds was also effective with a culture that identifies with Spain and has deep European roots. American sequencing strikes synchronic cultures as aggressive, impatient, and seeking to use customers as stepping-stones to personal advantage. If the relationship is genuinely to last, what is the hurry? Because the Mexicans did not agree that technological perfection was the key issue, they did not want to be on the receiving end of a detailed presentation timed to end just before the American departure. They wanted to experience a relationship they could partly control. In synchronic time, the demeanor of the American corporation during the presentation presaged its conduct in the future, and the Mexicans did not like it.

That said, the biggest advantage the French had was their willingness to spend two weeks dedicated to an agreement and leave it up to their hosts to use those two weeks in a flexible program aimed at synchronizing mutual efforts, rather than trying to agree on a schedule in advance. For the French and Mexicans, what was important was that they get to the end, *not* the particular path or sequence by which *that* end was reached. Also, the details of the equipment were less important to the Mexicans than the responsiveness of the supplier, since they could not know what problems might surface in the future. All they could really ask for, given this concern, was someone willing to alter a schedule to their convenience, and that the French showed they could do.

Moreover, the Americans had a narrower definition of how the negotiation should end. There should be a deadline when the Mexicans would say "yes." For the French, and synchronic cultures generally, there is no real "end," because the partnership continues. Instead of the *efficiency* of getting from A to B in the shortest possible time, there is the effectiveness of developing closer relationships long term. The Americans also made one more serious mistake. Anticipating that the Mexicans would be late returning from lunch, as they had been several times, the Americans caucused for half an hour among themselves. This action failed to show respect for the buyer. You "give them time" by waiting for them to join you. You do not use that time yourself in a way that makes you unavailable should they enter the room. A "readiness to synchronize" must be shown, as opposed to a mere delay in the sequence.

Planned Sequences or Planned Convergence?

In sequentially organized cultures planning consists largely of forecasts, which means extending existing trend lines into the future and seeing this future as "more of the same." Strategies consist of choosing desirable goals and then discovering by analysis the most logical and efficient means of attaining them. It is commonly believed that present and future are causally linked, so that rewards now produce future achievements, which produce greater achievements, which produce greater rewards. Deadlines are important because they signal the end of one link in a causal chain and the beginning of the next and keep you "on schedule."

Planning varies considerably between sequential and synchronic cultures. In sequential planning it is vital to get all the means or stages right and completed on time. "In Britain," an Italian researcher commented, "everything needs to be planned from start to finish. When the environment changes, everything needs to be recalculated from the start." For the more synchronic Italians the goals are what is most important, and the more paths you can devise to their realization, the better you fare against unforeseen events that block one path or another.

The 1990 Mundialito (Football World Cup) in Italy provides a relevant example of Italian organization. The challenge was to complete the championships by a certain date on which the finals would be staged. To the dismay of the British and other northwest Europeans, the Italians would periodically reorganize the entire program to bring about this result. To the surprise of these other cultures, though, the Italians were able to pull it off. The 1992 Olympic Games in Spain had many similarities to Italian planning. In Atlanta in 1996 it seemed that the sequential Americans had much more trouble in adapting to unexpected circumstances.

There is accumulating evidence that sequential planning processes work less well in turbulent environments. They are too brittle, too easily upset by unforeseen events. The fact that they tend to concentrate on the near future testifies to the vulnerability of long sequences. Synchronic plans tend to converge or "home in" on predetermined targets, taking into consideration fusions and lateral connections *between* trends that sequential planning often overlooks.

An intriguing example of a shift by a major corporation to a synchronic style of planning was the adoption by the Shell International Petroleum Corporation of *scenario planning in the 1980s*. In this exercise, scenarios for three alternative futures are written as if the writer were a contemporary commentator explaining how business had reached that point. In other words, past, present, and future are synchronized within the imagination, and three developments are traced from the past through the present into diverging futures and are written up as stories or narratives. For example, a scenario for 2003:

"In retrospect it was inevitable that California would be the launching pad for the electric car. So polluted had the Los Angeles area grown, that the world's strictest emission standards, originating in the 1980s, led to partly electric cars in 1995 and the fully electric car eight years later. Slowly the pall began to lift. The final breakthrough was the '1,000 mile electric' with batteries that were rechargeable overnight. Was this, at last, the end of the internal combustion engine?"[8]

In this type of planning we see sequential and synchronic thinking combined. It proves possible to reestablish forecasts within the scenarios, so that each "synchronic scene" has a different sequence of events.

Once again we find that differences in cultural orientation are not truly alternatives but are capable of being used in conjunction. The wise cross-cultural manager perceives *all* the ways preferred by different cultures. In scenario planning, sequencing and synchronizing work together.

Reconciling the Sequential and the Synchronic

It is frequently claimed that synchronic people are difficult to do business with, because they tend to ignore deadlines and are imprecise in appointments. Take the following example.

Jan Kuipers, a Dutch manager of a wholesale distributor of Italian haute couture, was getting more and more worried about late delivery times to his Dutch clients. The short Dutch summer did not allow delivery of high-priced goods a week late, which was the average delay from the Italian group. Kuipers had tried many ways of solving the problem, but with no result. He tried ordering early, but the Italians were not impressed. He then tried having them sign a contract so that they would take back the clothes unconditionally. Kuipers was now fighting the Italian transport firm, because the fashion partner denied any responsibility. What would you advise him to do to solve the late-delivery problem?

The Italian designers in Milan were giving a signal by consistently delivering late. It meant that they had no respect for the relationship. Italians are able to deliver on time, but they prefer to follow the subjective time of the relationship rather than the objective time of the clock.

While the Dutch, like Germans and Americans, would follow the clock, Italians are very much concerned about delivering in time for *you*. Jan Kuipers went to Milan and befriended the head of logistics. He discovered that in the Italians' view the contract intended to ensure on-time delivery was a reason for delivering even later. The problem never recurred.

Test Yourself

Consider the following problem:

Some managers are arguing about the best ways of improving cycle time and getting products to market when they are needed.

There were four possible views:

1. It is crucial to speed up operations and shorten time-to-market. Time is money. Enemies of tighter schedules and faster deliveries do too much talking and relating to each other.
2. It is crucial to speed up operations and shorten time-to-market. The faster the jobs are done, the sooner you can "pass the baton" to colleagues or customers in the relay race.
3. Just-in-time synchronization of processes and with customers is the key to shorter cycle times. The more processes overlap and run simultaneously, the more time is saved.
4. Just-in-time synchronization of processes and with customers is the key to shorter cycle times. Doing things faster results in exhaustion and rushed work.

Answers 1 and 4 show approval of, respectively, high-speed sequences and just-in-time synchronicity, but they reject the opposite orientation. Answer 2 approves of high-speed sequences and connects it to synchronic processes. Answer 3 approves of just-in-time synchronicity connected to high-speed sequences.

The following tables show practical tips for doing business in past-, present-, and future-oriented cultures.

RECOGNIZING THE DIFFERENCES

PAST ORIENTATION	PRESENT ORIENTATION	FUTURE ORIENTATION
There is much talk about the history and origins of the family, business, and nation.	Activities and enjoyments of the moment are most important.	There is much talk about prospects, potentials, aspirations, and future achievements.
People are motivated to re-create a golden age.	Plans are not objected to but are rarely executed.	Planning and strategizing are done enthusiastically.
Respect is shown for ancestors, predecessors, and older people.	Intense interest is shown in present relationships, "here and now."	Intense interest is shown in youthfulness and in future potentials.
Everything is viewed in the context of tradition or history.	Everything is viewed in terms of its contemporary impact and style.	The present and past are used, even exploited, for future advantage.

TIPS FOR DOING BUSINESS WITH . . .

PAST- AND PRESENT-ORIENTED PEOPLE (FOR PRESENT- AND FUTURE-ORIENTED INDIVIDUALS)	FUTURE-ORIENTED PEOPLE (FOR PAST- AND PRESENT-ORIENTED INDIVIDUALS)
Emphasize the history, tradition, and rich cultural heritage of those you deal with as evidence of their vast potential.	Emphasize the freedom, opportunity, and limitless scope for the company and its people in the future.
Discover whether internal relationships will sanction the kind of changes you seek to encourage.	Discover what core competence or continuity the company intends to carry with it into the envisaged future.
Agree to future meetings in principle, but do not fix deadlines for completion.	Agree to specific deadlines, and do not expect work to be completed unless you have set such deadlines.
Do your homework on the history, traditions, and past glories of the company; consider what reenactments you might propose.	Do your homework on the future, the prospects, and the technological potentials of the company; consider mounting a sizable challenge.

RECOGNIZING THE DIFFERENCES

SEQUENTIAL ORIENTATION	SYNCHRONIC ORIENTATION
People engage in only one activity at a time.	People engage in more than one activity at a time.
Time is tangible and measurable.	Time is continuous and diffuse and there is less concern for watching the clock.
People keep appointments strictly; they schedule in advance and do not run late.	Appointments are approximate and subject to "giving time" to significant others.
Relationships are generally subordinate to schedule.	Schedules are generally subordinate to relationships.
There is a strong preference for following initial plans.	There is a strong preference for following where relationships lead.

WHEN MANAGING AND BEING MANAGED

SEQUENTIALLY ORIENTED PEOPLE	SYNCHRONICALLY ORIENTED PEOPLE
Employees feel rewarded and fulfilled by achieving planned future goals as in management by objectives.	Employees feel rewarded and fulfilled by achieving improved relationships with supervisors and customers.
Employees' most recent performance is the major issue, along with whether their commitments for the future can be relied on.	Employees' whole history with the company and future potential is the context in which their current performance is viewed.
Plan the career of an employee jointly with him or her, stressing landmarks to be reached by certain times.	Discuss with the employee his or her final aspirations in the context of the company; in what ways can these be realized?
The corporate ideal is the straight line and the most direct, efficient, and rapid route to your objectives.	The corporate ideal is the interacting circle in which past experience, present opportunities, and future possibilities interact.

Notes

1. F. Kluckhohn and F. L. Strodtbeck, *Variations in Value Orientations* (Westport, CT: Greenwood Press, 1960).

2. É. Durkheim, *De la division du travail social*, 7th ed. (Paris, 1960) (1893).

3. E. T. Hall, *The Silent Language* (New York: Anchor Press, Doubleday, 1959).

4. R. Carroll, *Cultural Misunderstandings: The French-American Experience* (Chicago: University of Chicago Press, 1987).

5. T. Cottle, "The Circles Test: An Investigation of Perception of Temporal Relatedness and Dominance," *Journal of Projective Technique and Personality Assessments*, no. 31 (1967): 58–71.

6. T. J. Cottle and P. Howard, "Time Perception by Indian Adolescents," *Perceptual and Motor Skills*, no. 28 (1969): 599–612.

7. M. Buber, *I and Thou*, ed. W. Kauffman (New York: Scribners' Books, 1970).

8. Shell International, Group Planning Department, London.

How We Relate to Nature

THE LAST dimension of culture we shall consider in this book concerns the role people assign to their natural environment. This relationship, as with the other dimensions, is at the center of human existence. Human beings have from the beginning been besieged by natural elements: wind, floods, fire, cold, earthquakes, famine, pests, and predators. Survival itself has meant acting *against* and *with* the environment in ways to render it both less threatening and more sustaining. Constant action was originally an inescapable necessity.

People's economic development can be viewed as a gradual strengthening of their devices to keep nature at bay. In the course of human existence there has been a shift from a preponderant fear that nature would overwhelm human existence to the opposite fear that human existence may overwhelm and degrade nature, so that, for example, a genetic storehouse of incredible richness in the Amazon rain forest may be bulldozed to oblivion before we have even discovered it.

Controlling Nature or Letting It Take Its Course

Societies that conduct business have developed two major orientations toward nature. They either believe that they can and should *control* nature by imposing their will on it, as in the ancient biblical injunction "Multiply and subdue the earth," or they believe that humans are part of nature and must *go along* with its laws, directions, and forces. The first of these orientations we shall describe as *inner-directed*. This kind of culture tends to identify with mechanisms; that is, the organization is conceived of as a machine that obeys the will of its operators. The second, the *outer-directed*, tends to see an organization as itself a product of nature, owing its development to the nutrients in its environment and to a favorable ecological balance.

The American psychologist J. B. Rotter, working in the 1960s, developed a scale designed to measure whether people had an *internal locus of control*, typical of more successful Americans, or an *external locus of control*, typical of relatively less successful Americans, disadvantaged by their circumstances or shaped by the competitive efforts of their rivals.[1] The questions he devised we used in building our cultural databases to assess our respondents' relationship with natural events, and the answers suggest that there are some significant differences here among geographical areas. These questions all take the form of alternatives; leaders and managers were asked to select the statement they believed most reflected reality. The first of these pairs is as follows.

A. It is worthwhile trying to control important natural forces, such as the weather.

B. Nature should take its course, and we just have to accept it the way it comes and do the best we can.

Figure 10.1 shows the percentage of respondents who chose A, which are the inner-directors. No country produces a totally internalized reaction to this statement; the highest score is only 68 percent, but we see considerable variations among countries and, again, no marked pattern by continent. Only 19 percent of Japanese believe it is worth trying to control the weather, as few as 22 percent of Chinese, only 21 percent of Swedes, but 36 percent of the British. The British, Germans, and Americans are above the middle of the range but are by no means among the top scorers. If the alternatives are made to appear more personally related, however, we get a different result. Figure 10.2 (page 176) shows the percentage of respondents who chose A when asked to choose between the following.

Percentage of respondents who believe it is worth trying

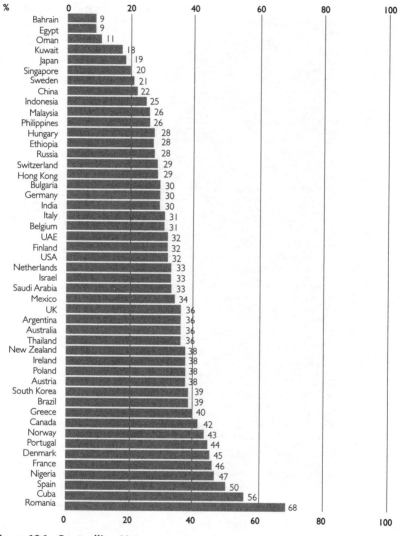

Figure 10.1. **Controlling Nature**

A. What happens to me is my own doing.

B. Sometimes I feel that I do not have enough control over the directions my life is taking.

On this basis a number of countries appear almost completely internalized; in the US, for instance, 82 percent of managers believe they

Percentage of respondents who believe what happens to them is their own doing

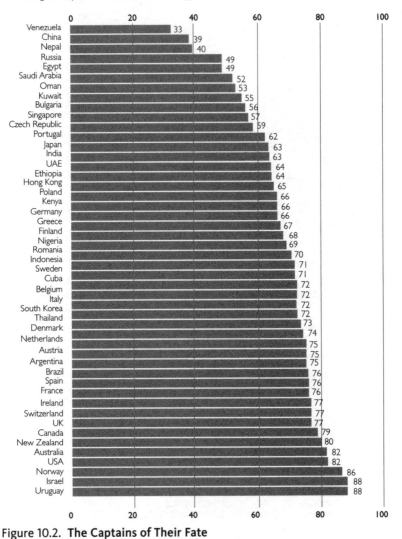

Figure 10.2. **The Captains of Their Fate**

control their own destinies, as do 76 percent of the French. Most European countries score high, in fact, though not the Russians, on whom 45 years of Communism may have had some effect. Similarly, the Chinese now rank much lower than the Japanese, although in Japan as in Singapore managers are far less likely to believe in internal control than are managers in North America or Europe.

Control and Success

The extremes of possible relationships between humans and nature are perhaps best instanced by contrasting the ancient Greeks with 20th-century Americans. For the Greeks the world was ruled by natural godlike forces: beauty (Aphrodite), truth (Apollo), justice (Athena), passion (Dionysus). These forces would contend for human allegiance and were often in conflict, leading to tragedy. Virtue was to achieve *harmonia*, harmony among the natural forces acting through you. Those who wanted their own will to triumph, such as Oedipus or Jason, were frequently confounded in a struggle with their fates. The post–Industrial Revolution society, on the other hand, has made heroes of entrepreneurs, whose struggles to tame nature are not expected to end in tragedy. This is especially the American view, shaped by the experience of discovering a new continent of immense size and small indigenous population and turning a wilderness into a new nation. Success is identified with control over outside circumstances.

However, internal versus external loci of control do not necessarily distinguish the successful from the less successful in non-American cultures. There are ways of adapting to external influences that can prove economically effective. To accept direction from customers, market forces, or new technologies *can be more advantageous than opposing these influences with your own preferences.* The "obvious" advantages (to Americans) of being inner-directed may not be obvious at all to managers in Japan or Singapore, and the advantages will be at least less obvious in Italy, Sweden, or the Netherlands, for example. Outer-directed need not mean God-directed or fate-directed; it may mean directed by the knowledge revolution or by the looming pollution crisis, or by a joint-venture partner. The ideal is to fit yourself advantageously to an external force.

In the original American concept of internal and external sources of control, the implication is that the outer-directed person is offering an excuse for failure rather than a new wisdom. In other nations it is not seen as personal weakness to acknowledge the strength of external forces or the arbitrariness of events.

In outer-directed behavior the reference point lies outside of people. A handy example is the history of the Sony Walkman, already described in Chapter 1. In an interview, Sony's Akio Morita explained that he conceived of the notion of the Walkman while he was searching for a way to enjoy music without disturbing others. This impetus is in sharp contrast to the normal motivation for using a Walkman in northwestern Europe and North America, where most users do not want to be disturbed by other people. In our continuing research in marketing (see for example *Marketing Across Cultures*) we find this same construct for consumers wanting an iPod and now iPad, as well as the role of headphones for MP3 players.[2]

The preponderant inner-directedness of North America and parts of northwestern Europe may help to explain why we Northerners have to go out of our way to teach "customer orientation" and "scanning the business environment." To outer-directed cultures, such as Japan and Singapore, this concept comes so naturally that it is not necessary to teach it. It is also noteworthy that outer-directedness does *not* preclude rivalry or competition but rather can help to give it form and style. To be directed by a customer or by the force of an opponent, as in *indo* (Japanese wrestling) and judo, is not to lack combativeness but to use another's powers in a more effective combination or harmony (*wa*). The ending *do* in *judo*, *indo*, *kendo*, and *Bushido* means "way of." You follow the way of the sword (kendo) or the warrior (Bushido), their practices and disciplines, until they become part of your nature. You may, as a result, be a more formidable competitor, not less. Like a surfer, you respond to the waves and keep your balance where others lose theirs.

In contrast to many Eastern sports, in which the opponent's force is harnessed to your own, Western sports such as American football and baseball idealize the zero-sum game, the clash of opposites, the rivalry of inner-directed wills, one-on-one—then, "If you can't beat 'em, join 'em." Even negotiations are "won" or "lost" depending on how much of what you originally wanted was gained, while compromise reduces the moral stature of all concerned.

Our Western contention that Asians "steal our ideas" is also shaped by our proprietary notions about what comes from *inside* of us and is therefore "ours." Asians may regard Western technologies as part of the environment, like fruit on a tree, which wise people pick and incorporate into themselves. Moreover, concepts such as *kaizen*, refinement, have high cultural prestige. To take something from the external environment and then refine or improve it is not "copying" but celebrating that environment, letting the finest forces shape your character. Even when the forces are violent and humiliating, such as devastation, surrender, and occupation by Americans, the Japanese prove masters at adapting to external circumstances and emerging on top. As they like to say, "A crisis is an opportunity."

Inner-Directed Mechanism: The Renaissance Ideal

The Western world is heavily influenced by Copernican and Newtonian views of the universe as a vast perpetual-motion machine that God wound up and left for his faithful to discover. To discover the laws of this universe, laws of time and motion, was to worship its creator. To understand the laws of the mechanism, it was necessary to predict and control the operation of nature's machinery—that is, to internalize natural law and then show that nature obeyed you. Against this background, to be inner-directed has become proof of scientific veracity. We hypothesize and deduce, and the principle is correct if the predicted result follows. Enlightened humanity is the master mechanic, the driver with a firm hand on the throttle.

While the early physicists left the description of human beings to religious authorities, this division of labor broke down in the 17th and 18th centuries. The person, too, became a machine, using reason to drive a somewhat reluctant body to obey rational dictates. According to Jacques Ellul, the earlier belief in magic was now replaced by *technique*, applied not simply to external nature but also to a person's head and body. "Technique," writes Ellul, "is the translation into action of man's concern to master things by means of reason, to account for what is subconscious, make quantitative what is qualitative, make clear and precise the outlines of nature, take hold of chaos, and order it."[3]

After the Renaissance, then, nature became objectified so that manipulation could be more easily demonstrated over passive entities. Quantification and measurement became central to science, including social science.

The Modern View of Nature: The Cybernetic Cosmology

While for the Greeks nature was a living organism and for the Renaissance it was a machine potentially controllable by human reason, in modern system dynamics or cybernetics both these views are transcended into a more inclusive concept of a living system that both nurtures the individual and can be developed by individuals dependent on that system.[4] There is a shift from trying to seize control *over* nature to identifying with its ecological self-regulation and natural balance. The manager *intervenes* but is not the *cause* of what occurs; the systems of organizations and markets have their own momentum, which we can influence but not drive. As the world fills up with economic actors and forces, we are simultaneously more influenced by external forces and yet more determined to create our own space among them. Figure 10.3 summarizes these changing views.

ERA	KIND OF NATURE	PRODUCTIVE FUNCTIONS	PHILOSOPHIES	FOCUS OF CONTROL
Primitive	Organic nature	Arts: to form	Natural; natural world	External control
Renaissance	Mechanism nature	Techniques: to transform	Mechanical; technical world	Internal control
Modern	Cybernetic nature	Applied sciences: to develop	Scientific; social world	Reconciliation of internal and external control

Figure 10.3. **Changing View of Nature**

How Important Is a Culture's Orientation to Nature?

Orientations to nature have much to do with how we conduct our day-to-day lives and manage businesses. Cultures may seek either to master nature, to accept and be subjugated by it, or to live in the most effective harmony with it. Nature is both controllable by people and liable to show sudden reversals of relative strength, becoming their master, not slave. Neither situation is very stable nor very desirable, since a subjugated nature may fail to sustain people on Earth.

A relationship closely analogous to humans and nature is that of organization and markets. A product may succeed not simply because we will it to, or because the special features designed into it delight customers. It may succeed for reasons *other than those that come from inside of us*, reasons that have to do with the way *other* people in the environment think rather than we ourselves. Are we then willing to take direction from customers, where this is not our original direction? Are we willing to change our minds when it becomes clear that customers' preferences are different from our own?

One powerful example of outer-directedness is the theory of evolution. According to evolutionary biologists, it is the environment that decides which creatures fit and which do not; so, by extension, markets decide, not managers. The business world sees not the survival of the fittest, driven by mechanisms determined to fight each other, but the survival of those best able to form a nurturing relationship with external niches and conditions. It may be for this reason that some outer-directed cultures are among the world's better economic performers. While the belief that the environment is all-powerful in deciding the future can lead to fatalism or resignation, the belief that we are all responsible can lead to scapegoating, blaming the victim, and a lack of compassion for those who have suffered misfortune.

An important aspect of inner-directedness is the notion of business *strategy*, which is a plan designed in advance to wrest competitive advantage from other corporations. The metaphor comes from the military sphere, and it is clear that either the organization prevails in its strategic intention or it is beaten by its environment. The seeming lack of interest in strategy per se by the Japanese and similar outer-directed cultures has been noted, and the whole "militaristic" concept of strategy criticized, by Henry Mintzberg. Mintzberg points out that, in any organization, those interfacing with customers have *already devised strategies for coping with day-to-day problems.*[5] The job of top management, therefore, is to assess these emergent strategies and give recognition, status, and formal sanction to those that have proved most valuable. This is an outer-directed process for adopting strategies *already initiated* at the organization's grass roots and is a further example of the need to let the environment shape *you.*

Managing Between Different Orientations to Nature

Paradoxically, Western and inner-directed managers trying to impose uniform procedures and methods on foreign and outer-directed cultures often "succeed" better than they expected, just because at least some of those cultures are accustomed to being heavily influenced by external sources and taking their cues from the environment. Still, it is a mistake to assume that *accepting* guidance from outside is the same as internalizing it or using it successfully. Some outer-directed cultures do not like to debate or confront, but this aversion does not mean that the directive in question is appropriate to their culture. The source of authority is seen as "natural" and will quickly be dissipated if the manager behaves in "unnatural" ways, for example by imposing his or her will for its own sake rather than because of a natural endowment of wisdom to sustain and nurture the organism. Other-directed cultures often regard nature as *benign.* If, therefore, you behave in ways interpreted as hostile, your "natural powers" will be forfeit.

At a Gabon subsidiary of a French oil company, the Dutch author discovered that a change management program initiated by headquarters was failing miserably. The French managers, when interviewed, could not really explain what was going on. The Gabonese seemed to agree completely with the drafted mission statement. They even accepted the operational steps that had been discussed and planned at length. When the plan had to be put into action, though, nothing happened. The employees behaved precisely as before. After careful inquiry it turned out that the Gabonese did indeed endorse the change but did not believe that it was for them as individuals to direct its implementation. The signal had to come from their French superiors, who alone had the natural authority to command action. When no command came, no action was taken. The idea that self-directed change would emerge from reasoned principles was *not* culturally shared.

It was the same with the pay-for-performance program initiated by MCC. Such a program assumes that each employee can behave in ways that increase the sales of computers, that he or she can personally induce greater effort and hence greater sales. This assumption was questioned by an Asian manager.

Mr. Djawa from Indonesia raised two objections to Mr. Johnson:

"Pay-for-performance does not work in our sales territories. It leads to customers being overloaded with products they never wanted and do not need. Furthermore, when things are not going well for our people, it is a mistake to hurry them or blame them. There are good times and bad times. Paying them for performance does not change inevitable trends."

This argument did not impress Johnson and his Western colleagues, whose response was, "We want to develop something at HQ that will motivate everyone. Are you saying that linking reward to success has no influence at all? Surely you must agree there is some connection."

"It certainly has effects," Mr. Djawa conceded, "but they tend to be swamped by economic booms and busts. Moreover, the customer needs to be assisted and protected from these fluctuations. It is not wise to push customers into buying more than they should. We need to ride out bad times together and then take joint advantage of good times."

Many of Mr. Djawa's Eastern and Latin colleagues concurred. Mr. Johnson was exasperated. "Why don't some of you suggest a method that *does* work?"

Here the Indonesians, seeing themselves as relatively more controlled by external forces, seek to join with customers and each other to "ride out" the inevitable waves. They can be motivated, but in directions consistent with their culture, and that is to make skillful adjustments to the ups and downs that they experience as "natural" and not caused by their own greater or lesser determination to prosper. They seem to regard the turbulence of their environment as a sufficient challenge to the members of their organization, without needing to attribute blame to those caught in a downturn, or reward those caught in an upturn. To do either would sap group morale by adding to the arbitrariness of events and tempt sales personnel to put their own advantage ahead of the customers'.

In contrast, the mechanistic view of people sees the salesperson cutting through the waves like a ship heading for its own planned destination and not being diverted from its path by poor weather. The test of good engineers or M.B.A.s is to do things right the first time and have their judgment vindicated by results. The good company promises "to put you in the driver's seat." Ideal mechanisms obey the will of their operators and enable them to overcome natural obstacles to achieve personal goals.

Is Modern Management a Battle Between Private Agendas?

One problem with the inner-directed person's seeking mastery over nature is that *everyone else* may come to stand for "nature." We all want power, but we can achieve it only if others are viewed as means to our ends. By definition, we cannot *all* direct the environment from within ourselves, since we ourselves constitute large parts of that environment. The invitation to others to "participate" is largely vitiated if, in fact, you are trying to steer them toward a conclusion you arrived at before the discussion began. Yet the relentlessly inner-directed manager has no other option. He or she is obliged to define social relationships objectively, as if moving pieces on a chessboard. This is what

Chris Argyris calls "Model I behavior," behavior designed to motivate the employee into doing what the manager formulated earlier.[6] Mr. Johnson, too, uses motivation in this sense, a method of persuading salespeople to sell more in any or all circumstances and regardless of what they say or want, or of what their cultures believe in.

The Hay method of evaluation of personnel is similarly inner-directed in identifying managers with their function. In this system it is not the employee who is being evaluated, but the efficiency with which he or she completes a task assumed to be directed from within the supervisor, within the organization. It is this relationship that gives authority its reason and legitimacy. Suppose the company exists to turn natural raw materials into products. It requires these functions to be fulfilled by a division of labor. It hires people who agree to perform these functions. They are directed by a chief executive officer who personifies the organization's inner-directed purpose. People trying to fulfill these functions are then paid according to the complexity and difficulty of the function, how well they have discharged it, and how they used their own (inner-directed) judgment. This arrangement is all logical, neat, and obvious, yet it treats physical and social environments as if they were objects and is not the way large parts of the world economy think. It is also blind to some of the most obvious social facts, such as that during a conversation both parties may change their minds and transform their joint thought processes into something new and better.

Reconciling Internal and External Control

For some considerable time there has been discussion in the business world regarding whether one should be led by technology push or market pull when developing new products. In an internally controlled culture people prefer to focus on technological innovation. What this can lead to we have seen at Nokia. Recently, this mobile phone manufacturer became the victim of its own successful technology push in the recent past. With the series of phones, indubitably the best ones at the time—it managed to find a new, supremely exclusive market: a market without customers. Apple's iPhone took over and the rest is history. In an externally controlled culture, instead, people focus mainly on the market. This also has its limitations. The client is not always fully aware of its own wishes. Sometimes listening to the client takes so long that a product is redundant as soon as it enters the market. Again, we may observe the power of reconciling the two cultures. The *push* of the technology may determine the choice of the clients to whom one wants to listen. The *pull* of the market may provide direction for the development of the technology.

We all make mistakes in life. Some three weeks ago the Dutch author asked his wife if he could borrow her car—a Mitsubishi Space Wagon—to pick up some loudspeakers in town. He had to stop at a pedestrian crossing. Just after coming to a stop, he heard a noise indicating that he had been hit from behind. He stepped out and saw that the length of the impressive Japanese car he'd been driving had diminished by at least 20 percent. Psychologically it felt as though the whole back of the car had disappeared in the crash. Pulling away from his car was a Volvo 200 series, better known as "the tank." Not a scratch could be seen on this vehicle even when examined closely. The driver, however, emerged with one hand covering a severe cut on his head. He apologized almost routinely: "There is not much left of your car, sir," he said, "but are you OK?" The Dutch author was fine, because he had hardly felt the collision.

The externally controlled Japanese evidently apply martial arts to safety. Japanese cars are designed to take the energy out of their opponent to their advantage. The Volvos and BMWs of this world seem to operate like an American football player: if I am stronger than you, I'll win and be safe. The end result, nevertheless, was that the driver of the Japanese car did not feel the collision, while the Volvo driver took it all.

The newest safety designs are built to reconcile flexibility and strength. The similarity with the Dutch poldering system is striking. Dikes are built to stop the water with great strength. If the pressure becomes too intense, doors are opened to relieve the pressure. In turn the next diking system takes the second overflow.

And doesn't your organization struggle to achieve a balance between technology push and market pull? Intuitively we know that if we push the technology to its extreme, we might end up in the ultimate niche market, best defined as that part of the market with no clients. But what if we just follow what clients desire? We might not deliver fast enough and will be at their mercy. The most effective organizations are those that are better at connecting the push of the technology to the pull of the market. Isn't it curious that, although the Americans are superior in both marketing techniques and developing innovative products, the Japanese wiped out the US consumer electronics industry? The Japanese seem to be especially adept at connecting what has been developed elsewhere. They also apply martial arts to essential economic laws.

Figure 10.4 shows that too much inner-directedness can lead to the lack of a market. Conversely, an overly developed customer focus risks

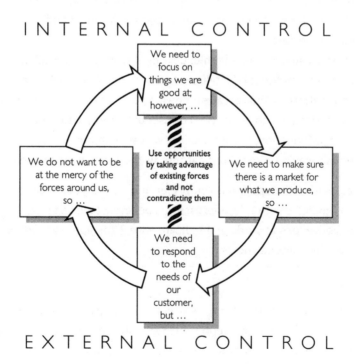

Figure 10.4. **Reconciling Internal and External Control**

leaving the organization at the mercy of market forces. Inner- and outer-directedness have to be reconciled.

Test Yourself

Several senior strategists were discussing whether strategy should be devised at the top of the corporation and "cascaded down," to be implemented locally, or emerge from the grass roots and successful interfaces with customers. The following views were expressed:

---

1. No one dealing with customers is without a strategy of sorts. Our task is to find out which of these strategies work, which don't, and why. Devising our own strategy in the abstract and imposing it downward only spreads confusion.
2. No one dealing with customers is without a strategy of sorts. Our task is to find out which of these strategies work and then create a master strategy from proven successful initiatives by commending and combining the best.
3. To be a leader is to be the chief deviser of strategy. Using all the experience, information, and intelligence we can mobilize, we devise an innovative strategy and cascade it down, to be vigorously implemented.
4. To be a leader is to be the chief deviser of strategy. Using all the experience, information, and intelligence we can mobilize, we create a broad thrust, leaving it to subordinates to fit these to customer needs.

Indicate with 1 the approach you prefer and with 2 your second choice. Similarly, indicate with 1 the approach you believe would be favored by your closest colleagues at work, and indicate with 2 the approach you believe would be their second choice.

Answer 1 affirms an outer-directed strategy and rejects inner-direction, while answer 3 represents the opposite. Answer 2 affirms a connection between an outer-directed strategy and an inner-directed strategy, while answer 4 affirms the opposite connection.

Summary

Cultures vary in their approaches to the given environment, between belief that it can be controlled by the individual and belief that the individual must respond to external circumstances. We should not, however, make the error of assuming that inner-direction and outer-direction are exclusive options. All cultures necessarily take *some* notice of what is inside or outside. To fail to do so would lead inner-directed cultures into a headlong rush to disaster, while outer-directed cultures would try to please everyone and dissipate their energies by overcompliance.

Inner-directed managers are never happier than when they have won over other people to their own way of thinking. This is the ideal they strive for, but it is one that may be deemed aggressive and uncouth in outer-directed cultures. Leaders in these latter cultures stress how much they have learned from their mistakes and from others' objections or criticisms. One reason staff suggestions enrich several Asian organizations and participation is so high is that listening rather than declaiming is seen as the more admirable trait. Such cultures do not clash openly. To negate what someone is saying is to ride roughshod over nature. The alternative is to take the proposal on board and alter its import subsequently if it remains unpopular.

The word *feedback* is a curious one in Western management jargon. It recognizes the need to periodically correct an ongoing thrust or function, but *rarely is feedback considered as important as the original direction*. Indeed, feedback is the means by which the original direction is *maintained*.

To participate fully in an outer-directed culture, inner-directed managers must accept that feedback can alter the whole direction of the organization. They must listen to customers and aim to fill their needs as opposed to win their allegiance.

Major change can come from both outside and inside. Once again we see that culture is about where a circle "starts" or where a manager conceives of change originating. To conceive of the organization as an open system operating within a larger system allows both inner-directed and outer-directed orientations to develop.

The following tables show practical tips for doing business in internally and externally oriented cultures.

RECOGNIZING THE DIFFERENCES

INTERNAL ORIENTATION	EXTERNAL ORIENTATION
People exhibit an often dominating attitude bordering on aggressiveness toward the environment.	People exhibit an often flexible attitude and are willing to compromise and keep the peace.
Conflict and resistance mean that you have convictions.	Harmony and responsiveness convey sensibility.
The focus is on self, function, one's own group, and one's own organization.	The focus is on the "other," such as the customer, partner, or colleague.
People are uncomfortable when the environment seems "out of control" or changeable.	People are comfortable with waves, shifts, and cycles, if these are "natural."

TIPS FOR DOING BUSINESS WITH . . .

INTERNALLY ORIENTED PEOPLE (FOR EXTERNALLY ORIENTED INDIVIDUALS)	EXTERNALLY ORIENTED PEOPLE (FOR INTERNALLY ORIENTED INDIVIDUALS)
Playing "hardball" is legitimate to test the resilience of an opponent.	Softness, persistence, politeness, and long, long patience will get rewards.
It is most important to "win your objective."	It is most important to "maintain your relationship."
Win some, lose some.	Win together, lose apart.

WHEN MANAGING AND BEING MANAGED

INTERNALLY ORIENTED PEOPLE	EXTERNALLY ORIENTED PEOPLE
Get agreement on and ownership of clear objectives.	Achieve congruence among various people's goals.

Make sure that tangible goals are clearly linked to tangible rewards.	Try to reinforce the current directions and facilitate the work of employees.
Discuss disagreements and conflicts openly; they show that everyone is determined.	Give people time and opportunity to quietly work through conflicts, which are distressing.
Management by objectives works if all parties are genuinely committed to directing themselves toward shared objectives and if these objectives persist.	Management by environments works if all parties are genuinely committed to adapting themselves to fit external demands as these demands shift.

Notes

1. J. B. Rotter, *Generalized Expectations for Internal Versus External Control of Reinforcement*, Psychological Monograph 609 (1966): 1–28. (Some items have been designed by Centre for Intercultural Business Studies.)
2. F. Trompenaars and P. Woolliams, *Marketing Across Cultures* (New York: Capstone/Wiley, 2004).
3. J. Ellul, *The Technological Society* (New York: Vintage, 1964).
4. S. Moscovici, *Essai sur l'histoire humaine de la nature* (Paris: Flammarion, 1977).
5. H. Mintzberg, *The Structure of Organizations* (Englewood Cliffs, NJ: Prentice-Hall, 1979).
6. C. Argyris, *Strategy Change and Defensive Routines* (London: Pitman, 1985).

National Cultures and Corporate Cultures

WHEN PEOPLE set up an organization, they will typically borrow from models or ideals that are familiar to them. The organization, as discussed in Chapter 2, is a subjective construct, and its employees will give meaning to their environment based on their own particular cultural programming. The organization is like something else they have experienced. It may be deemed to resemble a family, or an impersonal system designed to achieve targets. It may be likened to a vessel that is traveling somewhere, or a missile homing in on customers and strategic objectives. Cultural preferences operating across the dimensions described in the previous chapters influence the models people give to organizations and the meanings they attribute to them.

This chapter explores four categorical types of corporate culture and shows how differences between national cultures help determine the type of corporate culture "chosen." Employees have a shared perception of the organization, and what they believe has real consequences for the corporate culture that develops.

Different Corporate Cultures

Organizational culture is shaped not only by technologies and markets but also by the cultural preferences of leaders and employees.

Some international companies have European, Asian, American, or Middle Eastern subsidiaries that would be unrecognizable as the same company save for their logos and reporting procedures. Often these subsidiaries are fundamentally different in the logic of their structure and the meanings they bring to shared activity.

Three aspects of organizational structure are especially important in determining corporate culture:

1. The general relationship between employees and their organization
2. The vertical or hierarchical system of authority defining superiors and subordinates
3. The general views of employees about the organization's destiny, purpose, and goals and their places in this regard

Thus far we have distinguished cultures along single (linear) dimensions: universalism-particularism, for example, and individualism-communitarianism. In looking at organizations, we need to think in two dimensions, generating four quadrants. The dimensions we use to distinguish different corporate cultures are *equality versus hierarchy* and *orientation to the person versus orientation to the task*.

This process enables us to define four categorical types of corporate culture, which vary considerably in how they think and learn, how they change, and how they motivate, reward, and resolve conflicts. This is a valuable way to analyze organizations, but it does have the risk of caricaturization. There is a tendency to believe or wish that all foreigners will fit the stereotypes one has of them. Hence, in our very recognition of "types" there is a temptation to oversimplify what is exceedingly complex.

The four types can be described as follows:

1. The Family
2. The Eiffel Tower
3. The Guided Missile
4. The Incubator

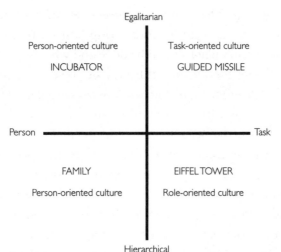

Figure 11.1. Corporate Images

These four metaphors illustrate the relationship of employees to their notion of the organization. Figure 11.1 summarizes the images these organizations project.

Each of these types of corporate culture is an "ideal type." In practice the types are mixed or overlaid, with one culture dominating. In many organizations the same corporate culture permeates everywhere, while in others there may be considerable variety among functional areas, such as the corporate culture of R&D compared with that of marketing and sales. Even so, this categorization into four extreme types is useful for exploring the basis of each type in terms of how employees learn, change, resolve conflicts, reward, motivate, and so on. Why, for example, do norms and procedures that seem to work so well in one culture lose their effectiveness in another?

The Family Culture

We use the metaphor of family for the culture that is at the same time *personal*, with close face-to-face relationships, but also *hierarchical*, in the sense that the "father" of a family has experience and authority greatly exceeding those of his "children," especially where these children are young. The result is a *power-oriented* corporate culture in which the leader is regarded as a caring father who knows better than his subordinates what should be done and what is good for them. Rather than being threatening, this type of power is essentially intimate and (it is hoped) benign. The work of the corporation in this type of culture is usually carried forward in an atmosphere that in many respects mimics the home.

The Japanese re-create within the corporation aspects of the traditional family. The major business virtue is *amae*, a kind of love between persons of differing rank, with indulgence shown to the younger and respect reciprocated to the elder. The idea is always to do *more* than a contract or agreement obliges you to do. The idealized relationship is *sempai-kokai*, that between an older and younger brother. Promotion by age means that the older person will typically be in charge. The relationship to the corporation is long term and devoted.

A large part of the reason for working, performing well, and resolving conflict in this corporate culture is the pleasure derived from such relationships. To please your superior (or elder brother) is a reward in itself. While this affection may or may not be visible to outsiders (the Japanese, for example, are often very restrained emotionally), it is nevertheless *there*, whether subdued Japanese-style or conveyed unmistakably by voice, face, and bodily gesture Italian-style. The leader of the family-style culture weaves the pattern, sets the tone, models the appropriate posture for the corporation, and expects subordinates to be "on the same wavelength," knowing intuitively what is required; conversely, the leader may empathize with the subordinates.

At its best the power-oriented family culture exercises power *through* its members' acting with one accord. Power is not necessarily *over* them, although it may be. The main sanction is loss of affection and place in the family. Pressure is moral and social rather than financial or legal. Many corporations with family-style cultures are from nations that industrialized late: Greece, Italy, Japan, Singapore, South Korea, and Spain. Where the transition from feudalism to industrialism was rapid, many feudal traditions remain.

Family-style corporate cultures tend to be *high context* (see Chapter 7), a term that refers to the sheer amount of information and cultural content *taken for granted* by members. The more in-jokes, the more "family" stories, traditions, customs, and associations there are, the higher the context and the harder it is for outsiders to feel that they belong or to know how to behave appropriately. Such cultures exclude strangers without necessarily wishing to do so and communicate in codes that only members understand.

Relationships tend to be *diffuse*. (Again, see Chapter 7.) The "father" or "elder brother" is influential in *all* situations, whether this person has knowledge of the problem or not, whether an event occurs at work, in the canteen, or on the way home, and even if someone else present is better qualified. The general happiness and welfare of all employees is regarded as the concern of the family-type corporation, which often provides housing and often considers the size of employees' families and whether their wages are sufficient for them to live well.

Power and differential status are seen as "natural," a characteristic of the leaders themselves and not related to the tasks they succeed or fail in doing, any more than a parent ceases to be a parent by neglecting certain duties. Above the power of the leader may be that of the state, the political system, the society, or God. Power is *political* in the sense of being broadly ordained by authorities, rather than originating in roles to be filled or tasks to be performed. This does not mean that those in power are unskilled or cannot do their jobs; it means that for such an organization to perform well, the requisite knowledge and skills must be brought *to* the power centers, thereby justifying the existing structure. Take the following testimony by a British manager.

"In Italy I was introduced to my counterpart, the head of applications engineering. I asked him about his organization, his department, and the kind of work they were engaged in. Within minutes he had given me a dozen names and his personal estimate of their political influence, their proximity to power, and their tastes, preferences, and opinions. He said almost nothing about either their knowledge, their skills, or their performance. As far as I could tell, they had no specific functions, or if they had, my informant was ignorant of them. I was amazed. There seemed to be no conception of the tasks that had to be done or their challenge and complexity."

It did not occur to the British manager that this "family model" is capable of processing complexity without necessarily seeing itself as a functional instrument to this end. The authority in the family model is unchallengeable in the sense that it is seen to depend not on tasks performed but on status ascribed. A major issue becomes that of getting the top people to notice, comprehend, and act. If older people have more authority, then they must be briefed thoroughly and supported loyally in order to fulfill the status attributed to them. *The culture works to justify its own initial suppositions.*

In our own research we tested to what extent managers from different cultures saw their leaders "as a kind of father" as opposed to someone who "got the job done." The results are shown in Figure 11.2, where we end up with one of the widest ranges of national variances of response, as well as a marked grouping of Asian countries toward the top of the chart. Another question asked of managers in the process of this research was to think of the company they work for in terms of a triangle and to pick the one on the diagram (Figure 11.3) that best represents it. The steepest triangle scores five points, and so on down to one.

The scores of nations where the leader is seen as a father (Figure 11.2) correlate closely with the steepness of the triangles in Figure 11.3 (page 200). The familial cultures of Turkey, Venezuela, and several Asian countries have the steepest hierarchies; the image combines attachment to subordination with relative permanence of employment. Nearly all of these are also to be found in the top third of Figure 11.2.

Family cultures at their least effective drain the energies and loyalties of subordinates to buoy up the leader, who floats on seas of adoration. Leaders get their sense of power and confidence *from* their followers, their charisma fueled by credulity and by seemingly childlike faith. All the same, skillful leaders of such cultures can also catalyze and multiply energies and appeal to the deepest feelings and aspirations of their subordinates. They avoid the depersonalization of management by objectives; management by subjectives works bet-

Percentage of respondents opting to be left alone to get the job done

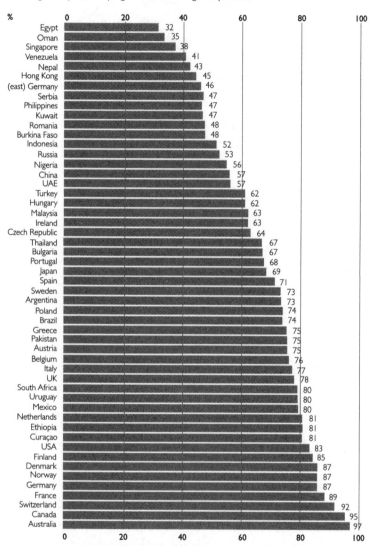

Figure 11.2. **What Makes a Good Manager?**

ter. They resemble the leaders of movements aiming to emancipate, reform, reclaim, and enlighten both their members and society, like the American civil rights movement; such movements also are essentially family-type structures, resocializing members in new forms of conduct.

Family cultures have difficulty with project-group organization or matrix-type authority structures, since here authority is divided.

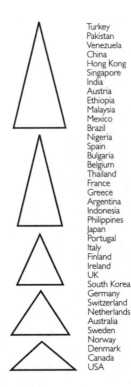

Turkey
Pakistan
Venezuela
China
Hong Kong
Singapore
India
Austria
Ethiopia
Malaysia
Mexico
Brazil
Nigeria
Spain
Bulgaria
Belgium
Thailand
France
Greece
Argentina
Indonesia
Philippines
Japan
Portugal
Italy
Finland
Ireland
UK
South Korea
Germany
Switzerland
Netherlands
Australia
Sweden
Norway
Denmark
Canada
USA

Figure 11.3. Company Triangles

Your function has one boss and your project another, so how can you give undivided loyalty to either? Another problem is that the claims of *genuine* families may intrude. If someone is your brother or cousin, this person is *already* related to your family back home and should therefore find it easier to relate closely to you at work. It follows that, where a role or project culture might see nepotism as corruption and a conflict of interest, a family culture could see it as reinforcing its current norms. A person connected to your family at home *and* your family at work has one more reason not to cheat you. Families tend to be strong where universalism is weak.

A Dutch delegation was taken aback when the Brazilian owner of a large manufacturing company introduced his relatively junior accountant as the key coordinator of a $15 million joint venture. The Dutch were puzzled as to why a recently qualified accountant had been given such weighty responsibilities, including the receipt of their money.

The Brazilians pointed out that this young man was the best possible choice among 1,200 employees, since he was the nephew of the owner. Who could be more trustworthy than that? Instead of complaining, the Dutch should consider themselves lucky that he was available.

The Eldest Child

Often employees in family cultures will behave like "the eldest child" left in charge while the parents are out, but relinquishing that authority as soon as a "parent" returns. The American manager of a plant in Miami encountered this relationship with his Venezuelan second-in-command. The Florida plant processed and packaged PVC. The process required high standards of quality control. The product had to be mixed in exactly the correct proportions, or it was dangerous. Any irregularity in mixing and blending had to be reported immediately after it occurred and the line concerned closed down at once, or unsalable product would accumulate. A decision to shut down was an expert one requiring detailed knowledge. Even a delay of minutes in taking action was extremely costly. It was better on the whole to shut down prematurely than to shut down too late.

The Venezuelan deputy knew beyond doubt when the product was satisfactory and when it was not. When his manager was away from the plant and he was in charge, he brought any line whose quality was failing to an immediate halt. His judgment was both fast and accurate. When the manager was there, however, he would look for him, report what was happening, and get a decision. In the time it took to do that, considerable product was wasted. However many times he was told to act on his own, that his judgment was respected and that his decision would be upheld, he always reverted to his original practice.

This was a simple case of a clash between the task orientation assumed by the American and the family orientation of the Venezuelan. The American had delegated the job of controlling the quality of PVC production. As he saw it, this was now his deputy's responsibility, whether he himself was in his office or away. It was required by the process. That view may make perfect sense, but for the deputy, his authority grew when he was left in charge and shrank the moment his "parent" returned. Decisions should be taken by the most authoritative person *present*. He would no more usurp the authority of his parents once they returned home than would any child left temporarily in charge.

Some well-known research by Inzerilli and Laurent, an Italian and a French researcher, showed the much higher appeal among Italian, French, and Japanese managers of the "manager who knows everything."[1] (See Chapter 8.) This was on the basis of posing the question: "Is it important for a manager to have at hand precise answers to most of the questions raised by subordinates?" We all realize that in the complexity of modern conditions it is becoming harder for managers to know even part of what their subordinates know as a group. Yet the supposition that your manager *does* know everything may require you to discuss everything with him or her, thus encouraging the upward movement of information to the apex of the organization, a process that contributes to learning. We must beware, therefore, of dismissing the family metaphor as primitive, pretentious, or feudal. Its intimacies can process complex information effectively, and wanting your "father" to have superior knowledge may have more desirable results than neither expecting nor wanting your boss to know very much. A visionary leader who mobilizes his or her employees around superordinate goals needs their trust, their faith, and their knowledge. The family model can often supply all three.

The results of the question posed in Chapter 7 on whether a company is responsible for providing housing (see Figure 7.6) also show those nations in which the family is a natural model. In these cultures there is almost no boundary for the organization's responsibilities to the people in its employ. These responsibilities even extend to where and how they are housed. Japanese employers make it their business as to whether you are married, how many children you have, and accordingly how much more you need to be paid. The company may help you find housing, help get your children into schools, offer you consumer products at reduced prices, make recreational facilities available, and even encourage you to take vacations with work colleagues. The belief is that *the more the company does for your family, the more your family will wish its breadwinner to do for the company.*

Thinking, Learning, and Change

The family corporate culture is more interested in intuitive than in rational knowledge, more concerned with the development of people than with their deployment or utilization. Personal knowledge of another is rated above empirical knowledge about him or her. Knowing is less hypothetical and deductive, more by trial and error. Conversations are preferred to research questionnaires, and insights are preferred to objective data. *Who* is doing something is more important than *what* is being done. If you invite the Japanese to a meeting, they will want to know who will be there before knowing specific details about the agenda.

Change in the power-oriented family model is essentially political, getting key actors to modify policies. Among favorite devices are new visions, charismatic appeals, inspiring goals and directions, and more authentic relationships with significant people. Bottom-up change is unlikely unless it is insurgent and seriously challenges the leaders, in which case major concessions may be made.

Training, mentoring, coaching, and apprenticeship are important sources of personal education, but these activities occur at the behest of the family and do not in themselves challenge authority but rather perpetuate it. Family-style cultures can respond quickly to changing environments that affect their power. Their political antennae are often highly sensitive.

A Dutch manager delegated to initiate change in the French subsidiary of a Dutch group described to us how impressed he had been at the precision and intelligence of the French managers' response to his proposals. However, he returned three months later to find that nothing had happened. He had failed to realize that it was also necessary to change the management team; the strategic proposals had simply been a front behind which the family continued to operate as before.

Motivating, Rewarding, and Resolving Conflict

Family members enjoy their relationships, so they may be motivated more by praise and appreciation than by money. Pay-for-performance rarely sits well with them, as is true of any motivation that threatens family bonds. They tend to "socialize risk" among their members and can operate well in uncertain environments. Their major weakness occurs when intrafamily conflicts block necessary change.

Resolving conflict often depends on the skill of a leader. Criticisms are seldom voiced publicly; if they are, the family is in turmoil. Negative feedback is indirect and sometimes confined to special "licensed" occasions. (In Japan you can criticize your boss while drinking his booze.) Care is taken to avoid loss of face by prominent family members, since these individuals are points of coherence for the whole group. The family model gives low priority to *efficiency* (doing things right) but high priority to *effectiveness* (doing the right things).

The Eiffel Tower Culture

In the Western world a bureaucratic division of labor with various roles and functions is prescribed in advance. These allocations are coordinated at the top by a hierarchy. If each role is played as envisioned by the system, then tasks will be completed as planned. One supervisor can oversee the completion of several tasks; one manager can oversee the jobs of several supervisors; and so on up the hierarchy.

We have chosen the Eiffel Tower in Paris to symbolize this cultural type because it is steep, symmetrical, narrow at the top and broad at the base, stable, rigid, and robust. Like the formal bureaucracy for which it stands, it is very much a symbol of the machine age. Its structure, too, is more important than its function.

Its hierarchy is much different from that of the family model. Each higher level has a clear and demonstrable function of holding together the levels beneath it. You obey the boss because it is his or her *role* to instruct you. The rational purpose of the corporation is conveyed to you through this person. He or she has legal authority to tell you what to do, and your contract of service, overtly or implicitly, obliges you to work according to those instructions. If you and other subordinates did not do so, the system could not function.

The boss in the Eiffel Tower is only incidentally a person. Essentially he or she is a role. Were the boss to drop dead tomorrow, someone else would replace him or her, and it would make no difference to your duties or to the organization's reason for being. The successor might of course be more or less unpleasant, or interpret the role slightly differently, but that difference is marginal. Effectively, the job is defined, and the discharge of it is evaluated according to that definition. Little is left to chance or the idiosyncrasies of individuals.

It follows that authority stems from occupancy of the role. If you meet your boss on the golf course, you have no obligation to let him or her play through, and the boss probably would not expect it. Relationships are *specific* (see Chapter 7), and status is *ascribed* (see Chapter 8) and stays behind at the office. This is not, however, a personal ascription of status as we see it in the family model. Status in the Eiffel Tower is ascribed to the role. This ascription makes it impossible to challenge. Thus, bureaucracy in the Eiffel Tower is a depersonalized, rational-legal system in which everyone is subordinate to local rules, and those rules prescribe a hierarchy to uphold and enforce them. The boss is powerful only because the rules sanction him or her to act.

Careers in Eiffel Tower companies are much assisted by professional qualifications. At the top of German and Austrian companies, which are typically Eiffel Tower models, the titles of professor or doctor are common on office doors. This practice is extremely rare in the US.

Almost everything the family culture accepts the Eiffel Tower rejects. Personal relationships are likely to warp judgments, create favoritism, multiply exceptions to the rules, and obscure clear boundaries between roles and responsibilities. You cannot evaluate your subordinate's performance in a role if you grow fond of that person or need his or her personal loyalty for yourself. The organization's purpose is logically separate from your personal need for power or affection. Such needs are distractions, biases, and intrusions by personal agendas on public ones.

Each role at each level of the hierarchy is described, is rated for its difficulty, complexity, and responsibility, and has a salary attached to it. There then follows a search for a person to fill it. In considering applicants for the role, the personnel department will treat everyone equally and neutrally, will match each person's skills and aptitudes with the job requirements, and will award the job to the best fit between role and person. The same procedure is followed in evaluations and promotions.

We tested the influence of the *role* culture as opposed to the more *personal* culture by posing the following dilemma to managers (Figure 11.4).

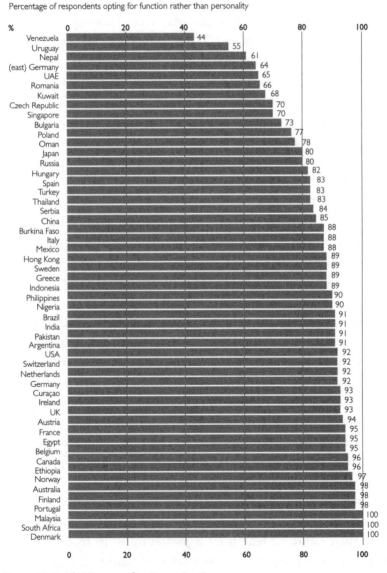

Percentage of respondents opting for function rather than personality

Country	%
Venezuela	44
Uruguay	55
Nepal	61
(east) Germany	64
UAE	65
Romania	66
Kuwait	68
Czech Republic	70
Singapore	70
Bulgaria	73
Poland	77
Oman	78
Japan	80
Russia	80
Hungary	82
Spain	83
Turkey	83
Thailand	83
Serbia	84
China	85
Burkina Faso	88
Italy	88
Mexico	88
Hong Kong	89
Sweden	89
Greece	89
Indonesia	89
Philippines	90
Nigeria	90
Brazil	91
India	91
Pakistan	91
Argentina	91
USA	92
Switzerland	92
Netherlands	92
Germany	92
Curaçao	93
Ireland	93
UK	93
Austria	94
France	95
Egypt	95
Belgium	95
Canada	96
Ethiopia	96
Norway	97
Australia	98
Finland	98
Portugal	98
Malaysia	100
South Africa	100
Denmark	100

Figure 11.4. **The Reason for Organization**

Two managers talk about their company's organizational structure.

A. One says: "The main reason for having an organizational structure is so that everyone knows who has authority over whom."

B. The other says: "The main reason for having an organizational structure is so that everyone knows how functions are allocated and coordinated."

Which one of these two ways usually best represents an organizational structure?

The nations most attracted to putting roles before people, largely North American and northwest European, opt by large majorities for B. Here *the logic of subordination is clearly rational and coordinative.* In option A it is left unspecified. The organization legitimates existing power differences.

The Eiffel Tower points to the goals to be achieved by the edifice, which is relatively rigid and has difficulty pointing in different directions. If, for example, the Eiffel Tower company needs to achieve goals inconsistent with hierarchical coordinated roles—say, inventing new products—then its structure tends to impede achievement. On the other hand, it is well designed to renew passports or check insurance claims, where the rules are devised in advance and consistent treatment is legally required.

In one of our workshops the head of strategic planning in a major German company gave a one-hour presentation on his company's strategic planning. He spent 45 minutes on how his firm was organized and the remaining 15 on strategic issues. Over lunch the Dutch author asked him why he had not wanted to devote 60 minutes to strategic issues. "But I did," was his reply. For him, structure *was* strategy.

Thinking, Learning, and Change

The way in which people think, learn, and change in the role-oriented, Eiffel Tower company is significantly different from similar processes in the family model. For employees in the Eiffel Tower, the family culture is arbitrary, irrational, conspiratorial, cozy, and corrupt. Instead of following set procedures that everyone can understand, and having objective benchmarks to which employees agree to conform, the family is forever shifting goalposts or suspending competitive play altogether.

Learning in the Eiffel Tower means acquiring the skills necessary to fit a role and, hopefully, the additional skills to qualify for higher positions. In Eiffel Tower companies, people—or "human resources"—are conceived of as similar to capital and cash resources. People of known qualifications can be planned, scheduled, deployed, and reshuffled by skill sets like any other physical entity. Manpower planning, assessment centers, appraisal systems, training programs, and job rotation all have the function of helping to classify and produce resources to fit known roles.

Change in the Eiffel Tower is effected through *changing rules*. With any alteration in the company's purpose must come changes in what employees are formally required to do. For this reason, the culture does not adapt well to turbulent environments. In theory, constant rule-change would be necessary, but this would in practice bewilder employees, lower morale, and obscure the distinction between rules and deviations. Change in an Eiffel Tower culture is immensely complex and time consuming. Manuals must be rewritten, procedures revised, job descriptions altered, promotions reconsidered, and qualifications reassessed. *Restructuring* and *rationalization* tend to be dreaded words in Eiffel Tower cultures. They usually mean wholesale firings and redundancies. Such companies resist change, and when it becomes inevitable, they suffer major dislocation as a consequence.

An American manager responsible for initiating change in a German company described the difficulties he'd had in making progress, although the German managers had discussed the new strategy in depth and made significant contributions to its formulation. Through informal channels he eventually discovered that his mistake was not having formalized the changes to structure or job descriptions. In the absence of a new organization chart, this Eiffel Tower company was unable to change. As with the Dutch manager earlier in this chapter, who had similar problems in dealing with a French family-style company, his assumption was that once an intellectual decision had been agreed to, instant action would follow. Both these managers came from task-oriented, guided missile cultures (the third type to be described here).

Motivating, Rewarding, and Resolving Conflict

Employees of the Eiffel Tower are ideally precise and meticulous. They are nervous in the absence of order and predictability. Duty is an important concept for the role-oriented employee. It is an obligation people feel within themselves, rather than an obligation they feel toward a specific individual.

Conflicts are seen as irrational, pathologies of orderly procedure, offenses against efficiency. Criticisms and complaints are typically channeled and dealt with through even more rules and fact-finding procedures.

The Family and the Eiffel Tower in Conflict

MCC, the company employing Mr. Johnson, whose problems we have been following throughout this book, is broadly speaking a task-oriented company, and many of Mr. Johnson's difficulties have arisen through clashes with colleagues whose expectations of companies are much closer to the family model. (The final installment of Mr. Johnson's story appears at the end of this chapter.) Another example of what happens when these two models find themselves side by side is the case of Heinz, a manager from a large German multinational. Experienced and outstandingly successful, Heinz was selected to help a Colombian packaging-material company get out of the red. All stakeholders, the Colombian government included, acknowledged that modernization and more professional management were needed. Heinz wanted to make the factory profitable and more efficient by introducing new production and quality standards.

The most important person in the company next to Heinz was Antonio, a Colombian, who was designated to take over Heinz's job after the German had completed his mission. After almost a year of working in Colombia, Heinz concluded that the activities in the factory had not improved significantly despite his best efforts.

The following are excerpts from a consultant's report in which Heinz and Antonio were interviewed separately.[2]

Antonio's Story

Antonio is very positive about Heinz's technical and organizational capabilities. The need to increase efficiency is undeniable, and the production processes still need much work. Heinz is absolutely right on this score.

Antonio is, however, shocked by the way Heinz is trying to impose his methods and ideas on the Colombians. He describes this action as turning them into robots, dehumanizing the whole organization.

He says Heinz seems obsessed with time and money. People hardly count at all. Heinz yells at workers for taking longer breaks than they should, forgetting that the previous week they worked overtime without extra pay, without complaint, and, of course, without thanks. He does not seem to realize that punctuality is not possible. The company has people reporting for work who walked when the bus broke down, and he shouts at them as they limp in at the gate. Antonio is amazed that they come to work at all.

Two men even waded a river to get to work when the floods washed the bridge away, and yet Heinz still wanted to dock their pay. Antonio refused to do this. He told Heinz, "Look, they have to *want* to come to work, to be appreciated here, or absenteeism will become far higher than it already is."

Heinz's Story

Heinz explains that the factory was a real mess when he arrived. There was no order, no procedure, no discipline, and no responsibility.

He complains that Antonio is always making excuses. Everything is a special case or an exceptional circumstance. He runs around like a wet nurse trying to discover why the employees are unhappy or disturbed. Heinz is forever telling Antonio to let them stand on their own two feet.

Employees think they can turn up to work when it is convenient for them, despite the fact that they know production cannot start until nearly all of them arrive. They wait for things to go wrong and then act as if they are making heroic gestures of self-sacrifice. He has told them repeatedly that he does not need them to stay late, that he just needs them to get to work on time.

"They have more colorful excuses than a tale of the Wild West. To hear them tell it, they come to work at all only because they love us. And they were late because their brothers missed an appointment or some bridge fell down or who knows what. We get 'scenes of village life' here every day."

Heinz adds that he has told Antonio that he does not want to bully or harass employees; he just wants to keep to agreements, deadlines, and schedules. He does not believe that is too much to ask.

In this rather extreme example, it should be noted that Heinz represents a very sophisticated Eiffel Tower culture and Antonio quite an unsophisticated family one. In the hands of a sophisticated family culture, like many Japanese companies, the consequences could be different. Nor are cultures necessarily exclusive. Families can "take on" the exacting rules of Eiffel Towers and become formidable competitors. The finest combinations lie beyond stereotypes and simple contrasts.

The Guided Missile Culture

The guided missile culture differs from both the family and the Eiffel Tower by being *egalitarian*, but it differs also from the family and resembles the Eiffel Tower in being impersonal and task oriented. You could say the guided missile culture is like the Eiffel Tower in flight.

However, while the rationale of the Eiffel Tower culture is means, the guided missile has a rationale of ends. Everything must be done to persevere in your strategic intent and reach your target.

The guided missile culture is oriented to tasks, typically undertaken by teams or project groups. It differs from the role culture in that the jobs that members do are not fixed in advance. People must do "whatever it takes" to complete a task, and what is needed is often unclear and may have to be discovered.

The National Aeronautics and Space Administration pioneered the use of project groups working on space probes; the groups resembled guided missiles in the sense that task completion was the end goal. To build a lunar landing module, it takes roughly 140 different kinds of engineers, each of whose contribution is crucial at an exact time that cannot be known in advance. Because every variety of engineering must work harmoniously with every other, the best form of synthesis needs to be discovered in the course of working. Nor can there be any hierarchy that claims that "A's expertise is greater than B's expertise." Each knows most about his or her part. How the whole will function needs to be worked out with everyone's participation. All are *equal*, or at least potentially equal, since their relative contributions are not yet known.

Such groups will have leaders or coordinators, who are responsible for sub- and final assemblies, but these generalists may know less than specialists in each discipline and must treat all experts with due respect. The group is egalitarian because it might need the help of any one expert in changing direction toward its target. The end is known, but the possible trajectories are uncertain. Missile cultures frequently draw on professionals and are cross-disciplinary. In an advertising agency, for example, one copywriter, one visualizer or artist, one media buyer, one commercial film buyer, and one account representative may work on a campaign that is yet to be agreed on by the client. All will play a part, but what part depends on the final campaign the client prefers.

Guided missile cultures are expensive, because professionals are expensive. Groups tend to be temporary, with relationships as fleeting as the project and largely instrumental in bringing the project to a conclusion. Employees will join other groups, for other purposes, within days or weeks and may have multiple memberships. This culture is *not* affectionate or mutually committed, but typifies the *neutral* cultures discussed in Chapter 6.

The ultimate criteria of human value in the guided missile culture are how you perform and to what extent you contribute to the jointly desired outcome. In effect, each member shares in problem solving. The relative contribution of any one person may not be as clear as in the Eiffel Tower culture, where each role is described and outputs can be quantified.

In practice, the guided missile culture is *superimposed* on the Eiffel Tower organization to give it permanence and stability. This is known as the matrix organization. You have one (Eiffel Tower) line reporting to your functional boss—say, electrical engineering—and another (guided missile) line of responsibility to your project head. This makes you jointly responsible to your engineering boss for quality engineering and to your project leader for a viable, low-cost means of, say, auto-emissions control. The project has to succeed, and your electronics must be excellent. Two authorities pull you in different, although reconcilable, directions.

Thinking, Learning, and Change

The guided missile culture is *cybernetic*, in the sense that it homes in on its target using feedback signals, and is therefore circular rather than linear. Yet the "missile" rarely, if ever, changes its mind about its target. Steering is therefore corrective and conservative, not as open to new *ends* as to new *means*.

Learning includes "getting on" with people, breaking the ice quickly, playing the part in a team that is currently lacking, being practical rather than theoretical, and being problem centered rather than discipline centered. Appraisal is often by peers or subordinates rather than by someone further up the hierarchy.

Change comes quickly to the guided missile culture. The target moves. More targets appear, new groups are formed, old ones dissolve. People who hop from group to group will often hop from job to job, so that turnover tends to be high, and *loyalties to professions and projects are greater than loyalties to the company.* The guided missile culture is in many respects the antithesis of the family culture, in which bonds are close and ties are characterized by long duration and deep affection.

Motivating, Rewarding, and Resolving Conflict

Motivations tend to be *intrinsic* in this culture. That is, team members get enthusiastic about, identify with, and struggle toward the final product. In the case of Apple the enthusiasm is about creating an "insanely great device." The product under development is the superordinate goal, for which the conflicts and animosities of team members may be set aside. Unless there is high participation, there will not be widespread commitment. The final consensus must be broad enough to pull in all those who work on the product.

This culture tends to be individualistic, since it allows for a wide variety of differently specialized people to work with each other on a temporary basis. The scenery of faces keeps changing. Only the pursuit of chosen lines of personal development is constant. The team is a vehicle for the shared enthusiasm of its members, but it is itself disposable and will be discarded when the project ends. Members are garrulous, idiosyncratic, and intelligent, but their mutuality is a means, not an end. It is a way of enjoying the journey. They do not need to know each other intimately and may avoid doing so. Management by objectives is the language spoken, and people are paid by performance.

The Incubator Culture

The incubator culture is based on the existential idea that organizations are secondary to the fulfillment of individuals. Just as "Existence precedes essence" was the motto of existential philosophers, so "existence precedes organization" is the notion of incubator cultures. If organizations are to be tolerated at all, they should be there to serve as *incubators for self-expression and self-fulfillment*. The metaphor here should not be confused with "business incubators." These are organizations that provide routine maintenance and services, plant equipment, insurance, office space, and the like, for embryo businesses so that these businesses can lower their overhead costs during the crucial start-up phase.

Note, though, that the logic of business incubators is similar to that of cultural incubators. In both cases the purpose is to free individuals from routine activities so that they can engage in more creative activities and to minimize time spent on self-maintenance. The incubator is *both* personal and egalitarian. In that regard, it has almost no structure at all, and what structure it does provide is merely for personal convenience: heat, light, word processing, coffee, and so on.

The roles of other people in the incubator, however, are crucial. They are there to confirm, criticize, develop, find resources for, and help to complete the innovative product or service. The culture acts as a sounding board for innovative ideas and tries to respond intelligently to new initiatives. Typical examples include the start-up firms in Silicon Valley, California, in Silicon Glen in Scotland, and on Route 128 around Boston. The companies are usually entrepreneurial or founded by a creative team that quit a larger employer just before the payoff on the new enterprise. Being individualist, such people are not constrained by organizational loyalties and may deliberately take a "free ride" with the current employer until their eggs are close to hatching. In this way larger organizations find themselves successively undermined.

Cultural incubators are not only small, innovative companies. They can be doctors in group practice, legal partners, consultants, chartered surveyors, or any group of professionals who work mostly alone but like to share resources while comparing experiences. Some writers on the subject see the incubator as the organizational wave of the future. Others see any decline of Silicon Valley as evidence that this culture cannot survive maturity and is but a temporary phase in starting up an organization from an ad hoc basis. Still others point to the rarity of incubator cultures outside the "enclaves of individualism" in the US, the UK, and the rest of the English-speaking world.

Just as incubators have minimal structure, so they also have minimal hierarchy. Such authority as individuals do command is strictly personal, the exciting nature of their ideas and the inspiration of their vision leading others to work with them.

Incubators often, if not always, operate in an environment of intense *emotional* commitment. However, this commitment is less toward people per se than to the world-changing, society-redeeming nature of the work being undertaken. The personal computer gave "power to the person"; gene-splicing could save crops, save lives, and rescue the economy and represents an odyssey into the unknown, wherein "the journey is the reward."

Incubator cultures enjoy the process of creating and innovating. Because of emotional commitment, shared enthusiasms, and superordinate goals, the incubator at its best can be ruthlessly honest, effective, nurturing, therapeutic, and exciting, depending as it does on face-to-face relationships and working intimacies. Because the association is voluntary, often underfunded, and fueled largely by hope and idealism, it can be the most significant and intense experience of a lifetime. It follows, though, that this experience is hard to repeat or sustain, since the project no sooner succeeds than strangers must be hired, and the founders' special relationships are lost. Incubators are typically limited in size by the leaders' "span of control," since it becomes problematic to communicate spontaneously and informally with more than 75 to 100 people.

Thinking, Learning, and Change

Change in the incubator can be fast and spontaneous where the members are attuned to each other. Roger Harrison has likened the process to an improvising jazz band, in which a self-elected leader tries something new, and the band follows if it likes the theme and ignores the theme if it does not.[3] All participants are on the same wavelength, empathically searching together for a solution to the shared problem. But because a customer has not defined any target, *the problem itself is open to redefinition*, and the solution being searched for is typically generic, aimed at a universe of applications.

American start-up companies with incubator cultures rarely survive the maturing of their products and their markets. This culture learns to create but not to *survive altered patterns of demand*. The "great designers" of the novel products continue to be the heroes of the company long after the focus has shifted to customer service and to marketing.

Motivating, Rewarding, and Resolving Conflict

Motivation is often wholehearted, intrinsic, and intense, with individuals working "70 hours a week and loving it" as the T-shirts at Apple Computer used to read in the company's earlier days. There is competition to contribute to the emerging shape of something new. Everyone wants to get his or her "hands on." There is scant concern for personal security, and few wish to profit or have power *apart from the unfolding creative process*. If the whole succeeds, there will be plenty for everyone. If it does not, the incubator itself will be gone. In contrast to the family culture, leadership in the incubator is *achieved*, not ascribed. You follow those whose progress most impresses you and whose ideas work. Power plays that impede group achievement will be reviled. Conflict is resolved either by splitting up or by trying the proposed alternatives to see which works best.

Which Countries Prefer Which Corporate Cultures?

As we have already said, these "pure types" seldom exist. In practice the types are mixed or overlaid, with one culture dominating. Nevertheless, in different national cultures one or more of these types will clearly dominate the corporate scene, and if we list the main characteristics of the four types, it becomes easy to refer back to the national cultural dimensions discussed in the preceding chapters. The following table shows how in the four models employees relate differently; have different views of authority; think, learn, and change in different ways; and are motivated by different rewards, while criticism and conflict resolution are variously handled.

CHARACTERISTICS OF THE FOUR CORPORATE CULTURES

	FAMILY	EIFFEL TOWER	GUIDED MISSILE	INCUBATOR
Relationships between employees	Diffuse relationships to organic whole to which one is bonded	Specific role in mechanical system of required interactions	Specific tasks in cyber-netic system targeted upon shared objectives	Diffuse, spontaneous relationships growing out of shared creative process
Attitude to authority	Status is ascribed to parent figures who are close and powerful	Status is ascribed to superior roles who are distant yet powerful	Status is achieved by project group members who con-tribute to targeted goal	Status is achieved by individuals exemplifying creativity and growth
Ways of thinking and learning	Intuitive, holistic, lateral, and error-correcting	Logical, analytical, vertical, and rationally efficient	Problem-centered, professional, practical, cross-disciplinary	Process-oriented, cre-ative, ad hoc, inspirational
Attitudes to people	Family members	Human resources	Specialists and experts	Co-creators
Ways of changing	"Father" changes course	Change rules and procedures	Shift aim as target moves	Improvise and attune
Ways of motivat-ing and rewarding	Intrinsic satisfaction in being loved and respected; manage-ment by subjectives	Promotion to greater posi-tion, larger role	Pay or credit for perfor-mance and problems solved; man-agement by objectives	Participat-ing in the process of creating new realities; manage-ment by enthusiasm
Criticism and conflict resolution	Turn other cheek, save others' faces, do not lose power game	Criticism is accusation of irrational-ity unless there are procedures to arbitrate conflicts	Constructive task-related only, then admit error and correct fast	Must improve creative idea, not negate it

The reader, however, should interpret this analysis cautiously. Smaller companies *wherever* located are more likely to take the family and incubator forms. Large companies needing structure to cohere are likely to choose Eiffel Tower or guided missile forms. In France, for example, smaller companies tend to be family and larger companies Eiffel Tower. In the US guided missile companies may dominate among large corporations, but the archetypal incubators are to be found in the Silicon Valley paradigm.

Summary

We have defined four broad types of corporate culture, which are closely related to the national differences described in earlier chapters. Just as national cultures conflict, leading to mutual incomprehension and mistrust, so corporate cultures collide. Attempts to "dice" the family with a matrix can cause rage and consternation. Getting cozy with subordinates in the Eiffel Tower could be seen as a potentially improper advance. Asking to be put in a group with a special friend is a subversive act in the guided missile culture. Calling your boss "buddy" and slapping him or her on the back will get you thrown from the Eiffel Tower, while suggesting in an incubator that everyone fill out time sheets will be greeted with catcalls. (If you really want to discover norms, *break them*; reading this chapter is intended as a less painful alternative.)

Yet the types exist and must be respected. Really successful businesses borrow from all types and ceaselessly struggle to reconcile them. We turn to this process in the final chapter. First, however, we should say good-bye to Mr. Johnson.

Back in St. Louis at the MCC management meeting, Mr. Johnson reported on the introduction of pay-for-performance. It had been resisted widely, and where it had been tried, in parts of southern Europe, the Middle East, and Asia, early results showed it had failed. The group listened in silence.

The atmosphere was distinctly cool. "Well," the CEO responded, "how do you plan to cope with these problems, Bill? I'm sure we don't need the HR function to tell us that there are a lot of different people and opinions in the world."

Johnson had by now decided that he had nothing to lose, so he voiced a concern he had felt for many months: "I realize we make machines, but I sometimes ask myself if we are letting the metaphor run away with the organization. These are people, not microprocessors or integrated circuits that can be replaced if they don't work."

"I wish we *could* operate more like a computer," interrupted the finance manager. "We hire quality people to do as we tell them and to function in ways they are trained. Either they do this or we get somebody else. What's wrong with that?"

The CEO was trying to calm things down. "I have to disagree there," he said. "I see this company as more of an *organism*. If you go to Barcelona and chop off heads, don't be surprised if the body dies. If we take out some subsidiary's right hand, we can't expect it to work well in the future. What I can't understand is why Bill can't get them to see that we're all one organism and that the hands and feet can't go off in all directions."

At once, all the exasperations of the last few months came to the surface. For a moment Johnson had thought that the CEO was supporting him, but it was the same old message: get the whole world to march in step with us.

"What I've been through in the last eight months," he told the group, "is about as far from a smoothly running computer or a living organism as you could get. I'll tell you what it's really like, because I was reading the story to my kids. It's like that crazy croquet game in *Alice in Wonderland* where she has to play with a flamingo as a mallet, waiters bending over as hoops, and hedgehogs as balls. The flamingo twists its head around to look at Alice, the hoops wander off, and the balls crawl away. The result is chaos."

He concluded, "Other cultures aren't part of a machine, or the organs of a supranational body. They're different animals, all with logic of their own. If we asked them what game *they* are playing, and got them to explain the rules, we might discover when we aren't holding a mallet at all, or even get the hedgehog to go in the right direction."

Was Mr. Johnson promoted, or was he given the job of overseeing the welfare of MCC pensioners? An educated guess is that he is running a small but fast-growing consultancy somewhere, specializing in cross-cultural management.

Notes

1. G. Inzerilli and A. Laurent, "The Concept of Organizational Structure" (working paper, University of Pennsylvania and INSEAD, 1979); "Managerial Views of Organizational Structure in France and the USA," *International Studies of Management and Organizations* 13 (1983): 1–2, 97–118.
2. D. R. Denison, *Corporate Culture and Organizational Effectiveness*, Wiley Series on Organizational Assessment and Change (Oxford: John Wiley & Sons, 1990), xvii, 267.
3. R. Harrison, "Understanding Your Organization's Character," *Harvard Business Review*, May–June 1972.

Bibliography

Hampden-Turner, C. *Corporate Culture*. London: The Economist Books/Business Books, 1991.

Handy, C. *The Gods of Management*. London: Souvenir Press, 1978.

Toward International and
Transnational Management

THIS BOOK has elucidated national and corporate culture differences, of which we have found a great many. So wide and pervasive are these variations that they would seem to confirm the doubt
expressed at the beginning as to whether universal or general principles of "how to manage" were feasible or useful.

Despite that caveat, among the implications of the research presented here is that universals exist at another level. While you cannot give universal *advice* that will work regardless of culture, and
while general axioms of business administration turn out to be largely
American cultural axioms, there are *universal dilemmas or problems of
human existence*. Every country and every organization in that country
faces dilemmas:

- In relationships with people
- In relationship to time
- In relations between people and the natural environment

While nations differ markedly in *how* they approach these dilemmas, they do not differ in needing to make some kind of response.
People everywhere are as one in having to face up to the same challenges of existence.

In this chapter we look at some of the specific problems faced by international management, in terms of structure, strategy, communications, and human resources, and consider a common approach to their solution.

Our research methods consist of stories, scenes, situations, and questions that put two moral and/or managerial principles in conflict. It is the researchers who force the managers to choose one over the other. In reality the answers managers gave may be considered as their first and second "foundation stones" in building the *moral edifice* that we present. Some managers, for example, felt that you had to give priority to a universal rule (universalism) and behave in particular instances accordingly. Some felt that you had to give priority to your affection for particular people (particularism) and develop whatever universals you could out of such obligations. Few were actually rejecting the alternative solution out of hand, and, as the figures show, it is rare for any national result to be anywhere near 100 percent in favor of any priority. Almost all our problems, as well as their solutions, are recognizable all over the world.

There is another important respect in which all the world's managers are the same: whichever principle they start with, the circumstances of business and of organizing experience requires them to reconcile the dilemmas we have been discussing. You can prosper only if as many particulars as possible are covered by rules, yet exceptions are seen and noted. You can think effectively only if you consider both the specifics and the diffuse wholes; the segments are as meaningful as the integrations. Whether you are at heart an individualist or a communitarian, your individuals must be capable of organizing themselves, while your communities are only as good as the health, wealth, and wisdom of each member.

It is crucial to give status to achievers, but it is equally crucial to back strategies, projects, and initiatives from people who have not yet achieved anything—in other words, to ascribe status to them in hope of facilitating success. Everyone should be equal in regard to rights and opportunities, yet any contest will produce a hierarchy of relative standings. Respect for age and experience can both nurture and discourage people who are young and inexperienced. Hierarchy and equality are finely interwoven in every culture. It is true that time is both a passing sequence of events and a moment of truth, a "now" in which past, present, and future are given new meanings. We need to accept influences from the depth of our inner convictions and the world around us.

In the final analysis *culture is the manner in which these dilemmas are reconciled, since every nation seeks a different and winding path to its own ideals of integrity.* It is our position that businesses will succeed to the extent that this reconciliation occurs, so we have everything to learn from discovering what paths others have taken.

Problems for the Cross-Cultural Manager

We are not the first to note these differences. Geert Hofstede did so in his international samples of IBM employees.[1] So did Inzerilli and Laurent in their research comparing Italian and French managers with those in the US, Japan, and Europe.[2] As we tracked the experience of Mr. Johnson of MCC from chapter to chapter, we found what these researchers have also noted, that favorite American solutions do not always solve the dilemmas of other nations. Since the US has been the principal source of management theory, this is crucial information for all students of business practice.

For example, the matrix organization is a clever reconciliation of the need to be organized by discipline and function on the one hand and the need to respond to projects, products under development, and customer specifications on the other. However, while this system solves American, British, Dutch, and Scandinavian dilemmas, it directly threatens and contradicts the family model described in Chapter 11, so that some Italian, Spanish, French, and Asian companies will have to devise a different solution.

Similarly, Peter Drucker's management by objectives is a justly famous reconciliation of an American dilemma and has rightly been adopted by like-minded nations. Conflict between equality and hierarchy, and between the individual and the community, is reconciled by getting individuals to pledge themselves freely to fulfill the key objectives of the community and the hierarchy. Voluntarily negotiated contracts join the person to the group. That is good, but not so good for nations that regard the performance of individuals as part of the relationship with the boss and that attribute excellence to the whole "family" or relationship.

Pay-for-performance is similarly an attempted solution to the achievement-ascription dilemma. Why not ascribe status and financial rewards to employees in proportion to their achievements? Again, this practice has broad appeal to those who put achievement first but none to those who put ascription first and seek to be the emotional "authors" of a subordinate's success. We discussed this problem in detail in Chapter 8, but it is so central to the issue that it bears an additional anecdote here.

An American computer company introduced pay-for-performance in both the US and the Middle East. It worked well in the US and increased sales briefly in the Middle East before a serious slump occurred. Inquiries showed that indeed the winners among salespeople in the Middle East had done better, but the vast majority had done worse. The wish for their fellows to succeed had been seriously eroded by the contest. Overall morale and sales were down. Ill will was contagious. When the bosses discovered that certain salespeople were earning more than they did, high individual performances also ceased. Obviously these were problems, but the principal reason for eventually abandoning the system was the discovery that customers were being loaded up with products that they did not need. Whenever A tried to beat B to the bonus, the care of customers began to slip, with serious, if delayed, results.

Centralization Versus Decentralization

The main dilemma that those who manage across cultures confront is the extent to which they should *centralize*, thereby imposing on foreign cultures rules and procedures that might affront them, or *decentralize*, thereby letting each culture go its own way, without having any centrally viable ideas about improvement, since the "better way" is a local pathway, not a global one. If you radically decentralize, you have to ask whether HQ can add value at all, or whether companies acting in several nations are worthwhile.

Decentralization is easier under some corporate cultures than others. To decentralize, you have to delegate. Of the four models described in Chapter 11, this can be done in the Eiffel Tower and the guided missile cultures but not so easily in the family model where the parent remains the parent. Stories are common of the difficulties that Japanese managers have in decentralizing and delegating to foreigners. The family communicates by a kind of in-house osmosis of empathy and bowing rituals that foreigners cannot easily share. Policies are made on telephone calls to Tokyo, because the intimate understandings between Japanese insiders are difficult to delegate.

As most of our case histories and anecdotes have shown, miscommunication is far more common than dialogue. Nevertheless, centralizing and decentralizing are, as with all the other dimensions introduced in this book, potentially reconcilable processes. A biological organism grows to higher levels of order and complexity by being more differentiated and more integrated. The more departments, divisions, functions, and differentiated activities a corporation pursues, the greater the challenge, and also the greater the importance of *coordinating all this variety*. As Paul Lawrence and Jay Lorsch demonstrated in the late 1960s, both overcentralized (overintegrated) and overdecentralized (overdifferentiated) companies underperform to significant degrees; differentiating and integrating need to be synergized or reconciled.[3] The corporation with the best integrated diversity is the one that excels.

Group management is often fooled by a foreign subsidiary's doing as it is asked by HQ but essentially performing a corporate rain dance. The local managers know it will make no difference to the rainfall, but if HQ wants a list of everyone's qualifications and salaries to compare the two, they will provide one. Never mind that the qualifications have probably been invented to fit the existing salaries. When these perfect scores arrive, HQ feels it is "in control" worldwide, but of course this is an illusion. The policy handbook says that "we pay no bribes," but in many countries, paid they will be. Relationships without presents are impossible.

The centralizing-decentralizing dilemma is often experienced as consistency versus flexibility of corporate identity. Is it more important for Shell to relate successfully in the Philippines by helping peasants to raise pigs, or should the strategy of being an energy company be used to maintain continuity? In practice helping pig farming has played a role in preventing oil pipelines from being blown up by Communist insurgents. If you are digging for oil in Nigeria anyway, why not find some water too and build some desperately needed wells?

Examples of this kind illustrate that the relationship between centralization and decentralization is a subtle one. It is not true that every differentiated activity takes you further from your core business simply because it is different. Water wells and pig farms may make all the difference between gaining business in less developed countries or losing it. *It is because we are all different that we have so much to exchange with each other.* In matters of culture, as in the relationship of the sexes, the difference can be the chief source of attraction. Italian design and Dutch engineering can lead to conflicts, as we have seen; they could also lead to a product made in heaven.

The ideal, then, is to differentiate in such a way as to make integration more effective, or to decentralize activities in such a way that an ever broader diversity gets coordinated by the "central nervous system" of your corporation. In matters of cultural diversity there is always a challenge, but where this challenge is met, valuable connections result.

Quality, Not Quantity, in Decentralization

It is not a matter of *how much* to decentralize, but *what* to decentralize and what to keep at corporate HQ. A company that does not centralize information cannot cohere at all, but this does not mean that decisions cannot be made locally. Arguably, technical specifications, such as the rules, standards, and procedures by which oil refineries are operated, can be decided centrally, but what mix of products to refine could be decided nationally, close to customers' changing demands. Pricing may also be a local decision, sensitive to the proximity of competitors and the degree of overcapacity. Financing decisions are normally allocated centrally or locally according to their size.

National companies often pay a standard overhead to headquarters and get "free" legal, financial, planning, and personnel services; this arrangement tends to protect the role of centralized functions. You have to pay, so you might as well use them. Alternatively, HQ staff may provide consultancy services to national companies on request. Under this system, unnecessary staff services at HQ will shrivel on the vine if no one wants them, an arrangement that tends to favor decentralization.

International and Transnational Companies

The issues of centralization and decentralization have been fully discussed by Christopher Bartlett and Sumantra Ghoshal in relation to their analysis of global versus multinational corporations and of international versus transnational corporations.[4] As they define them, global and multinational companies are both essentially centralized, in that their subsidiaries relate to the head company or country, even if not necessarily very strongly, rather than to the other companies or nations in the group. For these companies, there are unlikely to be many foreigners in the top management team, and the myth of the universal applicability of management techniques is likely to be strong. In contrast, in both international and transnational corporate structures, there is a significant attempt to overcome the dilemma of centralization versus decentralization; each of these in its own way sets out to manage diversity and gain competitive advantage from being located in different countries with special capacities. This book is aimed at those who are already operating on international or transnational levels, or aspire to do so.

The two forms take different paths to the reconciliation of centralizing and decentralizing. The international corporation moves out influence from its center to regions and nations, retaining a coordinative role, while the transnational corporation loses its center in favor of polycentric influences from different parts of its network.

The *international* corporation, of which IBM, Exxon, and Disney World are examples, breaks with the notion that national organizations are spokes around a wheel for all aspects of the business. This type of organization is somewhere in between multinational and global enterprises; some strategic areas are centralized, some are decentralized. It has a centralized main product or service, such as oil for Exxon and entertainment for Disney World. But there are slight adaptations in local operations, like the loyalty programs for Exxon and the serving of local beverages at the restaurants at Disney. National organizations have legitimate relationships with each other based on what it is that the customer wants and the best source of supply within the international system. HQ's role becomes not so much to instruct or to evaluate as to *coordinate*, to make sure that if one nation has embarked in a promising direction, other nations also learn from this experience. HQ facilitates this learning and possibly helps other nations to emulate the initiative.

As corporations move from a multilocal to an international form, the HQ behaves *less like a police officer and more like a consultant*. Functional and geographic chiefs are called coordinators, their authority stemming from the fact that they know what several functions, regions, or nations are doing.

The *transnational* corporation is polycentric, rather than being coordinated from the center. It consists of several centers of specialized excellence that will exercise authority and influence whenever they are qualified to do so by the challenge confronting the organization. The Swedish professor Gunnar Hedlund found this structure increasingly typical of some Swedish organizations; examples are IKEA and Ericsson. Bartlett and Ghoshal regarded transnationalism as an important direction, one that in cases such as Philips and Matsushita, among others, has become a reality. Jay Ogilvy, an American academic, has spoken of heterarchies replacing hierarchies.[5] Transnational corporations are likely to have top management teams that are a microcosm of the whole system, with German, Dutch, French, Italian, and Japanese executives at company HQ, in cases in which substantial businesses are located in those countries. These executives are not "delegates" or "representatives" in a foreign country, but full-time contributors to transcultural management, so that, say, the Italian subsidiary has its cultural traits not only within but also at the coordinating center. The best example is Applied Materials, where at one stage the top 100 consisted of more than 50 nationalities and the seven-person board had an American CEO, an Israeli COO, an Iraqi R&D head, a Chinese manufacturing person, a German marketing manager, and an Argentinean HR head (from Russian descent). Besides having a very multicultural top, transnational organizations are characterized by being able to combine best local practices into next practices that they globalize. Also these organizations are value-driven, and their values are often integrated opposites. If we take Pepsi-Co's values, they said "we strive for teams that consist of creative individuals" and we give "direct feedback, with diplomacy."

All these predictions of the future form of the successful transnational imply a flatter corporate structure drawing on a multiplicity of points of expertise. Hence, if a company is designing a new international sports car, the electronics might come from Japan, the engine and suspension from Germany, the design from Italy, the fiberglass shell from the Netherlands, and the mahogany wood finish from Britain, with the assembly to be done in Spain. National marketing departments will adopt different tactics to sell the car, while exchanging experience and drawing on each other's brand of management expertise. Each element in the "value-added chain" or loop would exercise authority on the issue of its own cultural strength. Robert Reich, the American political scientist, has argued that it does not really matter anymore who owns the company, be they American shareholders, Europeans, or Asians. What matters is where the most value is added in the transnational network.[6] Countries will prosper or stagnate by the skills they inject into these "value chains." In the economy of the future, knowledge is king, and influence flows from wherever that knowledge resides.

In the transnational company influence can be exercised by any nation on others and can start at any point, accumulating value as it goes and "circling" to reconcile cultural strengths.

What is important about transnationalism is that it follows the circular reconciliations sketched at the ends of Chapters 4 through 10; it combines the qualities of various cultures. The methodology of reconciliation is discussed in detail in Chapter 13.

You can join Italy's particularism to Germany's universalism, or join American individualism and inner-directed creativity to Japanese rapid communitarian exploitation of new products and other-directed skills of customer satisfaction. Where countries specialize in what they do best, the transnational circuits so formed could prove unbeatable. The remaining question is how the transnational organization is to survive the complete atrophy of its center.

Human-Resource Management in the Future

The main preoccupation of our analysis of cultural differences has been under the general heading of human resources. In the recruitment of the senior managers of the future, large companies seem at present to be at some disadvantage. The notion that it is desirable to gain "power" by climbing high in large organizations is currently somewhat out of fashion; autonomy is more sought after, and the attraction to recruits of internationalism is more likely to lie in the experience, knowledge, and investigation of multiple cultures. Recruits will want to plan their own careers in the international and transnational corporation of the future, and some career "ladders" may look more like "walkways." Companies that succeed in reconciling the centralization-versus-decentralization dilemma will have learned how to rotate their employees internationally (especially the highfliers), how to work in several languages, and how to make decisions at many points on the globe and to spread their effects.

Once the scarce commodity of intelligent managers has been attracted, the future transnational will set out to give these managers further training in cross-cultural awareness, starting with learning how to recognize a cultural problem, which, as we have observed, is often unidentified; it is often seen not as a problem but as "the stubbornness of south Europeans about incentive schemes." People who resist American universals are viewed as traditional, unbusinesslike, or even backward. More of this can be found in our book *Managing People Across Cultures*.

The Growth of Information

The Dutch author once gave a seminar in Thailand that saved a company $1.5 million. It was not, alas, the result of any insights he imparted. A French executive sitting next to a Thai executive of the same company discovered that the latter was about to build a pilot plant that would duplicate something the French had just completed. This is indicative of the frequent failure of internal corporate communications.

The development of information technology, however, presents new problems. IT has its own curious forms of absolutism. Given the high capacity, high speed, and high cost of computers, the impulse following their installation is to generate a great deal of information as quickly as possible, thereby reducing the cost per byte.

As a result, at HQ to know everything statistical about your subsidiary before it has even discovered the information itself is much prized. We have heard of subsidiary companies called up during breakfast, because of time differences, with complaints that tin wastage rates in the canning plants are up 50 percent.

This approach can have disastrous consequences for intercultural communication, and it militates against the development of international or transnational structures. The head of a national subsidiary is paid in part to use his or her discretion, free of oversight. If you seek a genuine cultural contribution from a foreign subsidiary, you cannot check up on it daily. Information should go first and foremost to those whose operations it concerns, with a lag before HQ gets it. This procedure gives time for local answers to be found and action to be taken.

A company will remain a centralized, directive, global organization so long as information is used for power and advantage. Because information depends on input, it is easily distorted. Subsidiaries punished for not meeting their forecasts will lower the forecast next time. IT can give an illusion of control that does not survive closer examination.

In the international and transnational structures, national operating companies communicate because they wish to and because the parallel activities of other companies in nearby markets are opportunities and resources. The IT philosophy in these structures states that every national company is free to take major initiatives without prior consultation but should keep the network informed of its actions. It has local autonomy but no right to secrecy about the exercise of that autonomy after the fact. All interested parties must know what has been done. Any interested subsidiary or centralized function can tap into the activities that concern it. This system allows for ad hoc project groups to take advantage of any number of converging lines of research or activity. The hallmark of the international or transnational structure is lateral connections between activities capable of being catalyzed to the advantage of the whole network. In this structure subsidiaries connect to subsidiaries. As with hounds hunting for a fox, anyone may pick up the scent, bay loudly, and have the others follow the new direction.

Software, moreover, may be more or less culturally compatible with how managers think. Diffuse ways of thinking and learning are often diagrammatic and configurative. Streams of words are more linear, specific, and sequential. "Windows" allow for selective viewing of information by those interested. The shape of software needs to be a microcosm of the larger structure and consistent with it. There is software for scenarios of alternative futures, for creative connections between ideas, for alternative applications of key technologies, and for spin-offs.

Implications for Business Strategy

Culture can all too easily put brakes on any movement to internationalize. Universalism tends to create global structures in which the values of the home country are celebrated worldwide. Individualism can produce multinational structures in deference to the individuality of each nation. Inner-directedness also contributes to global or multinational structures, depending on whether the inner-direction is toward a parent company (a global structure) or a national group (a multinational structure).

Equality, other-directedness, and achievement orientations will encourage internationalization, and it is notable that both the Dutch and the Swedes, who display these attributes, are quite successful internationally. Family-style corporate cultures may work well in their countries of origin but be difficult to transfer overseas. Eiffel Tower cultures will be rejected in nations with family-style traditions, especially if the "universals" are foreign. Guided missile cultures also offend family feeling with their on-again, off-again relationships and their "two fathers."

The principal implication for business strategy is a healthy respect for the "founding beliefs" of foreign cultures and the images they have chosen to create coherence. A "strange" culture usually has values neglected in ours, and to discover these values is to find lost parts of our own cultural heritage. Hence, family-style cultures can remind us that work is not necessarily alienating, impersonal, and self-seeking. We can benefit from such insights without putting our relatives on the payroll or feeling like children when the boss walks in. International and transnational structures allow us to *synthesize the advantages of all cultures while avoiding their excesses.* Families are eminently capable of nurturing independence and encouraging achievement. Managing across cultures gives you more possible pathways to your goal.

The only strategic system open to a genuinely international company will be the system described by Michael Goold as *strategic control.*[7] Here strategy is neither laid down by the center nor subject to strict financial parameters, but fed to the center by national companies. They propose, and the center coordinates, criticizes, approves, and adds its own funds. What occurs is a multicultural negotiation.

An international or transnational structure severely reduces its own powers unless it gives a free rein to certain national, cultural proclivities. Strategies tend to vary with national culture; hence, inner-directed, universalistic, specific, achievement-oriented cultures, typically the English-speaking ones, talk as if they were engaged in military campaigns, saturating consumers with a withering hail of commercials and generally conquering and occupying markets. In contrast, outer-directed, particularistic, diffuse, and ascription-oriented cultures, typically the Japanese, speak as if they were serenading customers before transacting business with them. They do not use the word *strategy* at all, although they clearly have a method of coevolving with customers. Individualist cultures with a sequential view of time, such as the US and Britain, are usually short term in their business strategies. Communitarian cultures with a synchronic view of time, such as Germany and Japan, are typically long term strategically.

An international or transnational structure that does not allow parties who are willing to postpone rewards for several years to do so could miss out on the secret of Asian and German economic strengths. Within the international or transnational structure a microcosm of international economic competition is going on. We would be foolish not to notice who is winning or why, and to fail to apply the lessons.

Local HR and Valuing Competences

One notable way of combining the universal values generated by the head office with local flexibility and the impact of national cultures arises in assessment procedures. HQ or global HR makes a list of what is to be appraised, but it leaves the priority of the items to the national operating company. Shell, for example, operated its HAIRL system of basic appraisal. The acronym stands for Helicopter (the capacity to take a broad view from above), power of Analysis, Imagination, sense of Reality, and Leadership effectiveness. We sought to discover if these components were equally important to various Shell operating companies and asked participants in several seminars to prioritize HAIRL for themselves. The results were tabulated as follows.

Netherlands	France	Germany	Britain
Reality	Imagination	Leadership	Helicopter
Analysis	Analysis	Analysis	Imagination
Helicopter	Leadership	Reality	Reality
Leadership	Helicopter	Imagination	Analysis
Imagination	Reality	Helicopter	Leadership

There is no inherent reason, it seems to us, why all nations should place equal weight on all values. If the Dutch want to stress realism, so be it. They find most of the oil by drilling where it really is and not where they imagine it to be. Prioritizing the values of assessment can tell us a lot about how cultures vary. It is the theme of this book that all cultures need to be both universalist and particularist, both individualist and communitarian, both ascriptive and achieving, both inner- and outer-directed. The difference lies in their priorities, where they "start." We have argued the essential *complementarity* of values. To post an individualist to communitarian Singapore can help to make that communitarianism more responsive to individuals, and the reverse would be true of posting a Singaporean to the US.

We should not forget that different priorities are not all equally successful. From studying different value priorities in different cultures comes vital clues as to how we can better manage our own affairs.

Local Freedom to Reward

It is similarly possible to have a universal rule that "success must be rewarded commensurate with its size," yet leave the form of that reward up to the national company. Our case study of MCC conveyed that message. That company was unable to accept that while it could have a central philosophy of pay-for-performance, it needed to decentralize its application. Managers around the world are in favor of the principle; the difficulty is that they all mean different things by "pay" and different things by "performance." It is entirely reasonable that a person in a communitarian culture should seek to reward the team members for his or her own successful efforts. They get the money the individual helped generate; he or she gets the respect, affection, and gratitude, which is not such a bad bargain. That the high performer in an individualistic society might like to attract rewards away from colleagues is also entirely reasonable. The solution is for communitarian and individualist cultures to give group rewards and personal rewards in accordance with their own judgments and results. After all, no culture pays salaries entirely as a bonus for individual effort; part is always fixed, so we are talking about relative emphasis. In a truly international or transnational corporation *every nation would be charged with finding its optimal mix between personal and group rewards*, with more of that reward for successful operations.

If we do this, we might be surprised. Do individuals in Western cultures create because of extrinsic rewards such as money, or because their peers encourage them? The answers could be instructive.

The question of hierarchical versus egalitarian pay structures could also be up to the national company. Relatively equal pay may improve cooperation. Relatively unequal pay may increase competition among employees. How much of each works best? The company should have a fixed ratio of its turnover to distribute as it sees fit. National companies might also be given the discretion to take lower salaries overall so as to reduce prices to customers, using a strategy of "increasing market share." The notion that everyone is motivated principally by monetary rewards needs to be challenged. Those willing to take long-term advantage of wage-control strategies should be encouraged. Corporate cultures based on the image of the family may not care so much about wage levels. People who work principally for each other's affection can be fiercely competitive on costs, as the Japanese showed in the 1990s. Pay-for-performance tends to be expensive.

Especially when people are poor, a group or communitarian orientation may be crucial for takeoff. A group-bonus scheme used by Shell Nigeria, for example, consisted of a water well and irrigation system for the town in which the employees lived, which not only materially benefited their homes and neighborhood but also raised their status in the community. It is arguable that such a scheme was far more valuable to individual employees than dividing the cost of the project among them and giving them the money instead.

The Error-Correcting Manager

Other cultures are strange, ambiguous, even shocking to us. It is unavoidable that we will make mistakes in dealing with them and feel muddled and confused. The real issue is how well we are prepared to learn from mistakes and how bravely we struggle to understand a game in which "perfect scores" are an illusion and reconciliation comes only after a difficult passage through alien territory.

We need a certain amount of humility and a sense of humor to discover cultures other than our own, a readiness to enter a room in the dark and stumble over unfamiliar furniture until the pain in our shins reminds us where things are. World culture comprises myriad ways of creating the integrity without which life and business cannot be conducted. There are no universal answers, but there are universal questions and dilemmas, and that is where we all need to start.

Notes

1. G. Hofstede, *Culture's Consequences* (London: Sage, 1980).
2. G. Inzerilli and A. Laurent, "The Concept of Organizational Structure" (working paper, University of Pennsylvania and INSEAD, 1979); "Managerial Views of Organizational Structure in France and the USA," *International Studies of Management and Organizations* 13 (1983): 1–2, 97–118.
3. P. R. Lawrence and J. W. Lorsch, *Organization and Environment: Managing Differentiation and Integration* (Homewood, IL: Irwin, 1967).
4. C. Bartlett and S. Ghoshal, *Managing Across Borders* (London: Hutchinson Business Books, 1990).
5. J. Ogilvy, *Global Business Network* (Ameryville, CA); personal communication.
6. R. B. Reich, *The Work of Nations: Preparing Ourselves for the 21st Century* (New York: Knopf, 1991).
7. M. Goold, *Strategic Control* (London: The Economist Books/ Business Books, 1990).

Reconciling Cultural Dilemmas

As we have explained throughout the book, every country and organization faces certain universal dilemmas. A nation's culture is expressed in the way people within it approach these dilemmas. Once we have learned to recognize differences and to respect that cultures have the right of self-determination, we need to consider how we can overcome problems of misunderstanding that can easily arise and leverage the business benefits of the different viewpoints by connecting those viewpoints and securing the benefits of both.

Awareness of Cultural Differences

An American CEO had exchanged customary, polite greetings with his Japanese opposite number, a ritual that the American felt had gone on far too long. They had at last come to the root of the problem, and the Japanese president was being evasive, ducking all the straight questions and repeating that "with goodwill and sincerity" all such questions could be satisfactorily answered.

As part of the initial greeting ceremony involving the Japanese delegation, the parties had exchanged *meishi* (business cards), and the American CEO, conscious of Japanese custom, had placed the cards on the table in front of him in the same pattern as the seating arrangement for the Japanese delegation. In this way he could call everyone by name, having a convenient reminder in front of him.

As the meeting grew more stressful and his impatience with evasive answers increased, he picked up one of the cards, absentmindedly rolled it into a cylinder, unrolled it again, and began to clean his nails with the edge. Suddenly he felt the horrified eyes of the entire Japanese delegation on him! There was a long pause, and then the Japanese president stood up and withdrew from the room. "We would like to call an intermission," the Japanese interpreter said. The American looked at the battered meishi in his hand. It was the one the Japanese president had given him.

This example aptly demonstrates the devastating effects that insufficient awareness of cultural differences may have. If the CEO had merely been following a long list of tips, or dos and don'ts, it is unlikely that "don't abuse the meishi" would have been on the list. After all, there are thousands of possible mistakes.

Some blunders are inevitable, but a *systematic* understanding of cultural differences would have enabled the CEO to foresee this pitfall and others. Had he been fully aware that the Japanese rarely answer directly; like to build a relationship before coming to the point; give their presidents very general duties, many of them ceremonial, so that they do not know the details; and regard meishi as symbolizing the status of the person referred to, as well as the quality of the relationship being created, then he would never have dreamed of mangling someone's meishi while that person was watching!

Cultural awareness, then, is understanding *states of mind*, your own and those of the people you meet. You can never be fully informed, since there is an infinite range of potential errors, but our seven dimensions of culture provide us with a frame of reference for analyzing ways in which people attribute meaning to the world around them.

One of the goals of cross-cultural training must therefore be to alert people to the fact that they are constantly involved in a process of assigning meaning to the actions and objects they observe. For cross-cultural training to be successful, it must not be limited to delivering more or less detailed information about other countries and cultures. If it is, even the most sophisticated model of cross-cultural differences will only enhance the particular stereotypes that the participants have adopted about another culture. So if the authors are approached by participants after a training course with comments like, "Thank you, Dr. Trompenaars. I already knew that I had difficulties working with the French; they are strange beings, and you have demonstrated it empirically. The information you just gave me proves that I am right," we know that something has gone wrong.

Increasingly, professionals in cross-cultural management who seek to develop cultural competence sense the need to go beyond the defense of their own model. It is legitimate to have a mental model. We are all creatures of our culture. The problem is to learn to go beyond our own model without being afraid that our long-held certainties will collapse. The need to win over others to our point of view, to prove the inferiority of their way of thinking, reveals our own insecurities and doubts about the strength of our identity. Genuine self-awareness accepts that we follow a particular mental cultural program and that members of other cultures have different programs. We may find out more about ourselves by exploring those differences.

The seven dimensions all indicate ways in which another culture may start from seemingly "opposite" premises, but this posture does not invalidate our own frameworks. It is simply a different approach from which we can learn. Milton Bennett, a cross-cultural researcher, has found that people encountering foreign cultures may *isolate* themselves and *separate* their norms and values from those of the foreign culture.[1] This response only impedes self-awareness. Both sameness and difference tell us who we are: "I am like A, but *not* like B."

Respecting Cultural Differences

An initial step toward developing respect for cultural differences is to look for situations in your own life in which you would behave like a person from another culture. Making this association is what helped a member of the purchasing department of a big European oil company who was negotiating an order with a Korean supplier. At the first meeting, the Korean partner offered a silver pen to the European manager. The latter, however, politely refused the present for fear of being bribed (even though he knew about the Korean custom of giving presents). Much to the manager's surprise, the second meeting began with the offer of a stereo system. Again the manager refused, his fear of being bribed having been heightened.

As he gazed at the piece of fine Korean porcelain presented to him on the third meeting, he finally realized what was going on. His refusal had not been taken to mean "Let's get on with business right away," but rather "If you want to get into business with me, you had better come up with something bigger." How embarrassing his refusal must have been for the Korean partner became clear to him when he recalled a similar situation in his own life. On one of his first dates with his wife, he had bought her a small present. From the expression on her face, he could easily tell that it was not quite what she had expected. Remembering this incident made him accept the fact that the Korean partner was simply trying to establish a relationship and had no intention of bribing him. To avoid similar misunderstandings in future encounters with Korean partners, the manager decided to try to communicate that he, too, was interested in good relationships but that he felt no need to exchange expensive presents. (One alternative he might have come up with would be to offer presents of little material value but that nevertheless signal appreciation and interest.)

This story illustrates how people can learn to appreciate and respect behaviors and values different from their own. Thinking about situations in your own life might help you understand that behaviors that seemingly differ are often different only in terms of the type of situation in which you observe them, not in terms of their function. This thought process will prevent you from prematurely valuing a behavior as negative and, more important, help you understand what the other person is actually trying to do. In understanding the other's intentions, and perhaps signaling your understanding, you take the first step toward developing a shared meaning with your partner.

Generally speaking, what is strong in another culture will also be present in some form in one's own culture. We speak of "guilt cultures" and "shame cultures," for example: those that try to make people feel guilty for breaking rules, and those that demand public apologies and subject the miscreant to the hostile stares of the group, such as with "loss of face." This example represents a significant difference between West and East, but who has never wished the ground would open up because of an excruciatingly embarrassing lapse?

Respect is most effectively developed once we realize that most cultural differences are in ourselves, even if we have not yet recognized them. For example, we often think that the Japanese are mysterious, even unreliable. You never know what they are feeling or thinking, and they always say "yes," even when they are negative about something. But don't we have situations in which the same happens to us? If your child has given a rather nervous and halting performance in her first solo in a school concert but must go on again after the intermission, you might well say, "Wonderful, darling" to give her confidence, even though you don't actually consider her performance to have been good.

Or suppose a minority employee who has been subject to discrimination in your company comes to see you in despair. You are worried that he might injure himself, sue the company, or attack his supervisor. It is likely that you would work on reestablishing your relationship with this employee, gaining his confidence, *before* suggesting that he might consider alternative forms of behavior. You would obviously be tactful and indirect in making these suggestions. You would be behaving in a "Japanese" manner, because the circumstances warrant it. So, then, perhaps circumstances in Japan make the sense of self so vulnerable that one usually tiptoes around another person's sensibilities. If we assume that most Japanese have a frail sense of self, their behavior makes excellent sense! We would be wise to do the same when in Japan.

Consider another case encountered by a German engineer in South Africa. We all work for money, and most of us have a sense of pride and duty in our work, but the money-duty continuum may be radically different in different cultures. The engineer gave his maid a Christmas bonus, and she promptly disappeared for two months, since as she saw it, she had no need to work. He was appalled. Of course, we don't know her motives: she may have felt no obligation to an employer she disliked, but a sense of duty to an employer she did like. Or perhaps working as a maid was only something she did in desperate circumstances. The engineer's wife concluded that she was "lazy," but that judgment came from her own frame of reference.

To sum up, both awareness and respect are necessary to developing intercultural competence. Still, even their combined power may not always suffice. In workshops people often ask, "Why should only we respect and adapt to the other culture? Why don't they respect and adapt to ours?" We will come back to this point when we discuss reconciliation.

Another, perhaps more interesting problem is that of mutual empathy, a term employed by Milton Bennett. What happens when one person attempts to shift to another culture's perspective when, concurrently, the other party is trying to do the same thing?

Motorola University once prepared carefully for a presentation in China. After considerable thought, the presenters entitled it "Relationships Do Not Retire." The gist of the presentation was that Motorola had come to China in order to stay and help the economy to create wealth. Relationships with Chinese suppliers, subcontractors, and employees would constitute a permanent commitment to building Chinese economic infrastructure and earning hard currency through exports.

The Chinese audience listened politely to this presentation but was quiet when invited to ask questions. Finally one manager raised his hand and said, "Can you tell us about pay-for-performance?"

What was happening here is becoming common. Even as we move toward the other person's perspective, that person has started to move toward ours, and we pass each other invisibly like ships in the night. Keep in mind that those Chinese who come to a presentation by a Western company may already be pro-Western and see Western views as potentially liberating. This dynamic is especially strong when a country is small and poor. When a drug salesperson from a US company meets with the minister of health from Costa Rica, the former's salary may be 10 times the latter's. This kind of encounter only hardens our prejudices: "See, they all want to be like us."

What must be recognized here is that foreign cultures have an integrity that only some of its members will abandon. In the Vietnam War the US found that the genuine nationalists among the Vietnamese were much tougher than its own opportunist allies. People who abandon their culture become weakened and corrupt. We need foreigners to be themselves if partnerships are to work. It is this very difference that makes relationships valuable.

This is why we need to *reconcile* differences; be ourselves, yet see and understand how the other's perspectives can help our own.

Reconciling Cultural Differences

Once we are aware of our own mental models and cultural predispositions, and can understand and respect that those of another culture are legitimately different, then it becomes possible to reconcile differences. Why do this? We are in the business of creating wealth and value, not just for ourselves but also for those who live in different cultural worlds. We need to share the values of buying, of selling, of joint venturing, of working in partnership.

Take two companies, one in the Netherlands and one in Belgium. The first was innovation oriented. The second relied on its strong traditional reputation and the prestige ascribed to it by Belgian culture. The status of the two companies was derived from achievement and ascription, respectively. They could have quarreled endlessly about their comparative "worth," but they did not. Rather, they jointly strove to establish a reputation for both innovation and quality, which they then achieved.

There are 10 steps that are useful in achieving reconciliation, which we present under the following headings:

1. The theory of complementarity
2. Using humor
3. Mapping out a cultural space
4. From nouns to present participles and processes
5. Language and meta-language
6. Frames and contexts
7. Sequencing
8. Waving/cycling
9. Synergizing and virtuous circling
10. The double helix

The Theory of Complementarity

The Danish scientist Niels Bohr proposed a theory of complementarity. The ultimate nature of matter is manifested both as specific particles and as diffuse waves. Nature reveals itself to us as a response to our measuring instruments. There is no one form "out there"; forms depend on how we perceive them and how we measure them.

Throughout this book, all our seven dimensions have represented continua with two extremes. Universalism and particularism are not separate, but different; they operate on a continuum between rules and exceptions. Things are more or less similar to the rule, or more or less dissimilar and hence exceptional. You could not even define rules without also knowing what exceptions were. The terms are therefore complementary.

It is the same for all seven dimensions. The individual is more or less separate from the group. "Being by yourself" requires a group if the difference is to register. There can be no specific part without a concept of the diffuse whole. Directing yourself from inside outward is necessarily in contrast to being directed from the outside inward. To say that we seek to integrate our values and that all cultures look for integrity and reconciliation implies recognition that values are holistic to begin with.

Using Humor

We often become aware of dilemmas through humor, which can signal an unexpected clash between two perspectives.

Values taken to extremes often suggest that the opposite value is really present, rather than the proclaimed one: "The more he talked of his honor, the faster we counted our spoons." "Why does the ascent of the preacher's rhetoric in TV evangelism so often accompany the descent of his pants?" the *New York Times* once asked.

Corporations that announce, "We trust our people" may end up breaking into employees' offices at night and rifling their desks, because the companies cannot be seen to be distrusting employees publicly but are secretly concerned about a spate of thefts. For the "lowdown" on what really happens in the corporation, look at the cartoons stuck on the walls of employees' offices. They often are incisive satires of the official line and reveal what the dilemmas really are.

Mapping Out a Cultural Space

Another effective process for exploring dilemmas is to turn their "two horns" into axes to create a cultural space. We can map some or all of the seven dimensions on this cultural space. The map is constructed through either interviews or questionnaires. Issues mapped recently include the following sampling:

A. Given the pluralism of local initiatives in Europe, is it possible to exercise any strategic leadership from US headquarters that is applicable to all the units concerned? (universalism-particularism dilemma)

B. Given the obvious desirability of getting our best products to the market according to the value of their achievements, is it possible to attain this goal while giving the autonomous R&D for high-potential products the space they need to mature? (achievement-ascription dilemma)

C. Given the need for a quick response to swiftly changing markets in the US, is it possible to keep ourselves committed to a long-term vision developed at our center in South Korea? (short-term–long-term dilemma)

Respondents drew attention to the first three dilemmas in words paraphrased here:

A. Universalism-Particularism Dilemma

- The markets in Europe could be served much better if our American headquarters could only understand the particular needs we have over here.
- If only Europeans could understand what it takes to become a truly global company.
- We know here in the US very well what different markets need, but we need to coeducate them in order not to fall into the trap of having happy clients but no margins for us. Economies of scale force us to limit our offerings.

B. Achievement-Ascription Dilemma

- If we in R&D could get some more time to work out our highly promising products without continuously being pushed by marketing, our products would be much better in the long run.
- You can't be innovative unless you are given some time to work things out. Customers need to leave you alone for a while.
- R&D people tend to deliver too-late products that the market frequently doesn't need. In marketing we should be more responsible and give R&D strict guidelines and deadlines.
- In our company we should have more trust in what we are developing. It is good stuff. Let's go for it wholeheartedly.

C. Short-Term–Long-Term Dilemma

- The Americans hinder our long-term achievements because of their drive for quarterly results. Our vision is often jeopardized by a quest for the quick buck!
- It seems as if in the Far East and in Europe there are no shareholders. The ease with which they accept quarterly losses would be unacceptable in the US.

Most of these remarks clearly show basic dilemmas that are inherent in cross-cultural debates. In intercultural encounters people frequently complain of excessive rivalry and an inability to harmonize the efforts of different units representing different cultures.

Dilemma A can be mapped between the pluralism of local initiatives on the horizontal axis and the universal truth of headquarters on the vertical axis. (See Figure 13.1.)

Dilemma B is between identification with customers' viewpoints on the horizontal axis, because it is the customer who buys the achievements of the product, whereas (on the vertical axis) R&D wants to be committed to the product by ascribing status to it, which allows its development without being hindered by clients' needs too early or too frequently. (See Figure 13.2.)

Dilemma C is between short- and long-termism. On the one axis the market demands a quick response, and US shareholders look for solid returns every quarter; on the other axis we find the long-term

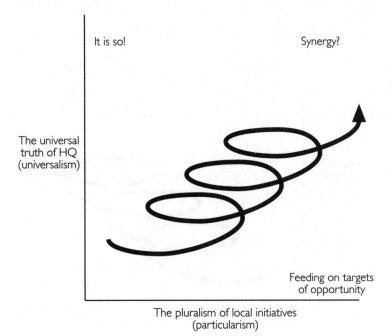

Figure 13.1. **Dilemma A**

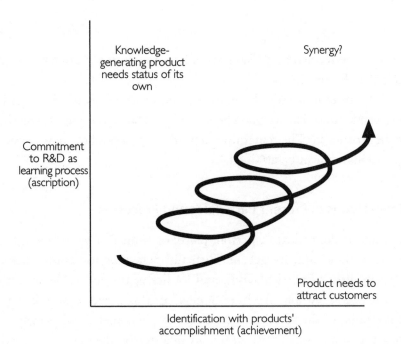

Figure 13.2. **Dilemma B**

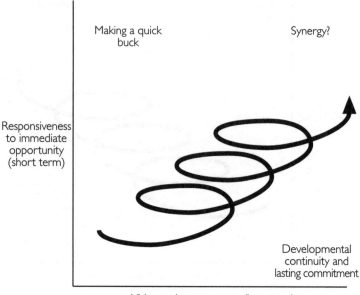

Figure 13.3. Dilemma C

needs to be framed by a vision that allows the short term to have meaning. (See Figure 13.3.)

The dilemma must be mapped before its reconciliation can be undertaken, so that we and clients have a clear definition of what has to be reconciled. The remaining steps in the process show how genuine reconciliation can be attained.

From Nouns to Present Participles and Processes

A noun is defined as "a person, place, or thing." A value, though, is none of these, and we get into difficulty when we use nouns such as universalism or particularism, and loyalty or dissent, to describe the horns of a dilemma. We have done so in this book because it is the convention of the social sciences to make phenomena look and sound physical, but it is still misleading. So, as a step on the road to reconciliation, we shall turn all nouns into present participles, ending in *-ing*, which transforms them into processes. Thus:

Universalizing or particularizing
Individualizing or communing
Specifying/analyzing or diffusing/synthesizing
Communicating neutrality or communicating emotion
Achieving or ascribing (status)
Sequencing time or synchronizing time
Directing oneself from inside or going with the flow of the
environment

Not all nouns can be made into present participles, but if we know what we want—to get rid of the "hard edges" and render the value as a process requiring the participation of people—then suitable words can be found. Since processes mingle in a way that things do not, we are now much closer to understanding that all seven dimensions are really continua, with a preponderance of one process at one end (yin) and a preponderance of the other process at the other end (yang). We have also softened the adversary structure of clashing nouns or "isms." This is what Edward De Bono calls "water logic."[2]

Language and Meta-Language

Since we are stuck with the structure of language, it is as well to consider how language achieves reconciliation. It does so by using a ladder of abstraction and putting one value (or horn of the dilemma) above the other—that is, by using both an object language and a meta-language and allowing them to dovetail.

Consider this famous quotation from F. Scott Fitzgerald:

"The test of a first-rate intelligence is the ability to hold two opposed ideas in the mind at the same time, and still retain the ability to function. You must, for example, be able to see that things are hopeless, yet be determined to make them otherwise."

The second sentence in the quote might appear to be a contradiction, but it is not. Contradictions cancel each other out: they are mean-

254 • RIDING THE WAVES OF CULTURE

ingless. What the author has done here is to dovetail the two clauses at different levels of language.

> Meta-level: "be determined to make them otherwise"
> Object level: "see that things are hopeless"

The object level is about things being hopeless. The meta-level is about the determination of the person who sees. The two statements are not contradictory because they do not apply to the same "things." The second statement in the sentence is about the person seeing, not about the things seen.

This premise applies equally to our seven dimensions. We could say, "The test of a first-rate manager is the ability to hold two opposed ideas in the mind at the same time, and still retain the ability to function."

You must, for example, be able to see that a *particular* customer request is outside the *universal* rules your company has set up, yet be determined to qualify the existing rule or create a new rule based on this case.

> Meta-level: Determined to qualify rule or create new one
> Object level: Particular request breaks existing rule

We could do the same for any of the seven dimensions. Take a small business unit that has enjoyed extraordinary success:

> Meta-level: Ascribe importance to this strategy company-wide
> Object level: Admire and reward this form of achieving

Top management has encouraged achievement in a particular unit and has ascribed universal importance to the strategy employed, so that other business units can benefit by emulating the particular achievement. Here particularizing and universalizing, as well as achieving and ascribing, have all been reconciled.

Frames and Contexts

In the preceding example of language levels, you could say that the meta-level frames the object level:

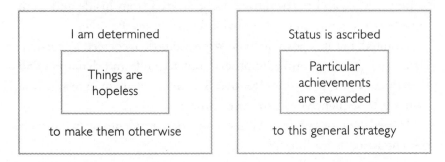

The usefulness of thinking in frames and contexts is that they contain and constrain the "picture" or the "text" within them. There is always a danger of people's value extremes "running away." "To see that things are hopeless" can lead to despair, unless framed by one's being "determined to make them otherwise." We might have concluded from the outstanding achievement of the business unit that top management should simply keep out of the unit's way, but that would have prevented the organization from learning based on a local success.

The important thing to grasp is that text and context are reversible, as are the picture and the frame. We could focus on a very intelligent person

and say: or we could say:

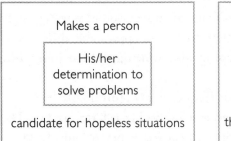
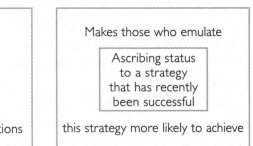

Sequencing

Values appear to clash and conflict when we assume that both must be expressed simultaneously. It isn't possible to be right and wrong, to universalize and particularize, to be steered from inside and from outside at the same time. One obviously precludes the other.

Granted, but it is possible to go wrong and then correct, to particularize and then generalize, to observe outer trends and dynamics and then direct yourself at your objective. So a major element in reconciling values is to sequence processes over time.

Indeed, one of the frames and contexts comments on what your present action is leading to: or:

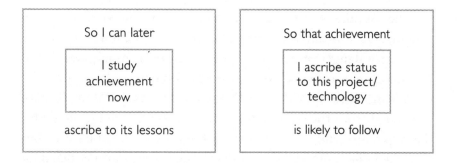

Waving/Cycling

Have you ever stopped to wonder what would happen to our values if, instead of assuming that they are things (e.g., colliding billiard balls), we assume that they are waveforms? Common sense assumes values to be like coins, jewels, or rocks. We could instead take the view that they are like water waves, electromagnetic waves, sound waves, or light waves. This change in assumptions makes an appreciable difference.

Consider the cycle of sleeping and waking, which looks like Figure 13.4.

Or consider music on various frequencies (Figure 13.5).

If we have two different frequencies, 50 Hz (Hertz) and 60 Hz, and we combine them, they form a beat frequency of only 10 Hz: a low-frequency wave has been created by harmonizing the two waves. The high-frequency sound is now "within" the low-frequency beat. If

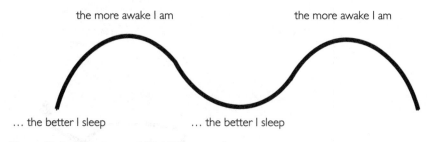

the more awake I am

the more awake I am

... the better I sleep

... the better I sleep

Figure 13.4. Sleeping and Waking

values are like sound waves, no wonder their harmony (what Southeast Asians call *wa*) can be more beautiful.

If the waveform is a legitimate expression of values, and if the values alternate like sleeping and waking, relaxing and exciting, erring and correcting, then we can draw the waveform between the axes as in Figure 13.6.

Here we first err, then correct, then err again, then correct again, and so on. The entire process is called an *error-correcting system*. We avoid both catastrophic mistakes (perhaps by using simulation) and the straitjacket of never making a mistake. If we want to learn fast,

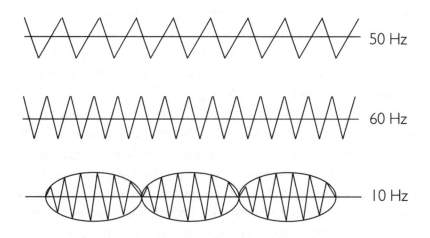

50 Hz

60 Hz

10 Hz

High-frequency sound + high-frequency sound
= low-frequency sound

Figure 13.5. High- and Low-Frequency Sound

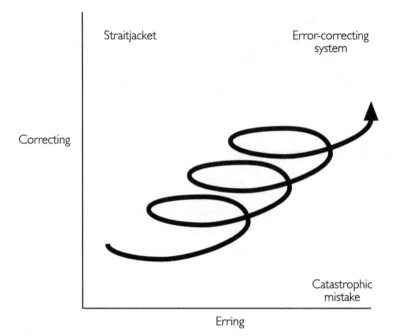

Figure 13.6. **Process of Continuing Improvement**

making many small errors that are corrected might be the best way. "Error," of course, is relative. If we call the bottom 35 percent of our performance "errors," we will go on improving. If we call only 5 percent "errors," we may come to ignore them or hush them up.

The notion of learning by error correction is so important that we include it in all our dilemmas, especially the seven dimensions. Suppose that we were to create a waveform between universalizing and particularizing. It might look like Figure 13.7.

This is a diagram of how particular exceptions are encountered and noted before they are encompassed within changed or reformed rules. No scientific law can ignore mounting anomalies. No legal statute can survive massive opposition. No corporate procedures can fail to account for a growing number of exceptions. In all such crises the old rules must be reformed or new ones created. The point is that if we want to improve the rules, we must be able to refute them. Nor can we properly appreciate what is unique and outstanding unless we know what the common standards are.

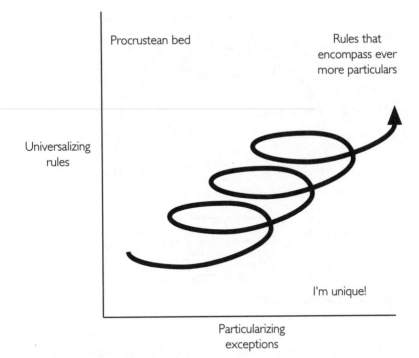

Figure 13.7. **Generating New Rules**

We have retained the idea of error correction by rendering our waveform as a cycle. The assumption is that we will periodically get things wrong and have to make a second "try" or circuit before improving on both axes.

Synergizing and Virtuous Circling

An important test of optimal reconciliation that includes both ends of the values continuum, but in even greater harmony, is the criterion of synergy. The word comes from the Greek *synergos*, meaning "to work with." When two values work with one another, they are mutually facilitating and enhancing. Thus, ascribing importance to a major project with France Télécom (now Orange) makes it more likely that your working group will be inspired to achieve that project; that your company has recently been seen to be achieving the project makes it far more likely that senior management will ascribe enhanced importance

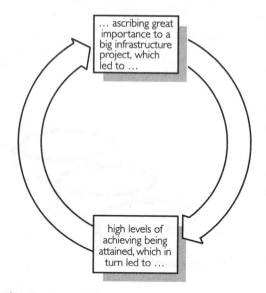

Figure 13.8. The Virtuous Circle

to it in next year's strategy deliberation. The virtuous circle looks like Figure 13.8.

Synergy is also present in nature. Steel alloys for jet engines are immensely stronger than the strength of all their components combined. The molecular chain in the alloy is simply a stronger structure.

The Double Helix

Finally we come to our model of models: DNA, the double helix molecular structure (Figure 13.9). Let us make it clear that we are

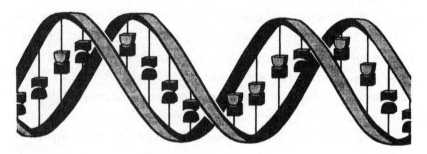

Figure 13.9. The Double Helix

using this model as a metaphor, not trying to borrow the mantle of biological science. But then, most of the social sciences, if not all, are based on metaphors. Since cultures are alive, we have consciously borrowed from the life sciences.

The double helix model helps to summarize the steps to reconciliation. The ladder of protein synthesis has four rungs. Similarly, we have a ladder of values synthesis with a series of rungs. The twisted ladder is full of *complementarities*. When the "pairs" come together unexpectedly, it can be *funny*. We can use the uprights on each side of the ladder as cultural space for *mapping*. The twisted elements of the ladder constitute a growth *process*. Each twist of the spiral speaks the *language* of growth and contains coded instructions. Each turn of the helix is framed and *contextualized* by the helix within and around it, containing and constraining. The process is *sequential*. It constitutes *waves and cycles*, with synthesis producing growth and *synergy*.

In short, the double helix helps summarize all of the preceding nine processes by which values are reconciled. It is a continuous process that repeatedly asks the question, "How can we get more of one extreme through connecting and combining it with more of the other?"

Notes

1. M. J. Bennett, "Towards Ethnorelativism: A Developmental Model of Intercultural Sensitivity (revised)," in R. M. Paige (ed.), *Education for the Intercultural Experience* (Yarmouth, ME: Intercultural Press, 1993).

2. E. de Bono, "I Am Right You Are Wrong," from *This to the New Renaissance: From Rock Logic to Water Logic* (London: Penguin, 1992).

When Two Worlds Collide

Culture Clash

In response to many requests from readers and client organizations, we adopt a more pragmatic approach in this chapter. The discussion therefore differs in style and format from that of other chapters because our aim is specifically to offer assistance to professional practice as well as explain the rationale. The framework is offered in some detail so that it can be taken as a starting point and adapted by readers to meet their individual needs.

Mergers, acquisitions, and strategic alliances are increasingly pursued not only to implement globalization strategies but also as a consequence of political, monetary, and regulatory convergence. Realizing the business benefits and creating wealth in an integration process is not easy, since it demands joining values that are not easily joined; two out of three deals do not achieve anywhere near the benefits that were originally anticipated.[1]

Organizations are commonly acquired on the basis of their inherent valuation rather than with the intention of achieving full integration. Increasingly however, motives originate from a range of other expected benefits, including synergistic values (e.g., cross-selling, supply chain consolidation, and economies of scale) or more direct strategic values (becoming market leaders, penetrating a ready-made customer base, etc.). The emphasis in the predeal and postdeal management is too often on ways to quickly exploit the new opportunities under a mechanistic systems or financial due-diligence mind-set.[2] It is assumed too often that delivering benefits simply requires the alignment of technical, operational, and financial systems and market approaches.

The evidence from our research and from practical experiences through our consulting reveals that next to paying an "optimistic" price, the real underlying failure to deliver the anticipated benefits arises from the absence of a systemic and structured methodological framework. The absence of a guiding framework means that senior managers do not know what to integrate or what types of decision are important to delivering the anticipated benefits. They have no rationale to allocate resources, prioritize actions, or achieve synergies.

While any integration program should include fundamental operational matters, much more attention and effort need to be given to managing the cultural differences between the new partners or businesses. Relational aspects such as cultural differences and lack of trust have frequently been reported as being responsible for 70 percent of integration failures as described in the business press.

Building trust is a cultural challenge in itself. Lack of trust is often caused by different views of what constitutes a trustworthy partner. Intercultural alliances involve differences in corporate cultures as well as national cultures, and even differences in the cultures of competing functional disciplines, such as R&D versus marketing. Problems can be due to more or less "overt" cultural differences, but also to the parties' differing perceptions about each other, arising from differing perceptions of corporate culture and national culture.

Thus, consideration must be given to leadership styles (including the need for personal transformation), management profiles, organization structures, working practices, and a wide range of perceptions in and of the marketplace. In short, culture is pervasive. Even when strategists and senior managers recognize the importance of culture, frustration continues, because they have no means of assessing or quantifying its causes and effects.

Ultimately success derives from enabling people with different cultural perspectives to engage in meaningful discussions around the newly created business. The methodology that we have developed and that is one of the cornerstones of this book includes "dilemma thinking," which is central to bringing people together to discover what they share and where they differ. We also follow Kelvin's edict that states, "If you can't measure something, you can't control it." Therefore, the integration process needs to be supported with validated instruments and tools that provide quantitative (and qualitative) diagnosis, monitoring of progress, and hard evidence to inform decision making and resource allocation. In this manner, any approach and associated actions can be based on needs that have been assessed and elicited rather than assumed.

Of course, some steps must be adapted to the particular needs of an organization in order to develop a program for integration to deliver positive outcomes. It is crucial that the knowledge that is embedded in this process is transferred to the organization, so that the ongoing and future operations continue to deliver growth goals through enhanced corporate success under the new leadership and management.

Different Types of Integration

A fundamental consideration for an integration process is whether one takes over or is being taken over. Some authorities argue that mergers do not exist; in the long run it is always an acquisition. Recall what Confucius said: "There is always one that offers the cheek and one that purses the lips." But let us consider the meta-dilemma that summarizes these two extreme paradigms of "acquiring" or "being acquired." (See Figure 14.1.)

Five categorical types of extreme behaviors in alliances or mergers can be distinguished:

Paradigm	Grid Reference	Epithet/ Metaphor
First, we have the alliance in which one of the partners sticks to its own values and proclaims, "My values first!"	Position 1/10	Bear Hug
The second type of response is to *abandon your own orientation and go native.* Here you adopt a "When in Rome, do as the Romans do" approach. That you are only acting or keeping up such pretences won't go unseen—you will be very much an amateur. Other cultures will mistrust you—and you won't be able to offer your own strengths to the merger marriage. Thus, the acquiring organization adopts the working practices and corporate culture of the organization it acquires.	Position 10/1	Runaway Company
Third we find the leadership in denial, avoiding and ignoring value dilemmas by operating at arm's length and assuming the synergy will take care of itself (not shown in Figure 14.1).	Position 1/1	Denial
Fourth there is the type of new partnership in which a compromise between values is found, with the new entity sometimes adopting the acquirer's way of doing things and sometimes that of the organization being acquired.	Position 5/5	Preserved Livestock
Finally, and for mergers/alliances that are more effective and that realize and exceed the expected benefits, we find the reconciling alliance, in which values are integrated to integrity.	Position 10/10	Riding High

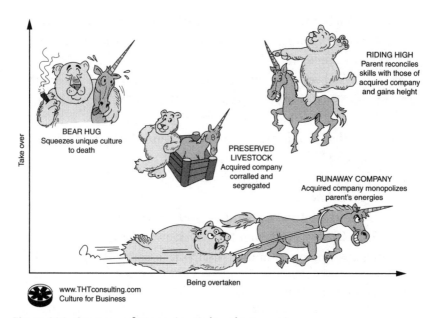

Figure 14.1. **Strategy of Managing Cultural Integration**

The extensive research evidence we have collected, and triangulated with real-world application through our consulting, reveals that the 10/10 paradigm in the top right corner is where a sustainable future that delivers the business benefits of the intended merger or alliance can be realized, if we apply a systematic methodology to reconcile the cultural differences.

We use the reconciling strategy of Riding High, in which the best of all worlds is combined synergistically. This process unfolds when there is at least as much attention for what organizations share as for what makes them different. The process is like a pendulum: it can swing at the bottom of diversity, because it has a nail that holds it together.

The quality of the pendulum rope signifies the quality of management and leadership. This leads to a process we call the Trinity Approach (developed by Allard Everts, who was one of our principal consultants).[3] It consists of three main perspectives:

Area 1: What binds and keeps us connected? What we *stand for* and decide to *go for*: this enables us to generate a Vision and Values framework.

Area 2: What separates and keeps us apart? How we deal with the dilemmas resulting from diversity in vision and (cultural) values between the partner organizations involved.

Area 3: What should we do to benefit from the first and manage the second?

- "Live" the Vision and Values framework and create common behavior.
- Reconcile business dilemmas and create win-wins.
- Develop key leadership behaviors: awareness, respect, courage, willpower, humility, discipline, and "walking the talk."

In this approach, integrating and redefining the culture and corporate values of any "NEWCO" (new company) is essential for the integration process, and in particular, when the new values support the re(de)fined vision and mission. This means that reconciling the differences builds a common platform for the future.

It is also important that the human side be fully integrated with the more technical and mechanistic aspects of the process. It is too easy to say why multiplicities of consultants of the established big consulting firms have hitherto set up NEWCOs for failure. The failure rates would be seen as even higher if one would focus on the human aspects.

Maximum performance from the integration is achieved only when strategic, structural, human-resource, and supplier and client processes are systemically aligned. In this wider context, our new approach is defined as a process of reconciling divergent goals, values, and structural, functional, and cultural differences for maximum performance.

In order to achieve these ambitions, it is necessary to design a process that we describe in three main phases:

Phase A: Creating the Compelling Business Case
Phase B: Developing the Implementation Strategy Through
    Objectives and Key Performance Indicators
Phase C: Realizing and Rooting the Benefits

We now discuss the key components of each phase.

Phase A: Creating the Compelling Business Case

This phase consists of five steps culminating in the creation of the compelling business case.

Phase	Focus		Steps
A:	Creating the Compelling Business Case	1	Re(de)fining the Vision and Mission
		2	Business Assessment
		3	Values Assessment
		4	Values in Practice
		5	Revisiting the Compelling Business Case for Integration

Again, evidence from our research and professional practice shows that it is essential to first create a compelling business case for the integration to become successful. The purpose of this initial phase in the process is to derive and explicate a clear idea of the vision and mission for the newly created entity. Therefore, when organizations integrate, it is important that the leadership's vision and mission are made explicit and, as needed, refined through extensive iteration. It is necessary to check if the re(de)fined mission is still inspiring and motivating. It is also important that the shared values and behaviors of the organization support that vision.

Historically, this process originates in the work of Collins and Porras, who have demonstrated that successful organizations need alignment between their "envisioned future" and "core ideology," together comprising the organization's vision.[4] In summary it looks like Figure 14.2.

Phase A—Step 1: Re(de)fining Vision and Mission

A well-conceived vision consists of the two major components cited: *core ideology* and *envisioned future*. Core ideology, the *yin* for Collins and Porras, defines what an organization stands for and why it exists. In successful organizations it is unchanging and complements

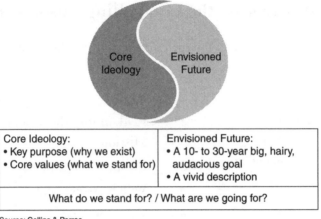

Core Ideology:	Envisioned Future:
• Key purpose (why we exist)	• A 10- to 30-year big, hairy,
• Core values (what we stand for)	audacious goal
	• A vivid description
What do we stand for? / What are we going for?	

Source: Collins & Porras.

Figure 14.2. **Building the Vision for the New Organization**

yang, the envisioned future. The envisioned future is what we aspire to become, to achieve, to create—something that will require significant change and progress to attain.[5]

Since a core ideology is not set but discovered, the seeking process itself is often an ideal way to communicate and explore the strengths of both organizations and how these strengths might be integrated in a way that is noncompromising. It can also reveal why an organization was purchased in the first place. And if the strategy is one of Riding High, the self-confidence of the members of the organization that was bought is also raised, including the essential commitment from the top.

Example

Not all organizations have visionary leaders such as Allessandro Profumo, CEO of the large Italian bank Unicredit, and Dr. Wolfgang Reitzle, CEO of the German company Linde AG. Each man's clarity on both vision and mission has been shown to be instrumental in turning significant international acquisitions into a success. Unicredit's vision is based on a determination to create a new way of banking by focusing on people as individuals and to enhance their potential and make their plans and ideas come true. Its mission is to create a new way of banking by striving to serve clients with innovative solutions.

Within Unicredit employees adhere to commonly held principles and a distinct set of values based on integrity as a primary condition of sustainability, which makes it possible to transform profit into value for all stakeholders.

In contrast, an alternative, top-down approach served what is now the world's largest gas-producing company, Linde AG. It was the vision of CEO Wolfgang Reitzle that Linde AG, a typical German-based engineering organization, had to become "the leading global gases and engineering group, admired for our people, who provide innovative solutions that make a difference to the world." Before acquiring the UK-based BOC Ltd., Linde AG was a standard German company made up of a variety of related and unrelated businesses (including a material handling business segment, one of the world's largest manufacturers of forklifts and warehouse equipment). Given the globalization of the markets, Reitzle was convinced that the size and approach Linde AG was adopting were not appropriate to materializing his stated vision. The organization needed to concentrate on the gas business, deepening its knowledge of the business, and become less German-centric. After the company made some major divestments, the BOC Ltd. organization was seen as a logical acquisition candidate, in that it was (perhaps?) somewhat less professional in the gas business than Linde but was undeniably international and shareholder driven. The only way to make a difference to the world through innovative solutions was to marry a candidate like BOC. The vision of Reitzle was the catalyst to make the right choice. The rest is history.

So, after the main vision and mission of the NEWCO have been re(de)fined, the context is created within which the leadership of the organizations is invited to assess its business and values. This is frequently a top-down process, as with the original decision that prompted the merger or acquisition.

It does not really matter whether you start with the yin or the yang—it is the connections that are built between them that are important. Which end you start from is itself often culturally determined.

Some synchronic cultures would begin with both simultaneously. We observe that most Asians would find it difficult to envisage starting from a single point on a circle.

Phase A—Step 2: Business Assessment

The beauty of assessing the business logic of the integration from the outset is that members of management are invited early on to put their minds to creating a new shared future and ask, "Why did we come together in the first place?"

This course of action is much better than the frequently observed behavior of looking at the differences first. Differences become more supportive of the integration process *after* the shared boundaries are defined.

Thus, in this step we start with defining the "big, hairy, audacious goal" (the BHAG) to help create the envisioned future. This goal is a bold mission to stimulate progress (such as: "to put a man on the moon"). The BHAG, according to the authors who coined this phrase, should meet the following criteria:[6]

1. Be clear and compelling
2. Act as a catalyst for team spirit
3. Have a clear finish line
4. Engage people
5. Be tangible, energizing, and highly focused
6. Be easy to understand by everyone

Audacious goals are inspiring and daring goals that can be reached only through extreme effort. Hamel and Prahalad call these *stretched goals*.

Here are some examples of BHAGs:

• Become a $125 billion company by the year 2000 (Wal-Mart, 1990)
• Democratize the automobile (Ford Motor Company, early 1900s)
• Become the company most known for changing the worldwide poor-quality image of Japanese products (Sony, early 1950s)

- Become number one or number two in every market we serve and revolutionize this company to have the strengths of a big company combined with the leanness and agility of a small company (General Electric Company, 1980s)
- Become the Nike of the cycling industry (Giro Sport Design, 1986)

At this second step the aim is to find the main areas where the integrated parties can develop business synergies within their newly defined BHAG. In fact, these might have been the main reason why the organizations partnered. It is a valuable exercise to ask the participants to combine both BHAGs (bold missions) and see whether there are some possible synergies.

To keep both or a variety of BHAGs is risky, since the end scenario might become unclear. A BHAG should never be treated like a "balanced scorecard" wherein different fields are given different key performance indicators (KPIs). The exercise should end with one vivid description that inspires all team players.

The BHAG should unite people and invite them to participate in its creation.

Business Assessment Through Capturing Business Dilemmas. We assess the business case for the integration of organizations by eliciting the business dilemmas within the context of the re(de)fined vision and mission.

This can be done effectively through a combination of face-to-face interviews and an online semistructured questionnaire we have developed that we call WebCue. Our premise is that in an integration process, differences in business and cultural orientations are often part of the problems that people encounter when working in a multiorganization environment. People everywhere have different ways of working and relating to each other that, in the end, will affect the success of the collaboration between members of the new organization.

The big picture: At this stage we can reflect that a genuine and successful integration process requires the four components of our underlying cultural framework:

1. Recognition of different business and cultural orientations
2. Respect for those differences
3. Reconciliation of both business and cultural dilemmas resulting from components 1 and 2
4. Realization and rooting, in which the business benefits of connecting different orientations are embedded throughout the organization

The following example illustrates how dilemmas capture the core challenge of an integration process.

If a large pharmaceutical firm buys a smaller company to take care of its lack of innovation capability, the dilemma looks like this:

ON THE ONE HAND	ON THE OTHER HAND
We need to increase the size of our organization for distribution and economies of scale	We need to develop the innovative powers of "small is beautiful" and exploit flexibility

---

If this is not seen as a dilemma, the question arises as to why the larger organization did not choose to grow organically.

The dilemma of centralization versus decentralization surfaces frequently in many integration scenarios. With Linde AG, a highly centralized, German-based organization, one of the main arguments for buying BOC Ltd. was its decentralized approach in international business, where leaders had the basic philosophy that it was desirable to delegate their authority as deeply as possible into the organization. With the Campofrio Group, a Spanish-based food company, which consisted of many locally operating brands, it is the same story.

The reconciliation of this key dilemma makes or breaks the success of the merger.

When a global organization is faced with the dilemma of whether to centralize or to decentralize business activities, there are four possible extreme choices.

Choice	Explanation
Centralize	One response is to centralize strategy. This is the "head office" dictates paradigm.
Decentralize	Another possible choice is to decentralize, to "go native."
Compromise	In compromise, each side gives up something to achieve a common goal, centralizing some things and decentralizing others.
Reconcile (Centralize and Decentralize)	Much more challenging and at first sight not what one might think is possible. . . . When two apparently opposing views are reconciled so that instead of "either-or" thinking or "and-and" thinking, there is a "through-through" solution, in which new value is created by combining the best of both.

Partners in pre- and post-merger discussions might assume that they have common points of view and similar value orientations and that they give similar meaning to things they are debating, without realizing that they are all talking from different perspectives.

Business Dilemmas in Mergers. In a merger, many business dilemmas are inherent in the intending marriage between different ways of working in the legacy organizations. You should worry when there are no dilemmas to be found!

You might wonder why the organizations are merging in the first place. With Linde and BOC, we observed the dilemma as shown here.

On the One Hand	On the Other Hand
We need to supply global (or standardized) products/services	We need to supply products/services that respond to local tastes and needs
We need to develop our people	We need to keep people focused on delivering results as central to the success of the joint NEWCO

The reconciliation of these dilemmas, in particular the first one, becomes crucial to the success of the NEWCO.

With Unicredit, when integrating the two acquired banks, the German Hypovereinsbank and the Austrian Baca organization, the following dilemma was crucial.

On the One Hand	On the Other Hand
The concern for moving to an integrated European bank as a "truly European bank"	The concern for maintaining close local relationships with clients/customers as a multilocal bank

In a similar logic, when Geodis-Wilson bought TNT Express, both companies active in transport and logistics, the following dilemmas came to the table.

On the One Hand	On the Other Hand
We need to achieve short-term financial objectives	We need to develop a mid- to long-term strategy
We need to grow *bigger* for economies-of-scale reasons and to match global customer requirements	We need to grow *better* so as not to slide behind the competition
We need to standardize our processes to raise productivity	We want to be flexible to answer to our customers' demands
We need a clear and focused IT strategy	We need to keep numerous disparate systems running in the short term
We must grow the business by acquisitions and increased efficiencies	We should keep employee motivation high during uncertain times

Of course, these generic dilemmas—what we call "golden" dilemmas—manifest in specific ways in the particular circumstances and context of the merger. (See Chapter 16.)

From a selection of golden dilemmas in our dilemma database (see Appendix B), potential business dilemmas that the new organization needs to reconcile are reviewed to help make the integration successful.

Reconciliation of Business Dilemmas. The process of reconciling the business dilemmas is essentially touching the core of the strategy of new organizations striving to integrate. Although we are discussing "business dilemmas" here, it should be remembered that all cultures share these dilemmas. As explained throughout this book, how the dilemmas are perceived, what meaning is given to various aspects, which side may be favored, and how they are initially approached is culturally determined.

If there is a conscious effort of the two organizations to seek synergy between the strengths of each of the legacy organizations, they have the highest chance of success. We guide our clients through our highly structured dilemma-reconciliation process (or DRP) described in Chapter 13.

In the integration process, Geodis-Wilson was clear about the need for combining the requirement to achieve short-term financial objectives (which was a major strength of TNT Express) and the requirement to develop a mid- to long-term strategy, based on the forte of the French mother company, Geodis. This reconciliation would make the organization much more resilient. The end result looked like Figure 14.3.

The beauty of the discussion framework was that the positives and negatives of both approaches were openly discussed without excessive value judgment. The reconciliation in "being more selective in their investment strategy" was highly appreciated by all participants. They thought it would prohibit the typical TNT Express reaction to "shoot from the hip" (because "money talks") or "shoot, shoot, aim" *and* avoid the typical French (or rather, Parisian) "aim, aim, aim, oh I forgot to shoot."

Selecting the investment decisions based on how they could harness short-term results while realizing the longer-term vision was an invitation to combine the best of both worlds and an excellent opportunity to avoid the stereotypes about the negatives of both legacy approaches.

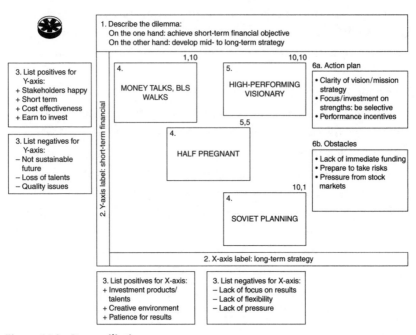

Figure 14.3. Reconciliation

Integrating Opposites as a Continuous and Creative Dialogue. Any integration process will be scattered with similar dilemmas in many areas, which can include HR, loyalty programs, IT, finance, and others. The process we have been describing generates a "creative space" where the ultimate solution can be significantly better than any initial one-dimensional solution. We would call this the area where synergies are realized.

Here we find an intense and rewarding process of dialogue involving the different organization units—both operating companies and holdings. Given the likelihood of future integration processes, recognition of the value of this dialogue offers a significant contribution.

We have found that people succeed in achieving these types of synergy, not because they are good at choosing one side over the other, but because they are able to reconcile seemingly opposing values. Integrating two desirable aims that were in tension creates a new, enriched reality. So it is not a matter of choosing whether a sales or a service culture would make a better company. The challenge is determining how to use a more sophisticated service culture in order to sell more, and vice versa.

In the case of Unicredit the choice was not between becoming an Italian bank with local characteristics or becoming a pan-European bank without anything Italian. The approach centered around how the NEWCO could become a pan-European bank with an Italian footprint and how the best NEWCO offer in Italy could be a springboard for the other European activities.

Organizations that are able to reconcile their differences will have created competitive advantage. If they cannot, they will be among the 70 percent of the mergers that fail. More important, the DRP invites the parties to become involved in a creative dialogue rather than just complaining about each other in the corridor.

Approaches to Discovering the (Key) Purpose. To find the purpose of the new organization, one must think beyond everyday occupations. If one has no other aim than what one already does daily, then there is no potential for growth, and irrevocably there is a risk of standstill. And as sensei Kenshiro Abbe, Seventh Dan, reminded us, "立って静止画に後れを取ると同じです" (standing still is the same as lagging behind).

How does one discover the (key) purpose of an organization, its higher goal? Although no quick fix exists, we can try different approaches to discovering the ultimate nature of the organization. These can be applied separately or in combination. In the following framework we have summarized the different approaches as consecutive steps.

It is fruitful to begin with discovering the specific characteristics of the organization. This is done by referring back to the findings from the original assessment of (combined) business opportunities and trying to find which behavior and communication patterns are and need to be specific to the newly created organization.

Then it is time to ask what ambitions people have for the new organization, what motivates their colleagues, and what is making a difference vis-à-vis the competitors and other stakeholders. One has to be careful that the purpose is formulated in a clear and concise way and that it is not expressed in simple slogans or clichés. It concerns the raison d'être of the company. A slogan per se is OK, provided it does not vulgarize or trivialize. The purpose as expressed should not become too cryptic either. A purpose is no cryptogram; it must be able to inspire people immediately.

Finally, the process of rolling out the purpose by calling on more members of the organization, regardless of which legacy companies were their origins, creates bonding around what the NEWCO wants to share. As in the case of Campofrio and Smithfield, the acquired company, the validating series of rounds contributed significantly to increasing the commitment and engagement of the purpose, because of the extended participation and involvement at many levels. That example helps illustrate why we advise companies to avoid choosing the extant purpose of one of the legacy organizations. If it is still so good a purpose that it should be applied for the NEWCO, then it will bubble to the surface anyway.

Phase A—Step 3: Values Assessment

Now that the (bold) mission and the (key) purpose have been formulated, it is time to discover the values of the organization(s).

Values are the elements that in their unique constitution support both the purpose and the mission. It is in purpose and mission where values and norms originate and certain types of behaviors are activated. Values define the good and bad, whereas norms define the right and wrong. Behaviors are just expressions of those norms and values.

Values are highly functional and should be linked to the mission of the organization, not just be a set of hobbyhorses of the CEO. Obviously, when two or more organizations come together, you cannot ignore the deep structure that their values represent. It is naive to say that one set of values is superior to the other, so the other just needs to adapt. All values have a reason for existence that cannot be ignored. Cultural diversity expresses itself in viewpoints and values, in operational priorities, and in ways of doing things. In our experience working with organizations facing complexity caused by cross-border mergers, acquisitions, and strategic alliances, we have found that issues rooted in cultural differences can be usefully formulated as dilemmas, since it is in this manner that such tensions can be openly revealed.

Because culture is a key human driver of organizational performance, in any integration process people from diverse backgrounds differ in the specific solutions they choose and offer for universally shared business topics. Thus, we find differences in management styles, decision-making processes, communication styles, client orientations, reward mechanisms, and many other areas.

The Organization Values Profiler (OVP). We discussed in Chapter 11 how profoundly a corporate culture bears on an organization's effectiveness, because it influences how decisions are made, how human resources are used, and how the organization responds to the environment.

In order to elicit the values of the existing organizations that will challenge and influence the merger or acquisition, we use our Organization Values Profiler (OVP) model. This 48-item instrument enables us to identify the possible similarities and differences of the organizational cultures involved. The OVP is a multifunctional instrument that enables respondents to review and examine the interpretations they give to relationships with each other and with the organization as a whole.

Unlike our other corporate culture diagnostic tools and our own four-quadrant model (see Chapter 11), the OVP goes beyond simple diagnosis and serves as the basis for the reconciliation of the key tensions that owe their origin to a merger, an acquisition, strategic change, diversity, globalization, or a similar source. It is also intended to be free of cultural bias, so that it is applicable to a diverse range of organization cultures across the world. We have seen too many models that display an Anglo-Saxon or US signature and that have been validated only in the national cultures where they were developed.

The OVP is able to diagnose the different corporate cultures of the parties engaged in the integration process and will clearly show the value dilemmas that the NEWCO is facing. It is an organizational culture scan based on the degrees of formalization and flexibility and on the degrees of hierarchy and openness to the environment.

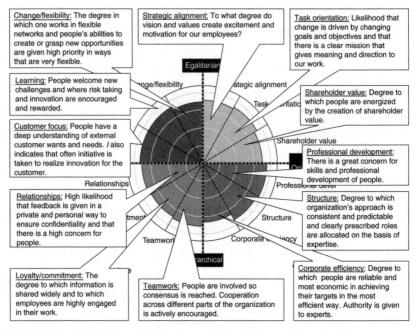

Figure 14.4. OVP Segments

It still has our underlying four-quadrant model of corporate culture described in Chapter 11, but it subdivides each quadrant, leading to a full 12-segment model. (See Figure 14.4.)

The four underlying quadrants represent how the organization orients itself to four basic processes in terms of task/strategy/mission, role/efficiency/consistency, power/human relations/involvement, and person/learning/adaptability. Within each of the subsegments we explore specific aspects that together determine the major orientations.

Additionally, our questionnaire has been designed in such a way that it reflects our underlying philosophy that bipolar scales (i.e., more of one alternative meaning less of the other alternative) are fundamentally inappropriate for the type of assessment we are seeking.

As in all our work, we undertook extensive formal research and field-testing to finalize the questions, including statistical analysis (Cronbach alpha reliability analysis) and triangulation with face-to-face and online semistructured interviews.

Respondents can score any subcomponent high or low within the set of subcomponents that collectively combine to form the construct being assessed. In this way, it is possible to score high on all four quadrants and all 12 segments. No longer is an organization of only one stereotype. This reflects our conceptual framework in which an integrated organization harnesses the strengths of all extremes and is not restricted to choosing between opposing options.

By using cross-validating questions, we have verified whether opposites and contradictions within one corporate culture have been reconciled. So, for example, we ask respondents to rate statements such as, "There is a clear and overt strategy for the future" (Guided Missile) and "Through our short-term thinking we are quick on our feet" (Incubator). They are validated by a (combination) reconciling question, such as, "We are able to meet short-term demands without compromising our long-term vision" (Reconciliation). We reiterate, the dilemmas are shared by all cultures, but how they are approached and what meaning is given to them is culturally determined.

Another example is the tension between task (Guided Missile) orientation and people (Family) orientation, which we explore first with two contrasting questions: "There is a lot of teamwork" and "People strive for self-realization" and then the validating question: "We have teams that consist of creative individuals."

In this way, the OVP shows how healthy an organizational culture can be by covering all 12 segments *and* the reconciliation between those segments.

External validation (i.e., against departmental or functional performance indicators) shows that the higher the scores on *all* segments, the higher the score on the validating reconciliation questions correlates directly with higher long-term performance of the organization. See Figure 14.5.

Low-performing organizations score low on all segments. Industry "followers" have an average score, while "market leaders" score high on all segments; they have an integral culture reconciling all contradictions in their business.

We can also explore "current" and "ideal" situations by asking respondents to indicate two sets of ratings for their own organization.

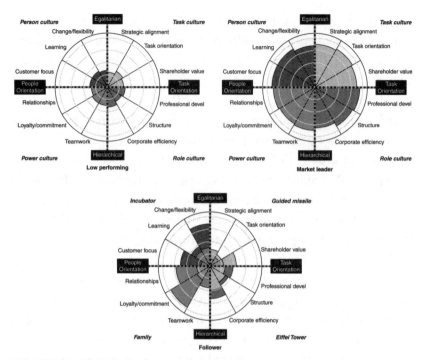

Figure 14.5. OVP Results

Alternatively, we can compare the value orientation profiles of both parties in a merger.

A cultural values assessment that compares the organizations that want to integrate will identify opportunities and obstacles to cultural change. It will help define the necessary guidance in the development of personal alignment, group cohesion, and structural alignment processes. This provides the foundation for identifying key performance indicators that will be used in the final step of values management.

The value dilemmas that were selected from the interview and Web-based processes are triangulated with the dilemmas raised from the OVP (see step 4).

Let us take the example of the integration process of the German Linde AG and the British BOC Ltd. The top 150 leaders were asked to complete a version of our Internet-driven OVP. The results, as displayed in Figure 14.6, were both revealing and insightful.

Even at first glance the contrasts between cultures are obvious. Linde is a German-based, highly professional organization with an

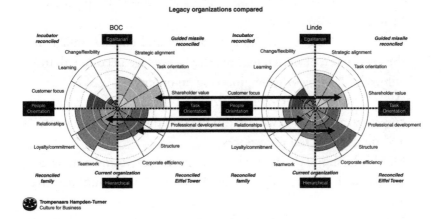

Figure 14.6. **Legacy Organizations Compared**

excellent R&D division, centralized in its governance, and highly successful after focusing on the gas business and divesting lots of unrelated businesses under the direction of a strong, visionary, and powerful leader, Dr. Wolfgang Reitzle. In contrast, BOC was a highly successful global player with a multinational management team, rather project based, practical in its approach, and empowering people wherever possible, with a highly committed and loyal population.

Linde's success could best be summarized by a highly professional, disciplined, and mission-oriented organization (a Guided Eiffel Tower), while BOC's strength was a combination of dedicated and empowered people around a clear set of global goals for the sake of shareholder value (a Guided Family). When we compared the corporate cultures from the OVP, dilemmas captured from the semistructured open-question format of our online WebCue questionnaire, and the face-to-face interviews, the results were fully convergent and reinforcing.

Six key dilemmas evolved:

1. We need to cut costs wherever we can for the sake of our shareholders' return versus we need to invest for long-term sustainability
2. We need to supply global (or standardized) products/services versus we need to supply products/services that respond to local tastes and needs

3. We need to develop our people versus we need to keep people focused on delivering results
4. We need to focus on the human element and take advantage of the experience of managing diversity versus we need to enhance a culture of leading-edge engineering autonomy
5. We need to develop looser controls and greater management empowerment versus we need to develop tight top-down controls and more restricted procedures
6. Our leadership style should be more participative and empowering versus our leadership style should be more decisive and directive

Dilemmas 3 through 6 were clearly value dilemmas, and the success of the future Linde Group would be highly dependent on their reconciliations.

What About the Personal Values of the Key Players? Once the dilemmas are formulated and validated by the differences in corporate and possibly other relevant cultures, it is time to see how the personal values of the top leadership of the respective organizations help to reconcile the dilemmas at stake.

This process begins by profiling the personal values of the leadership group and their direct reports and then getting the commitment of the leadership group to values and behavioral change.

For assessing the personal values of key players, we use our Personal Values Profiler (PVP), which offers important insights into the relationships employees have with their organization.[7] A variant of our PVP is our CVP (Corporate Values Profiler). This is essentially the same tool, but respondents are asked to indicate what values should drive the organization.

In the new workplace of the coming decade, what matters for the individual and what matters for the organization need increasingly to be congruent. Differences between the PVP and CVP results may reveal changes in the industry or functional discipline over time. For example, imagine a young woman choosing nursing as her career because she perceives that working as a nurse will be congruent with her personal values (PVP profile). However, after many years, she finds the reality of working in a city-center publicly funded hospital to be more about being verbally and physically abused by drunks and drug addicts and being concerned about getting sued for any practice that does not accord with strict (Eiffel Tower) guidelines. The need for efficiency and conforming to procedure would be reflected in the CVP and quite different from her PVP results. Her response to her current situation might be low motivation and performance, or she might opt to leave and work for a private health clinic or cosmetic surgeon that would be a close match to her PVP results.

The PVP provides understanding of matters concerning personal resistance or support in regard to change, the capacity for stability, sustainability, and innovation. These matters can exert a decisive influence on the overall ability of the organization to deal with the challenges and dilemmas it faces.

This PVP/CVP combination is usually cross-linked to our OVP (Organization Values Profiler) to provide further important comparisons to analyze the corporate culture. In our arena of mergers and acquisitions, we need to be alert for any mismatch between the values that will support the key purpose of the NEWCO and the PVP results of key players.

While the PVP/CVP and OVP are designed to be semistructured and rather deductive in nature, the "simple," more open Internet-based questionnaire and the validating interviews are principally inductive. The value dilemmas that are selected from the interviews and Web-based process will validate the dilemmas raised from the OVP and PVP/CVP.

Final Selection of Values. Finally, a definitive decision on the core values must be made in the context of the envisioned future and key purpose of the organization. These values need to be instrumental to the achievement of the goals set for the organization, and they need to fit the purpose.

There are several possible approaches to selecting the core values for an organization. For example:

- Values as helping key business dilemmas to be reconciled
- Values as helping key cultural dilemmas to be reconciled
- Values as giving life to purpose
- Values as extensions of personal values

Values arise from functionality and are fed by success. *The quality of a core value can be best demonstrated by its relevance to helping solve the key dilemmas that business leaders face.* The core values need to support the dilemma-reconciliation process.

Therefore, the most preferred method (because of its elegance) for deriving the core values is to end the process of reconciliation of business dilemmas with the question, "What values and behaviors do we need to develop to reconcile this dilemma?"

Values as Constructs to Aid the Reconciliation of Key Cultural Dilemmas. Next to vibrant discussions about functionality, it is also satisfying to see all parties involved, engaging around a shared reality they want to create together rather than focusing only on differences. It is obvious that there are also some opposites possible when we look at the cultural side of the integration. These value clashes could lead to problems if not dealt with appropriately. An approach similar to the one used for the business dilemmas can be unfolded.

Values as Extensions of Personal Values. In some cases the original organizations have so many different histories and so many vested interests that values to drive the future of the organization can best be defined from a clean sheet. Rather than have people brainstorming about what existing values would best fit the NEWCO, we often advise the joint top leadership to respond to the PVP. This will elicit the personal values of the leadership and compare them with an initial set of values that they individually believe to be appropriate for the organization. Ideally, there should be a match between the two, of course—and there usually is. Presumably that is why they are with the organization in the first place! Depending on the situation, it may be most effective to start with the top leaders' own values and to reason from there.

Phase A—Step 4: Values in Practice

Here we begin to translate value constructs into what they mean in practice on a day-to-day basis by identifying what behaviors are appropriate to bring about living the values. It is a three-part process:

1. Giving direction to acceptable and unacceptable behaviors
2. Imagining the future
3. Making crucial decisions

While the OVP, PVP, and our Intercultural Awareness Profile (IAP, which is based on the Seven Dimensions) are focused on diagnosing the main orientations of the key parties and individuals involved and where they agree and differ in their approaches to shared dilemmas, this fourth step focuses on what the newly created organization needs to *share*. It revisits the complete overview of the dilemmas that need to be addressed, in terms of both business and culture, in order to create a sustainable high-performance culture.

As we have said earlier, the "value" of a "shared value" is the degree to which it helps you to reconcile the basic business and cultural dilemmas the organization is facing while integrating toward the NEWCO. High performance is achieved when all the key dilemmas are reconciled. A sustained high performance is achieved when there is a mindset embedded throughout the organization to continually review, elicit, and address evolving dilemmas.

So what does our combined organization consider of value? The definition of an organization's core values is based on what drives its people and what binds them. Core values are the timeless tenets of an organization. Together with its key purpose, they reflect what the organization stands for and tell this story to the outside world.

Process and Tools for Translating Values to Behavior (V2B). It happens too often that management or other key staff make remarks about the glossy posters on the walls and fancy brochures in desk drawers expressing the beauty of the organization's core values and mission, adding that if people would just apply the content to the way they behave, then these items would be of use. Cynicism too often dominates here.

This is why there is a need to introduce a means by which people define concrete behaviors that they want to see and do not want to see, starting with intact teams. The end product can be expressed as a "charter of behavior."

The objective is to improve common understanding, trust, communication, cooperation, and effectiveness in a team. The creation of a charter of behavior not only helps teams to spell out a limited number of desirable and undesirable behaviors but also initiates actions in the team as individual team members help to "live" the behaviors in the charter.

The process involves translating every core value to desirable and undesirable behaviors, using a facilitating structured work sheet. From here, the team collects the individual statements, which are then discussed, and the importance of each statement is evaluated by the group, culminating in a final selection.

The whole process thus results in the selection of desirable and undesirable behaviors for the team and, finally, the production of a charter.

The V2B process uses the energy released by values that are genuinely shared within the organization, such as the core values that capture what the organization stands for. Typically, core values reflect what binds and connects those working for the organization and are part and parcel of the corporate identity. However, they often fail to energize management and employees. This is because core values are often too abstract to give guidance in real-life situations. They need to be interpreted or "translated" to expose their relevance in daily work. This is what is happening in the V2B process, and this is why the charter is important to bring it all to life.

The V2B process builds on the powerful centuries-old adage "Don't do upon others what you don't want to be done upon yourself." Team members explore in depth the behavior pattern they mutually expect from each other. From this they then jointly create a charter capturing a limited number of observable desirable behaviors for further embedding and "living," along with undesirable behaviors they need to avoid.

Where cooperation between two teams needs improvement, a so-called external V2B process is needed. Here both teams create an external charter, capturing the behaviors each team expects from the other (e.g., suppliers or another department). After exchanging and explaining these external charters, both teams will create action programs to better "live" the desirable behaviors.

Phase A—Step 5: Revisiting the Compelling Business Case for Integration

This final step of the first phase is aimed at keeping everyone aligned in the same direction. At this stage members of the leadership team have enough information to develop a detailed implementation program. They have completed the following prerequisites:

- Customized the communication of the implementation program so that it aligns with the key drivers of the total population
- Established a clear sense of collective direction: vision and mission
- Identified the core values, principles, and purpose
- Agreed on a set of behaviors and drivers that guide their day-to-day decision making and actions

Before implementing a process of whole-system integration involving culture change, it is important that the CEO and the board have elicited and clarified the compelling reasons for the integration.

A convincing link must be made between the performance issues and the cultural issues. The CEO and his or her team should present a clear, overt story line so that the reasons for the whole system integration and change effort are readily understood and supported by the executive and employee populations. This goes beyond just improving current performance; it is about how they can position themselves to take advantage of value differences and build long-term resilience and sustainability.

In summary, after the previous steps, the following will have been made clear:

1. A defined joint visionary framework and purpose
2. The cultural and value differences and similarities on the personal, team, and organizational levels
3. The main business and cultural dilemmas that need to be reconciled
4. The main core values and behaviors that enable the reconciliations to be successful

These are all the ingredients necessary to address the second phase of the implementation of the NEWCO's strategy and the objectives and key performance indicators.

Phase B: Developing the Implementation Strategy Through Objectives and Key Performance Indicators

This second phase consists of two basic steps and begins to apply the results of the diagnosis and analysis undertaken in the preceding phase.

The focus now shifts to planning for implementation to realize the business benefits of the merger/alliance.

Phase	Focus	Steps	
B:	Developing the Implementation Strategy Through Objectives and Key Performance Indicators	6	Survey of Key Drivers
		7	Developing the Implementation Strategy Through Objectives and Key Performance Indicators

We view the development of an organizational identity renewal in this wider context as the process of reconciling divergent goals, values, and structural, functional, and cultural differences. Our approach is to synthesize strategy, structure, operations, people, and culture into a single integrated whole, which also includes the economic, social, and cultural context in which the new organization functions. Taking the perspective of the company as a whole, we seek to identify how these elements can be aligned and reconciled to generate maximum performance. This includes the complete spectrum of issues, much more than just hard values and financial diligence. Thus, the dilemmas involving all drivers, including shareholders, employees, business processes, clients/customers, suppliers, and society at large, need to be satisfied.

Phase B—Step 6: Survey of Key Drivers

It is necessary to validate the key drivers for the following reasons:

1. To customize the design of the *communications* surrounding the integration process, particularly the compelling reason for change
2. To customize the methodology and content of the cultural integration process
3. To provide executives and managers with personal feedback for coaching purposes

By validation, we mean to objectively assess the drivers and thus not proceed simply on the basis of assumed drivers. There is a motivation-through-participation aspect as well. We use the process of validating a key purpose and its core values to *align all participants in the process.*

To give the core values context, it is important that the leadership team validates the organization's BHAG (big, hairy, audacious goal) and fundamental reason for being, or key purpose. Because the key purpose needs to serve as a guiding star at the horizon, which the organization will ever pursue but never reach, it cannot just be superimposed by the top; it must be coproduced with involvement of as many people as is practical.

Since purpose and values are what guide and inspire and what give meaning to all the work being done within the integrated organization, they need to come from those involved and inspired.

Once the purpose has been drafted by the very top, it needs to be validated by the layers below. Therefore, the expression of the purpose must avoid overly sophisticated language, in order that it can be understood and enriched through constructive criticism.

As explained earlier, the OVP gives an overview of the dominant values of the organization, both current and ideal, and maps the major differences between the organizations involved on those orientations. In contrast, the PVP gives an overview of the dominant personal values of the leadership of the organization. Tensions between the results of the OVP and PVP are a potential source of cultural inertia. In the modern workplace, it is essential to reconcile what matters for the organization and what matters for the employees.

Any such tensions must be analyzed and key drivers selected to best close the gaps between current and ideal situations and between personal and organizational values.

Cultural inertia needs to be reconciled *at* each level (leaders' personal values and organization values) as well as *between* levels (what leaders value and what middle management values). Otherwise, we can end up with extreme scenarios, such as a denial culture in which the leadership thinks all is OK, but there is a widening gap with middle and operational management, and leaders deny such a gap exists.

Phase B—Step 7: Developing Implementation Through Objectives and Key Performance Indicators

At this point the CEO and leadership teams have sufficient information to develop a detailed implementation program. They know the compelling business reasons for the integration program; they customized its communication and key drivers for the executive and employee population; they have a clear sense of collective direction—the vision, mission, and purpose; they know the shared core values and behaviors they aspire to; and they have a clear picture of where the parties currently are.

It is vital to set targets for the integration process in performance, cultural, and leadership improvements and capture them in indicators making up a variety of scorecards.

However, as noted earlier, we want to go beyond "balanced scorecards," since "balance" implies that if you have more of one, you have less of the other. That is not very fruitful when we are trying to get synergies between organizations. The benefit of reconciliation lies in integrating differences and connecting points of view. These are more powerful ways of facilitating implementation and enabling the leaders to focus on delivering reconciliations. So we base our performance indicators on our Integrated Scorecard, in which we develop key *reconciling* indicators (KRIs) rather than simple KPIs.

Adopting an approach around delivering S.M.A.R.T. objectives is tantamount to abandoning the whole idea of reconciliation. In this scenario, we would have used our dilemma thinking only for diagnosis. Following an approach based on KRIs brings the benefit of reconciliation right through to the final achievement of a high-performance culture and mind-set change.

We can categorize indicators into three types:

1. "Causal" indicators that relate to values and behaviors
2. "Output" indicators that relate directly to performance
3. "Outcome" indicators that relate to the end results

Causal Indicators. These targets are set for values and behavior improvement at both the group and individual levels. This improvement would be reflected by a balanced OVP profile of the NEWCO displaying a full complement of 12 segments showing that all the key dilemmas were reconciled, leading to high performance. Similarly, measures at the individual level of the leadership would show improvement.

We use the PVP and OVP for monitoring progress on the behavioral and value levels and scan semiannually the decrease in cultural inertia. The output of the V2B charters (as discussed in step 4) is also taken as a reference point to see whether the intact teams and their individual members are making progress on causal indicators that relate to values and behaviors.

On the individual level it is important that the appraisal process reinforces the desired shared values and behaviors. It should be much more than checking the completion of previously agreed-on deliverables as in conventional change management of a merger, because this practice lacks the behavioral component.

The manager should also check whether the individual has lived his or her corporate activities according to the espoused values and behaviors. In more comprehensive approaches this could be linked to the team feedback on how the V2B process has been lived by the individual.

Consider a set of values of one of our clients:

1. Striving for teams that consists of creative individuals
2. Striving for local learning so that it can be rolled out globally
3. Striving to continuously develop leading-edge products and services that serve client needs
4. Striving to develop shareholder value to further develop people

Assessing whether these values are being lived cannot be achieved using a method based on a linear scale.

The following questions appropriate to the foregoing values serve to illustrate what needs to be assessed.

Question 1: What are supporting values that help you reconcile working in teams with creative individuals?
Question 2: What are the key reconciling indicators that can help you say, "This is clear evidence of progress"?
Question 3: What are the key behaviors that can help you say, "This is clear evidence of this value"?

In this exercise we should note particularly the second question. First, what is a key reconciling indicator? It is a behavioral output that indicates that you have lived the value. And it can't be specific enough. Our Web-based version of our Integrated Scorecard provides access for individual use by middle managers as well as their superiors. This Internet-based tool also provides updates of the KRIs and indicates how the organizational leadership can help make progress.

Output Indicators. We define output targets as indicators of performance improvement, such as productivity, efficiency, innovation, and employee and customer satisfaction. These measures need to be aligned with the ongoing monitoring in the organization.

The unique offering of our approach over and above conventional change management consists of an online system of semiannual measures of the major dilemmas created by striving for the stated goals and the progress in achieving reconciliations.

Outcome Indicators. Here we define outcome indicators as targets of performance improvement that are relevant to the newly created organization such as market share and profitability.

Phase C: Realizing and Rooting the Benefits

After completion of all the preceding activities, we have arrived at the third and last phase.

Phase	Focus	Steps	
C:	Realizing and Rooting the Benefits	8	Developing Systemic Alignment
		9	Value and Culture Awareness Programs
		10	Continuous Reevaluation: Monitoring Change Toward the High-Performance Culture

This part of the process is aimed at keeping everyone aligned.

The challenge now is to help the CEO and leadership team in making the vision, mission, values, and behavior pervasive throughout the organization in two basic steps.

Phase C—Step 8: Developing Systemic Alignment

There are three major components to the integration process in bringing about a shift in the individual and collective behaviors of all those involved:

- Personal alignment
- Group cohesion (values alignment and mission alignment)
- Structural alignment

The purpose of the efforts regarding personal alignment and group cohesion is to give the integration process a head start by focusing on the alignment of values with the vision and mission of the top team and those who report to the top team (top 100 or so). These executives are the guardians of the high-performance culture to be created. We have found that the pursuit of enhanced personal alignment and group cohesion needs to be integrated into the initiatives that the organization has unfolded.

Phase C—Step 9: Value and Culture Awareness Programs

From the organization level at which we stop the cascade of personal alignment and group-cohesion programs, we replace it in the tiers below by a value and culture awareness program. The objective is to make the employees aware of the major differences in corporate and national cultures and how to take advantage of those differences within the shared envisioned future and core values and purpose of the organization.

Sustaining the Initiatives. In some situations it is more effective to start with the value and culture awareness program before addressing personal alignment and group cohesion, after appropriate adjustments are made. To monitor progress, a set of Integrated Scorecards is developed to help guide and monitor the major value tensions among personal, cultural, and core values.

Phase C—Step 10: Continuous Reevaluation: Monitoring Change Toward the High-Performance Culture

The progress and speed of the integration process depends largely on the specific situation. Each situation will require tailored plans, interventions, and monitoring systems. Once you move into full-fledged preparation and beyond, there are some checklists available to monitor the progress of implementation on the individual, company, and unit levels. These checklists can be integrated in ongoing surveys as employee surveys, engagement surveys, and the like.

Using a combination of the online check on progress on the reconciliation of main dilemmas, the OVP, and the instruments measuring the KRIs in HR systems, along with any other related programs, it will be possible to monitor regularly, and, where necessary, interventions can be made on the spot.

Conclusions

Today's world of business is complex, and simplistic approaches to integration do not work, which is why too many mergers fail to realize the expected benefits.

We have described our range of comprehensive solutions to help organizations reach a high-performance culture and realize and sustain the business benefits of their mergers, acquisitions, and alliances.[8]

We emphasize that we have sought to demonstrate that the goal is not just avoiding conflict, misunderstanding, and embarrassment because of differences, but using these differences to the NEWCO's advantage and thereby delivering the business benefits of the integration through connecting these different viewpoints.

Notes

1. *Economist* 9 (January 1999).
2. KPMG Consulting M&A Report 1999.
3. We owe very much to Allard Everts, who worked as a senior consultant at Trompenaars Hampden-Turner.
4. Collins, J. and Porras, J., *Built to Last*, (New York: HarperBusiness, 1994).
5. Ibid., "Building Your Corporate Vision," *Harvard Business Review*, September–October 1996.
6. Ibid., 73.
7. See www.ridingthewavesofculture.com for further details.
8. For further information and for our complete discourse on this topic we refer the reader to *The Global Tango: Reconciling Cultural Differences in Mergers and Acquisitions,* by F. Trompenaars and M. Nijhoff Asser, published by Infideas, Oxford, UK, 2010.

The Diversity of Diversity

As well as differences among nations, other variables contribute to the way in which people approach dilemmas. In this chapter we explore these differences and try to answer many questions we have received about whether cultures are converging or diverging and in what ways. We also give consideration to issues such as gender, age, ethnicity, and functional diversity.

Ongoing Evidence

As explained throughout this book, and as detailed in Appendices A and B, we have continued to collect primary data about cultures with our diagnostic questionnaires. This information is captured in several databases. In addition to the specific diagnostic questions discussed regarding the seven-dimensions model, we have included basic biographical and other categorical data for the respondents. We are, therefore, able to report the results of our ongoing database mining in which we have looked at other potential sources of value differences. The major effort was to assess the significance of eight potential sources of difference: country or national culture, type of industry, religion, job or function, age of respondent, corporation, education level, and gender. We have also extended our sample base to younger respondents, including students, as it has become clear that generational differences are increasingly important.

We measured the relative amount of variety (entropy) between these subclassifications and the database as a whole. For example, how much difference is associated with being a woman, working in the energy industry, being a marketing professional, being a US citizen? Is one's national culture the most or the least important of these variables? Because lower entropy implies more order, the relative importance of different classifications is in inverse proportion to their entropy. In the following table, the rank orders are given for each classification.

National culture of origin is the most important difference for every dimension. Religion looms large for universalism, individualism, specificity, and achievement. The Protestant religion, for example, treats the Bible as "the law of God," codified instructions for salvation. It invites individuals to work for their own salvation, to offer God their work, and to eschew all but the most specific and unadorned religious symbols. Type of industry is also important. Are you engaged in a continuous-process manufacturing system or customizing complex services for particular clients? Job or function is moderately relevant, while gender, education, age, and corporation show small differences overall.

Such findings should not be misinterpreted. What they mean is that a person's being female or male is not now used as a competitive advantage for a company, not that a company founded and run mostly by women will not find such an advantage in the future. By the same token, low scores on corporate differences do not mean that corporate culture is unimportant, only that, on average, differences are not systematic and tend to cancel each other out.

No sooner do we change the circumstances than important differences start to appear. Cultures tend to appear and disappear from our horizon, depending on circumstances. Any difference, even the smallest, could become significant as the search for competitive advantage continues and pathfinders are imitated.

Religion, ethnicity, and other variables may also combine, so that American Jews, for example, are more likely to enter law, medicine, social science, the media, universities, and garment making than are other ethnic groups. By becoming a majority or significant minority in certain key jobs and industries, these various cultures reinforce certain

VARIETY IN VALUE DIFFERENCES

ENTROPY	UNIVERSALISM-PARTICULARISM	INDIVIDUALISM-COMMUNITARIANISM	NEUTRAL-AFFECTIVE	SPECIFIC-DIFFUSE	ACHIEVEMENT-ASCRIPTION	TIME	INTERNAL-EXTERNAL
Lowest	Country	Country	Country	Country	Country	Country	Country
	Industry	Religion	Industry	Industry	Industry	Industry	Industry
	Religion	Industry	Job	Religion	Religion	Job	Religion
	Job	Education	Religion	Age	Job	Religion	Education
	Age	Age	Corporate	Gender	Age	Gender	Job
	Corporate	Gender	Age	Education	Education	Age	Age
	Education	Job	Gender	Job	Corporate	Education	Gender
Highest	Gender	Corporate	Education	Corporate	Gender	Corporate	Corporate

key values common to them all. Our data mining may show only that large patterns, national cultures, are more salient than smaller cultures, such as people of a particular age cohort or job description. The larger patterns are able to organize more values more consistently.

Changing Cultures?

We stress that the cultural constructs throughout this book seek to structure the experiences of managers and form a conceptual model for such business readers and students of business. Our aim is to help leaders and managers of enterprises to be more effective in dealing with different cultures. The quantitative aspects of our work are not oriented toward guidelines for tourists, or anthropologists seeking to measure cultures, that might lead to a simplistic prescriptive series of "dos and don'ts."

Even so, we are frequently asked about our database scores and if they show trends, and this issue merits some discussion.

We all recognize that most societies are increasing in diversity. Many nations now describe themselves as being "multicultural" as a result of immigration and migration. If we were to simply assemble 20 participants (managers) from a client company who are all from the same country in a training workshop, the group would likely be more diverse than in the past. It might comprise second-generation immigrants and/or ethnic minorities but who would all describe themselves as having the same nationality.

So if the reference data scores that we publish suggest to a marketer who is planning a new product launch that one culture is more individualistic than another, then do we mean it "was" or "is now" or "is expected to be in the future"? And do we mean for the culture of the original inhabitants, or the new evolving mixed society?

Of course, there is no such thing as the culture of the original inhabitants. The "English" never were a purebred "English" culture, one that has been suddenly influenced by an increase in immigration in the last century. Two thousand years ago they were warring tribes from the different cultures of Saxons, Picts, Scots, and Celts. The Romans came in 55 B.C. The Normans came in 1066. Similarly, in the

Netherlands there were broad changes in the population around the fourth century during the "Grote Volksverhuizing" (great movement) and again after the time of the Reformation. And the Dutch, with their long-standing tradition of tolerance and their seafaring skills, welcomed more migrants pro rata over a longer period than many other nations. As a final example, both the populations and cultures of the United States and Australia are built on immigration from many countries.

Acculturation through synthesis and the resolution of tensions over time gives rise to a constantly evolving culture. Our world has changed even more quickly in the last 50 years through modern technology, advances in communications, and globalization, and so we need to ask if cultures are continually evolving in parallel with these trends and, if they are, whether that evolvement is accelerating.

At first glance, we have observed some changes in the (raw) database "scores" based on the answers given by respondents to many of our questions, and it is tempting to interpret them as fundamental changes in cultures. On this subject, exhaustive analysis has led to new understandings that offer more insightful explanations.[1] Space limitations prevent a thorough treatment here, so only the highlights are included, and the reader is referred to www.ridingthewavesofculture .com for further discovery.

At the onset we need to acknowledge the ideographic-nomothetic issue, which has become more significant over the last few years.

- **The nomothetic perspective:** This is what we can define as your own fundamental value orientation in the context of your work situation: how you strive to deliver your job targets, how you contribute to company goals, how you act at work both on your own and in your work teams. This is the "work" part of your "work-life" dichotomy.
- **The ideographic perspective:** This is what we can define as your own fundamental value orientation. It refers to you as a person and comprises the meanings that you give to your own career, your competencies, how you go about solving your day-to-day family problems, and how you prefer to act at home and with your family. This is the "life" part of your "work-life" dichotomy.

Our diagnostic questionnaires include items that probe both aspects. When we ask about "quality of life" (Figure 5.1), we are asking essentially about an ideographic orientation, whereas "what kind of job" (Figure 5.2) is more of a nomothetic orientation. Both are concerned with exploring the dimension from individualism through to communitarianism.

We combine a number of such questions in order to summarize a culture with a single dimension score. Our database mining has revealed that there is some increasing divergence between these two components (nomothetic and ideographic) over the last 15 years, and in many cases we have significant and reliable data for such trends. We emphasize, however, that the rank order (by country) on our scales remains virtually the same. Comprehensive analysis of our scales, adjustments to weighting based on reliability studies, and revisions of our algorithms that allow for kurtosis enable us to continue to offer reliable country scores from our database for our various training and interactive models. Thus, the degree of universalism on our linear profile scale for Dutch nationals shows little variation over this period. (See Figure 15.1.)

However, if we examine subcomponents, especially with a diagnosis that differentiates between the ideographic and nomothetic, then we can observe shifts over this time frame. (See Figure 15.2.)

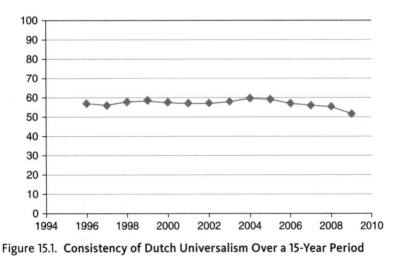

Figure 15.1. Consistency of Dutch Universalism Over a 15-Year Period

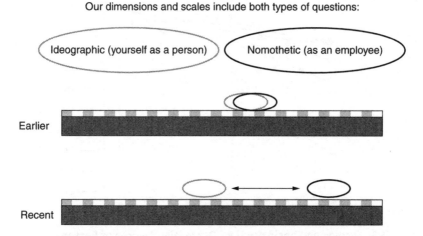

Figure 15.2. **Increasing Divergence Between Ideographic and Nomothetic Cultural Orientations**

One explanation of this effect—simply to clarify and illustrate the debate (albeit validated by interviews)—is that a respondent may be fundamentally individualistic, but (because of all those team-building courses at work!) he or she now spends a majority of time working in teams, has learned to interact successfully with others, and sees benefits that might not have been evident initially. So nomothetically, the person may be less individualistic.

Example of longitudinal changes: decreasing individualism at work (nomothetic).[2]

Example of longitudinal changes: increasing specificity (i.e., decreasing degree of personal involvement) with boss at work (nomothetic).[3] (See Figures 15.3 and 15.4.)

Of course, what these linear scales do not reveal are changes in the propensity to reconcile each end of the dimensions scales.

Example: Eurovergence

So is the world of values converging or diverging over time? If we reflect on political developments, we might conclude from the behavior of the Basques in Spain, the Catholics in Northern Ireland, and the

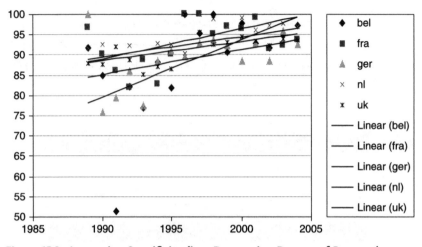

Figure 15.3. Increasing Specificity (i.e., Decreasing Degree of Personal Involvment) with Boss at Work (Nomothetic)

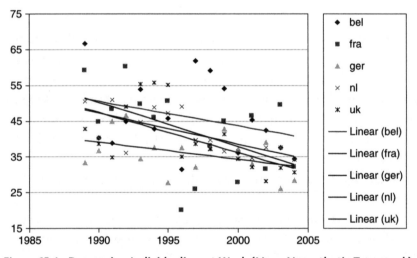

Figure 15.4. Decreasing Individualism at Work (More Nomethetic Teamwork)

Albanians in Kosovo that cultures have an irresistible urge to diverge from each other.

While evaluating these relationships, it is also appropriate to analyze European developments. In general, it appears that the cultures of Europe known in the Middle Ages were in fact much more similar than they are now. Royal families were also much related and interbred. The introduction of the euro seems to have caused a stimulus for some cultures to dig in even deeper. The British tend to emphasize even more loudly, "we *and* the Europeans," as if they have never been part of Europe. Even the Dutch, one of the least Euro-skeptic nations, demonstrate ethnocentric behavior: after a historic soccer match a Danish minister proclaimed, "If you can't join them, beat them."

The Dutch author often comments that in his opinion, the European Summit at Nice in 2001 was at the very lowest level of European convergence. But what can you expect when the French are in the chair? The beginning of Chirac's first term as president (1995) symbolized the essence of French culture. He organized one nuclear test after another to show the world that France was still in charge. And when the world protested, he demonstrated how bad his English was: he took the word "pro-test" literally and kept on testing.

Perhaps the question of whether the world is converging or diverging in its value systems has been wrongly posed. The evidence from our longitudinal research indicates that managers in countries such as the Netherlands, the US, the UK, and France have not changed significantly over the last 20 years, especially in terms of the rank order on our component or composite dimension scales. However, we do see some movement toward communitarianism on some nomothetic components as described previously, if we apply discriminant analysis.

In exploring such trends, it is important to compare like with like, because we know that the spectrum of respondents from our samples is also changing. Thus, the question, "How many years have you worked abroad?" enables us to select the less-global, less-traveled managers. Similarly, managers working in their own country for what is essentially an indigenous employer also tend to reflect their original national characteristics.

We add that Japanese managers seem to have changed dramatically, particularly toward individualism (nomothetic), but it has also become apparent that variety by age and gender has decreased in our samples, reflecting greater participation in business of a more diverse range of managers.

Given our expectations and general observations of changes in society, it is not surprising that over the last few years, Japanese managers have drawn increasing attention to the role and contribution of successful women. The logical response of many Western women is that it was about time that they caught up with this trend.

What also intrigues are the central European cultures. These are occasionally described as "oscillating" cultures. Take Romania or Russia. After the fall of the Wall, they shifted to extreme individualistic orientations from extremely collectivistic values. This shift also led to pathological extremities that in turn stimulated collectivistic nostalgia. A Russian expatriate once indicated, out of envy for the richness of French grammar, that his language needed only three tenses: a nostalgic past, a bleak present, and an uncertain future. But again, these attitudes are explained more by nomothetic effects.

In the 25 years since we started our research, we have found that almost all countries show a larger diversity within their boundaries (the multicultural society), although France less so.

The Cricket Test

The dynamic of fan loyalty in regard to cricket matches helps us to illustrate what we have found from our data mining. The original "cricket test" was a question posed by UK politician Norman Tebbitt to second- and third-generation immigrants born in the UK of Pakistani grandparents: "Who would you support to win if England were playing Pakistan in the World Series?" Most answered Pakistan, even though they declared themselves to be of UK nationality and totally assimilated into UK culture and to identify with UK culture. The cricket test is decidedly toward the extreme of the ideographic.

An analysis of the broad spectrum of 90-plus countries represented in our core cross-cultural database indicates no single paradigm of converging or diverging values except some increasing divergence between ideographic and nomothetic aspects. The data reveal a mixed pattern of categories of tendencies. In Europe there is some degree of convergence (nomothetically), while in other regions and countries people seem to reemphasize their identity by pushing back from this shift to a more central tendency (especially ideographically).

Because (in business) we will all be making our PowerPoint presentations using the company's standard template with corporate logos, driving similar makes and models of company cars approved by our transport manager, conducting business in the "European way," in which the language is international English, all the while spending our euros, we may tend to think that Europe has converged. However, when we get home, turn on the TV, watch football, interact with our families, spend money on consumer purchases, and socialize with our friends or attend a family wedding, we enjoy and live our cultural heritage.

In conclusion, some convergence of cultures can be observed at the extreme nomothetic perspective and some reidentification and return to recent history at the extreme ideographic perspective.

We also caution readers and researchers that simple changes in the wording of diagnostic questions, in both written questionnaires and oral interviews, can sometimes shift the (absolute) responses. For example:

> Question 1: "Are you basically an individualist, who likes doing things on your own?"
>
> Question 2: "*At work*, are you basically an individualist, who likes doing things on your own?"

The simple addition of the context "at work" in question 2 shifts the focus to the nomothetic and may result in a different response. Without appropriate cross-validation and correlation studies, such response changes may be misinterpreted.

Ideographic versus nomothetic aspects of culture were studied in detail by one of our doctoral students, Dr. Nicola Broom.[4]

Review of Cultural Differences Deriving from Variables Other than Nationality

This section presents some examples of specific variables and associated value differences. We have made an effort to compare "like-for-like" cases and control for other variables.

Gender Differences Worldwide

The following table provides profiles of gender differences worldwide based on interviews with male and female managers. That the differences appear to be small is, in itself, highly significant.

Why are the male and female scores so close? The women we studied were trying to make their way as managers in a predominantly male world and trying to escape the stereotypes with which women often find themselves labeled. If you were a woman in such an environment, would you adopt professionally neutral behavior, or easily burst into tears? The truth is that the way to the top in any organization is to adopt its most salient values and eschew its least salient. If anything, women in North America and northwest Europe need to work harder than men to show they are achieving individuals, measuring themselves by specific criteria and by universal yardsticks.

That said, some differences do exist, mostly on issues for which stereotypes are weaker. Women are consistently more outer-directed than men, feeling less personal control over the direction of their lives, and they are much more synchronic in their relationship to time, telescoping past, present, and future and doing things simultaneously or in parallel rather than in sequence. We suspect this difference may remain because there are no stereotypes around synchronicity as there are, for example, around female intuition (diffusion). Hence, no conscious effort is being made to live up to masculine values of sequential thinking. Women admit to being slightly more emotional than men, but even women are trying not to be emotional. If we isolate American scores (shown in the following table), we see that American men admit to showing more emotion: it is now politically correct to do so.

GENDER PROFILES

WORLD SAMPLES	MALE	FEMALE
Universalism-particularism	66	64
Individualism-communitarianism	50	52
Neutral-affective	59	56
Specific-diffuse	71	72
Achievement-ascription (of status)	60	61
Internal-external (control)	62	54
Time orientation: past/present/future	1.28/1.93/2.76	1.23/2.03/2.70
Sequence-synchronicity	5.7 (low)	4.4 (high)

ENGLISH-SPEAKING DEMOCRACIES AND NW EUROPE	MALE	FEMALE
Universalism-particularism	70	73
Individualism-communitarianism	53	56
Neutral-affective	59	57
Specific-diffuse	71	72
Achievement-ascription (of status)	60	61
Internal-external (control)	62	54
Time orientation: past/present/future	1.25/1.90/2.76	1.07/2.04/2.85
Sequence-synchronicity	6.2	5.1

LATIN CULTURES (SOUTH AMERICA, SOUTHERN EUROPE, CARIBBEAN)	MALE	FEMALE
Universalism-particularism	63	61
Individualism-communitarianism	45	46
Neutral-affective	56	53
Specific-diffuse	66	67
Achievement-ascription (of status)	52	51
Internal-external (control)	61	55
Time orientation: past/present/future	1.39/1.89/2.68	1.34/2.01/2.61
Sequence-synchronicity	5.7	5.4

ASIAN CULTURES	MALE	FEMALE
Universalism-particularism	59	54
Individualism-communitarianism	37	39
Neutral-affective	64	62
Specific-diffuse	60	56
Achievement-ascription (of status)	48	43
Internal-external (control)	51	43
Time orientation: past/present/future	1.06/2.08/2.83	1.12/2.13/2.66
Sequence-synchronicity	5.7	4.8

There is some evidence that the French want their women to be different, while Americans want their women to be the same. The American female manager is more individualistic than the male, the French female significantly less individualistic. One might ask whether organizations should seek to promote women because they are "just as good" as men, or because they are "significantly different" and corporations want the benefit of that difference. These are two good but very different reasons for promoting women.

Clearly there is no such thing as a "female culture" in the middle and upper reaches of major corporations, where our work has been done. We have not yet been able to assess situations in which women form a critical mass and make the rules of the corporation. Nor is there such a thing as a "female culture" globally. Nearly all our female respondents were outnumbered, some heavily. There could and will be a female culture when sufficient numbers join certain corporations and set the strategies of those companies. The Body Shop, the natural and ethical beauty brand, for example, is a largely female culture and is almost certainly different from male-domi-nated corporations.

We must also be wary of expecting that women managers in the West would uphold the "weaker," less popular end of the value dimensions—that is, be particularist, not universal; diffuse, not specific; ascriptive in getting status from their husbands and not achieving personally; warm rather than cold; and so forth. If men specialize in being tough and women specialize in being tender, the oppression of tenderness by toughness will not cease. Women do not play "soft" roles in US corporations, because they know they would lose if they tried! They would be seen as less "American" and hence less central to cultural life. Theirs is certainly a wise precaution.

In all this, we must not forget the emphasis on reconciliation in earlier chapters. The point is not to be tough or tender, but to be tough on problems and tender with people; not to choose between rules and particular exceptions, but to make sure that the exception proves the rule, the community nurtures its individuals, and ascribed values are achieved. The importance of women in the workforce is that, provided they are not exploited, they are capable of revealing values that are different from and yet complementary to those of men, thereby creating a synthesis of values. A strategy for both men and women is to learn to command all the value dimensions, to be individualistic enough to generate a group that develops individuals, to be universalistic enough to cover all particulars, yet to realize when an exception is so crucial that only a new universal will suffice.

Age and Generational Differences

In part our database conceals some of the differences due to "age." This is because most of our respondents are middle and senior managers in business and do not represent the full age spectrum of societies. We have not explicitly surveyed children or senior citizens to make comparisons, but recently we added students (from many nationalities) as representatives of younger age-groups.

Further, because our database contains many more cases as it continues to grow since we last reviewed this variable, with now many more longitudinal studies, we can begin to quantify such differences.

In this effort we need to differentiate (for example) between aging and ages. Thus, we might be interested in any of the following:

The cultural differences between senior managers aged 55 and junior managers aged 25 at the same period (say, 2012)

The cultural differences between managers aged 55 in 1992 and managers aged 55 in 2012

The cultural differences between a manager 15 years ago and the same manager now

The first case is what we can describe more as generational differences. What are the cultural values of the iPod/iPad generation, Generation X, and the baby boomers? All parents have strong opinions about the lifestyle and values of their children and their children's friends, compared with their own beliefs, contrasting even more with those of their own parents.

The main effects we observe involve an increasing difference between ideographic and nomothetic. Generally, from an ideographic perspective, younger people are more particularistic, more communitarian, more diffuse, and more ascription oriented (witness the rise of the celebrity culture). They are much more short term. Differences in inner- versus outer-directness follow individual rather than national trends. Thus, some younger people follow a more entrepreneurial philosophy and seek higher education to get what they want, while others are frustrated with their lack of progress after graduating, increased housing costs, changes in the meaning of family, and the breakdown in personal relationships, and they thereby may become more outer-directed. In extreme cases they may turn to religion, or to self-destruction, such as through excessive alcohol or drug taking. Such changes offer challenges to employers in the "war for talent" (retention and recruitment of employees) as well as to altruistic politicians with a concern for their "fellow man."

Considering such changes in cases in which cultures are customers, rather than employees, invites marketers to study the changing characteristics of their buyers, which we have discussed in *Marketing Across Cultures*.[5]

Because we normally keep our database anonymous to comply with the requirements of data protection as well as ethics, we have not tracked many individual managers over time to see how they have developed during the course of their careers, other than a few specific trials when they had agreed to participate. Nevertheless, we can draw inferences from comparative cases, often triangulated with interviews, and we are aided by the fact that in many situations we are still offering training programs to the same clients from years before. We generally observe a shift toward the centers of each dimension as a manager grows older. In their youth, people often have more extreme preferences, which become mellow with time. However, the observed effects are misleading in that they are really due more to the restrictions of modeling such changes with linear scales. What actually happens with age (i.e., gaining more experience in doing business and managing with other cultures) is an increase in the capacity to reconcile those differences and to develop cross-cultural competence over one's career.

Age and generational differences were studied extensively by one of our doctoral students, Dr. Kerstin Reich.[6]

Cultural Differences and Ethnicity/Diversity

An ethnic group is a social group whose members have a common cultural tradition, a common history, and a common sense of identity and exists as a subgroup in a larger society. The members of an ethnic group differ with regard to certain cultural characteristics from the other members of their society. The ethnic group may have its own language, religion, and other distinctive cultural customs.

Extremely important to the members of an ethnic group is their feeling of identification as a traditionally distinct social group. The term is usually, but not always, applied to minority groups. Ethnic groups should not be confused with, or taken as synonymous with, racial groups, although it is possible for an ethnic group to be a racial group as well (e.g., African Americans). Conceptually, ethnicity is a complex process, with multiple stages and multiple outcomes. The process begins with contact, when newcomer ethnic groups arrive but try to maintain their old culture and identity. In acculturation, ethnic identities emerge amid broadening exposure to the larger society and culture. Adaptation sees the group members trying to maintain their ethnic identity but slowly giving way to the dominant culture. The decreasing number of foreign-born members of the group are accommodated and gradually integrated, finally being assimilated into the mainstream society and culture.

Commonly recognized American ethnic groups include American Indians, Latinos, Chinese, African Americans, and European Americans. Other examples from the American ethnic experience would include Italians, Jews, the Irish, Chicanos, Puerto Ricans, and Poles. In some cases ethnicity involves merely a loose group identity, with little or no cultural traditions in common. This is so with many Irish and German Americans. In contrast, some ethnic groups are coherent subcultures with a shared language and body of tradition.

Cultural traditions manifest in daily life, but especially on significant occasions such as weddings or the birth of a new a family member.

Because these terms are used in various ways in changing situations, it is not entirely clear how "interethnic" diverges from "cultural difference." Ethnicity is, among other designations, any of the following: a "source of cultural meaning"; a "principle for social differentiation"; an act of "communicating cultural distinctiveness"; a "property of a social formation"; and an "aspect of interaction." Whatever the designation, it is commonly agreed that ethnicity is observable.

The concept of ethnicity has proven useful to domestic government agencies and international organizations trying to help ethnic minorities in polyethnic societies to advance themselves. Rather than treating the inhabitants of a developing country as culturally homogeneous, for instance, most international aid agencies now try to take into account the values, institutions, and customs of various ethnic groups, targeting relief or assistance to their particular needs.

People may show that they are proud of their specific ethnic group in a variety of ways:

- Behaving in a distinctive manner
- Living near one another
- Attending special functions
- Performing traditional rituals (e.g., wedding ceremonies)
- Wearing distinctive clothing

Ethnicity is in many contexts the single most important criterion for collective social distinctions in daily life; ethnic distinctions are rooted in perceptions of differences between lifestyles. However, even more important (and usually overlooked) is that ethnic groups often share the same meaning as their ancestors in the inner layer of culture. It is all too easy to notice the outer layers and fail to respect not only these observable differences but also the right of all people to interpret the world in the way that they choose. As with national cultures, the seven-dimensional model of culture helps us to understand these deeper differences.

The challenge for members of ethnic groups is to reconcile their own cultural heritage, and what they prefer to retain, with the norms and values of the dominant society and culture in which they live and the opportunities that derive from adapting.

The challenge for the larger community is to integrate everyone into a multicultural society.

Diversity: A Business Necessity

Diversity fundamentally means "variety." Today more than half of the US workforce consists of minorities, immigrants, and women. The challenge for business leaders, therefore, is to build and manage a diverse workforce now that employee diversity has evolved from sound public policy to a strategic business imperative.

Why should companies concern themselves with diversity? Until recently, many managers answered this question with the assertion that discrimination is wrong, both legally and morally. Today, though, managers are voicing a second notion: that a more diverse workforce will increase organizational effectiveness. It will lift morale, bring greater access to segments of the marketplace, and enhance productivity. In short, they claim, diversity is good for business.

Diversity strategies and practices are integral to facing challenges caused by economic development, mobility, and migration. They link values, ethics, and corporate responsibility to organizational effectiveness, performance, and progress by focusing on the changing nature and needs of the workforce, customers, clients, suppliers, and other stakeholders.

Most people assume that workplace diversity is about increasing representation based on one or more of the following categories:

• Race
• National origin
• Gender
• Class

In other words, it's about recruiting people from previously under-represented groups.

This undertaking often reflects a simplistic notion of equality and fairness, or a company recruits people who it thinks can relate to the customer. As an upshot, African-American M.B.A.s often find themselves marketing to inner-city communities.

Diversity goes beyond simplistic approaches. Diversity should be seen as the rich, varied perspectives and approaches that members of different groups contribute.

Diversity in the US

Some years ago in Orlando, Florida, we helped conduct a survey among (potential) participants in the city's annual national conference of the Society for Human Resource Management (SHRM) in collaboration with the Ruth Institute (Philadelphia). More than 1,000 HR specialists responded to a 60-item questionnaire developed to measure basic cultural differences. We have collected more data from more recent SHRM and other major HR conferences, and the results continue to show similar patterns as summarized in this section.

Ethnic diversity exhibits far greater differences than does gender, perhaps because women can more easily approximate men (and vice versa) than black Americans, Hispanics, American Indians, and Asian Americans can approximate Caucasians. Moreover, ethnic groups go home to their own kind. Men and women tend to go home to each other.

A voluntary association of HR specialists is significantly different from American managers as a whole. The functions people perform in a corporation, as well as their willingness to confer with those from other organizations who perform the same function, would appear to generate a diverse culture and subgroup within US business. Our SHRM sample was significantly more concerned with groups and teams (communitarianism); more inclined to base people's achievements on who they are, such as women, Native Americans, or blacks (ascription); more diffuse, such as in multiplicity of relationships; more

externally controlled by the needs of clients; and more synchronic in
conceiving of time.

This characterization resonates with the judgment that HR activities in the US are one of the places where the countercultural advocates
of the early 1970s found a working home, and that people in such a
role have a distinctive outlook shaped by the cultural rebellions of the
1960s and early 1970s. Much of the ad hoc radicalism of these times
was influenced by sympathy for oppressed minority groups, concern
for the environment, heightened awareness of injustice to women, and
similar catalysts. HR initiatives are one way of pursuing remedies in
these arenas without disruption or loss of income.

We might also note that the number of ethnic minorities with
a middle-class lifestyle and a good job was probably higher in this
sample than among US business as a whole. Problems with black,
Hispanic, Asian, or Native American workforces are often dealt with
by hiring a supervisor or an HR specialist from the ethnic group concerned, so that cultural conflicts can be resolved at managerial levels.
In short, SHRM respondents constituted a cultural mosaic, with members of minority groups not only more senior and more numerous than
in US business culture at large but also more assertive and influential.
Members of ethnic groups had reason to believe that they represented
to management the cultures from which they came.

All such considerations probably contributed to the differences we
found and the tendency of members of minority groups to remain true
to their traditions. We will go through the seven dimensions in turn.
The following table summarizes the first six.

DIVERSITY WITHIN THE SHRM CONFERENCE

	BLACK/ AFRICAN	NATIVE AMERICAN	ASIAN/ PACIFIC ISLANDER	WHITE/ CAUCASIAN	HISPANIC	OTHER
Universalism-Particularism	51	41	43	65	63	58

Individualism-Communitarianism	52	43	29	71	62	47
Neutral-Affective	35	62	71	44	32	39
Specific-Diffuse	45	32	29	67	34	45
Achievement-Ascription	52	48	56	78	61	55
Internal-External	43	22	34	69	61	46

Universalism-Particularism

You will recall the car accident that we discussed in Chapter 4. On the responses to this dilemma, differences were relatively small (see Figure 15.5). The participants at HR conferences largely share the US's high universalism, although by a significantly smaller margin: 91 to 95. Men and women are identical, both seeking to succeed or otherwise according to a common set of rules. Caucasians and Native Americans tend to pull up the universalist scores. Black Americans, Asians, and Hispanics tend to pull these down, with a minority espousing particularism and exceptionalism, believing perhaps that the "level playing

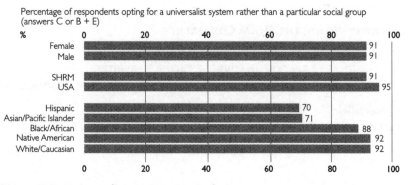

Figure 15.5. **Universalism Versus Particularism**

field" is not as fair to those of their race as is commonly supposed. In Figure 15.5 we see the percentage of respondents who would consider that their friend had no right to expect any help in court after the accident, and those who would allow the friend some right but not lie in court.

However, even among Hispanic and Asian minorities there is no major challenge to the US legal system and the need to serve it by truthful witness, even when people of your own ethnic group are facing punishment. The question used was about the traffic accident and refusing to cover up the fact that your close friend was speeding. Asians and Hispanics within the US are closer to the scores of Southeast Asia, Spain, and Latin America (Figure 4.1 in Chapter 4), but only halfway there. They are clearly divided between American universalism and the greater particularism of their traditional culture.

The Group Versus the Individual

Each of us must decide what we owe ourselves and what we owe the groups that raised us, that educated us, and that employ us. Do we start with what "I want," or do we consider our obligations? From our database, a sample of US managers answered the following question:

Two people were discussing ways in which individuals could improve the quality of life.

A. One said: "It is obvious that if individuals have as much freedom as possible and the maximum opportunity to develop themselves, the quality of their life will improve as a result."

B. The other said: "If individuals are continuously taking care of their fellow human beings, the quality of life will improve for everyone, even if it obstructs individual freedom and individual development."

Which of the two ways of reasoning do you think is usually best, A or B?

Here, in contrast to universalism-particularism, the difference between SHRM and US managerial culture as a whole is massive. Only 55 percent of human-resource professionals at the conference chose the individualist option, compared with 79 percent of US managers generally, a difference of 24 percent—larger than that between most national cultures. This is probably a result of the social conscience that motivates much HR work and the desire to develop the careers of minority aspirants. It is of interest that Caucasians are more socially oriented than Hispanics, perhaps defining themselves as "change agents" for a more inclusive society. Native Americans and Asians are more socially than individually oriented. Females are marginally more individualistic than males, perhaps fearing that they will be taken advantage of if they are too altruistic.

Female individualism is characteristic of the US. In most other countries men are significantly more individualistic. Female "liberation" has been defined in the US as making it in a male competitive arena. Consequently, women tend to score even more like men.

To Show or Not to Show Our Emotions

There are valid reasons for showing our emotions—how else can other people keep us happy and know what we want? There are also valid reasons for emotional restraint and neutrality: for reserving our expressions of feelings for important occasions, not making demands, not ruffling feathers, being attuned to soft signals. There is no "bet-

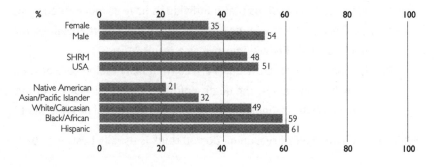

Figure 15.6. **Neutral Versus Affective**

ter way." Cultures have conventions about how much or little you show and draw their conclusions about your mood, pain, and pleasure accordingly. We posed the following question:

Please indicate the degree to which you agree or disagree with the following statement (a = strongly agree, b = agree, c = undecided, d = disagree, e = strongly disagree): In retrospect I very often think I have given away too much in my enthusiasm.

We can see from Figure 15.6 that among HR professional men, showing more emotion is considered good—54 percent report wearing their hearts on their sleeves. They are improving their EQ (emotional quotient) and showing the sensitivity practiced by facilitation. Good HR men should be "in touch with themselves." Women eschew affectivity in much larger numbers: 65 percent choose neutrality, only 35 percent affectivity. They probably calculate that for them to succeed, the stereotype of the "hysterical woman" must be left even further behind. Once again, we see that American women are on a different path from that of women in most of the rest of the world, who admit to being more affective than men.

Among ethnic minorities, Hispanics judge themselves as more excitable based on the norms of their US culture, closely followed by black Americans. Asian Americans and Native Americans are emphatically neutral and rarely give themselves away. HR professionals as a group may also be fighting the "touchy-feely" stereotype. They are less affective than US managers as a whole.

How Far Do We Get Involved?

Closely related to whether we show emotions in dealing with other people is the degree to which we engage others in specific areas of our lives and single levels of personality, versus diffusely in multiple areas of our lives and at several levels of personality at the same time.

In specific-oriented cultures a manager segregates the task relationship he or she has with a subordinate from other dealings. That may sound perfectly reasonable, but in some cultures every life space and every level of personality can permeate all others. Ethnic differences are evident under the headings of specificity and diffuseness. The range is illustrated by responses to the following situations:

A boss asks a subordinate to help him paint his house. The subordinate, who doesn't feel like doing it, discusses the situation with a colleague.

A. The colleague argues: "You don't have to paint the house if you don't feel like it. He is your boss at work. Outside he has little authority."

B. The subordinate argues: "Despite the fact that I don't feel like it, I will paint it. He is my boss, and you can't ignore that outside of work either."

In specific societies status is confined to the job at hand and does not extend to situations in general. If I meet my boss in the bowling alley, where he is a novice and I am a champion, I will treat him like the novice he is, not rudely but realistically. Back at work, he instructs me.

The scores on this question are summarized in Figure 15.7. The really extraordinary difference is between US managers as a whole—89 percent of them reject the boss's diffuse authority and its influence beyond the workplace—and SHRM members, only 52 percent

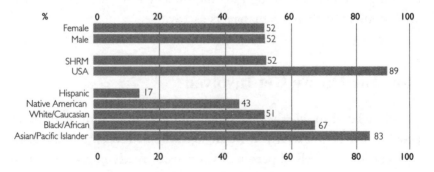

Figure 15.7. Specific Versus Diffuse

of whom reject diffuse thinking. What makes SHRM members so different? Why do they have a strong tendency toward diffuseness even in a situation as seemingly open and shut as this one?

One reason might be that HR management is not, in fact, a specific function or task within corporations, in the way that sales, R&D, and finance are. HR personnel are responsible for employees in whatever department they work. There is no part of the organization in which human processes operate where HR is not involved. HR representatives may be called in and consulted on any human problem affecting the company. Because their authority is diffuse and crosses boundaries, so does the way they think.

Once again there is no male-female divide on this topic. A small majority would decline to paint their boss's house, but 48 percent of both genders would agree. Members of minority groups who belong to the SHRM are even more diffuse in their thinking. We have seen that "human resources" pervade every department, but so does being black, being Asian, being an American Indian, and being Hispanic. In so far as being a minority person is a problem, that problem diffuses everywhere, and the solution—nondiscrimination—diffuses everywhere too. Being Hispanic is not simply a problem in accounting; it is a challenge in general for that person in all departments.

Minority groups also bring their own cultures to the US. Hispanics and Asians come from more diffuse cultures such as Mexico, Puerto Rico, Colombia, the Philippines, and Taiwan. It takes time to assimilate, and it may not be wise to try. Highly cohesive ethnic groups, specifically the Japanese Americans and Jews, have been among the most successful in the US, and they have generally kept their cultures intact.

Is High Status Earned
Through Achievement or Ascribed?

All societies give certain members higher status than others, signaling that unusual attention should be focused on such people and their activities. While some societies accord status to people on the basis of their achievements, others ascribe it to them by virtue of age, class, gender, education, position, project, or bearing. Hence, the curator of a museum, surrounded as she is by beautiful things, has taste, refinement, and sensibility ascribed to her. It is, in contrast, hard to say what she has achieved—perhaps a successful exhibition—but her association with the museum is probably stronger. A star salesman of aluminum siding, though, is identified by his sales record and the bonuses he earns. Status comes, if at all, from his success at selling and very little else. Status, thus, either is achieved by success at some task or calling or is ascribed to people because the culture they live in likes what they are.

Achievement-oriented cultures justify their hierarchies by claiming that senior people have "achieved more" for the organization; their authority, justified by skill and knowledge, benefits the organization.

Ascription-oriented organizations justify their hierarchies by "power to get things done." This may consist of power over people and be coercive, or power through people, which is participative. There is a high variation within ascriptive cultures, and participative power has well-known advantages. Whatever form power takes, it is intended to advance the values to which status has been ascribed and thereby help the organization realize its vision through managers who personify it.

Ascribing cultures tend to accord status to "natural" characteristics that "naturally" evoke admiration, such as older and wiser people, those with dignity and presence, beautiful and elegant women, highly qualified experts, and those running projects generally thought to be important: the Head Start program, the Peace Corps, the Equal Employment Opportunity Commission.

Within HR doctrine there is also a strong current of opinion that members of minority groups must accept their ethnicity, as being blacks, Asians, Native Americans, Hispanic Americans, or whatever the qualifier. In order to do this, ascription would need to be placed first: "I am a black American and achieve as a black American, holding open the door to fellow blacks and acting as a role model for them."

It is commonly believed among HR professionals that without this ethnic identification, the success of minority members merely reinforces the dominant achievement ethos, so that successful blacks,

Percentage of respondents who (strongly) disagree that men and women are treated differently

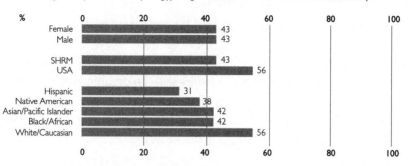

Figure 15.8. Achievement Versus Ascription

Hispanics, or women are used to prove that no further assistance is needed for those groups. The best of them will achieve on their own.

This may help explain the much higher achievement ethic among American managers in general than among HR professionals attending the conference. The scores are shown in Figure 15.8 in response to the statement, "In our society men and women are treated significantly differently."

Those who thought that treatment was significantly different would attribute this difference to ascriptive norms; those who denied this difference would attribute women's lower pay and position to their nonachievement, a fair and logical consequence. The figure shows the extent to which "different treatment" was rejected. Forty-three percent of both men and women regard the opportunities of men and women to achieve to be roughly equivalent. Women do not complain more than men about difference in treatment, perhaps because at least some women are confident of achieving and see this anticipated achievement as their route to the top, versus protesting against inequality.

It is a different story for nonwhites, who complain of discrimination (against women) in far larger proportions than do Caucasians or American managers in general. Sixty-nine percent of Hispanics, 62 percent of Native Americans, and 58 percent of black and Asian Americans see the playing field as not level for women and almost certainly not level for themselves.

Control or Be Controlled:
American Belief in Inner-Directedness

The next dimension concerns the idealized relationship between humans and the environment. Cultures with an organic view of nature see human beings as immersed within and therefore part of the larger ecosystem. To survive, we "go with the flow," adapt to natural forces, and allow ourselves to be outwardly directed.

Other cultures have a more mechanical view of themselves as controlling, mastering, and subjecting nature, as one might plough a field or clear a forest and harness natural laws to do one's bidding. Such a view is directed inward and "puts you in the driver's seat," to quote a Hertz advertisement. Francis Bacon declared that "knowledge is power." Through scientific advances we demonstrate to each other that nature can be predicted and controlled: we even "master" business administration and "call the shots."

As mentioned in Chapter 10, the American psychologist J. B. Rotter developed a scale designed to measure whether people had an internal locus of control, typical of more successful Americans, or an external locus of control, typical of relatively less successful Americans, disadvantaged by their circumstances or shaped by the competitive efforts of their rivals.[7] Outer-directed people tend to bewail their "bad luck" and cry foul.

We used the questions he devised to assess our SHRM and US managers' relationship with natural events. The answers suggest that there are some significant differences here among geographic areas. These questions all take the form of alternatives; managers were asked to select the statement they believed better reflected reality. The first of these pairs was as follows:

A. Becoming a great success is a matter of hard work; luck has little or nothing to do with it.

B. Getting a good job depends mainly on being in the right place at the right time.

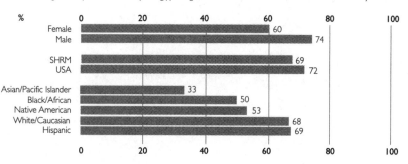

Figure 15.9. **Internal Versus External**

Figure 15.9 shows the percentage of respondents who chose answer A, the inner-directed choice. These scores are in line with what we find elsewhere in the world: males believing that much more of their destiny is in their own control. Females seem to be significantly more outer-directed.

HR specialists are somewhat less inner-directed than US managers as a whole, 69 percent to 72 percent. Perhaps they experience the necessity of having to consult widely and to "grow" people rather than direct them. Perhaps they had been consulted on cases of injustice to minorities. Still, the difference is small. Female HR personnel are considerably more outer-directed: 60 percent to 74 percent. Women may feel that their careers depend largely on being liked and on unknowable responses from men. Hispanics are marginally more inner-directed than Caucasians, a reflection possibly of the macho tradition of the irresistible man. But Asians, African Americans, and Native Americans, true to most of the cultures from which they come, are preponderantly outer-directed (between 33 percent and 53 percent), and this may be more a matter of aesthetics than of oppression, of being in harmony with the universe.

Ethnic minorities tend to be criticized whatever they do: for being "too pushy" if inner-directed, or "too passive" and quiet if outer-directed. Women are also caught in this trap. Being stereotyped as gentle "by nature," they easily offend men if they are inner-directed or assertive. Even in HR positions they feel generally less secure and

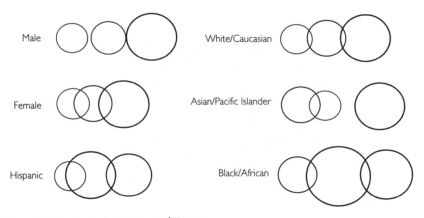

Figure 15.10. **Past, Present, and Future**

more at the mercy of outside events and unforeseeable contingencies. This may be a realistic reflection of their lower pay and seniority.

How Is Time Organized in the US?

If only because managers need to coordinate their business activities, they require some kind of shared expectations about time. Just as different cultures have different assumptions about how people relate to one another, so they approach time differently.

This orientation is about the relative importance a culture gives to the past, present, and future. As we quoted Saint Augustine in Chapter 9: "The present has . . . three dimensions: the present of past things, the present of present things, and the present of future things."

The question posed was Tom Cottle's circles test used earlier in the book, but modified in Figure 15.10 for different ethnic and minority groups.

While the differences in the relative sizes of the circles were not significant for men and women, the degree of overlap was. In fact, it is the most startling contrast in this chapter. Men think sequentially, viewing past, present, and future as passing us in a straight line like a train. Women think of past, present, and future as synchronized and merged within the mind as interactive, parallel processes. Perhaps women have been free to deviate so widely from men in this respect because no negative stereotypes have been brandished to bring them into line.

This particular characteristic of female mental processing is not a topic of reproach or ridicule; we have not yet discovered the extent of its ramifications. What it does suggest, though, is that American women, at least, have an integrative capacity and orientation not exhibited by most men, and it raises the provocative question as to whether they may not be more adept at dilemma reconciliation, getting the two ends of our various dimensions to work together. Certainly this will be our next hypothesis for testing. Women, subject to demands from men and children, may simply be more adept at responding to simultaneous inputs.

We can also see from our database that women most resemble Asian Americans and indeed the cultures of Japan and Southeast Asia generally in their orientation to time. (See Chapter 9.) In light of especially high scores on satisfaction for North American women posted to Southeast Asia and Latin America, and as recently reported by Nancy Adler, we may be witnessing a coincidental meeting of the minds and a possible advantage for women working overseas.[8]

There is a tendency for ethnic groups subject to the most discrimination, blacks and Hispanics, to regard the present as most important. This may reveal a strong desire to "make it" now and an impatience with slow emancipation, but without further investigation we cannot be sure.

Functional Diversity

Although not as strong as international differences, differences among functional areas are still significant and dominant.

A manager at the Dutch multinational Philips once told us that in the 1980s Philips was known as a company with outstanding research-and-development activities (patents in small audiocassettes, Video System 2000, and basic compact disc technology are just a few examples) and an impressive marketing and sales operation. Despite these excellent credentials, Philips was close to bankruptcy in some crucial business areas in the early 1990s. The problem, according to this manager, was that functional discussions of manufacturing, marketing, and R&D were not well coordinated.

In a related matter, consider Western medicine. It seems to work quite well within medical specialties, but in light of the more than a thousand known iatrogenic (doctor-caused) diseases, many patients turn to holistic medicine, such as homeopathy, despite the fact that the efficacies of such practices are not confirmed. What are called "side effects" in Western medicine are the displacement of symptoms from one specialty to another.

The whole pattern of Western cultures shows greater emphasis on differentiating functions than on integrating them. We hear quite a bit about the "division of labor" but too little about its integration.

To highlight functional differences, we use the case of a large chemical company that has had problems launching a new product, owing to miscommunication among functions. Some typical comments from three functions illustrate the problem.

> **Marketing:** If manufacturing would just once get its act together, we could serve our customers so much better and more quickly. In manufacturing they take too much time to readjust their setups.
>
> **R&D:** Marketing people in general and their sales force in particular sell before the products have been tested properly. They do the quick and dirty stuff, and we get the blame if it is not up to standard.
>
> **Manufacturing:** Both R&D and marketing have no clue about what our problems are. We are continuously put under pressure from both sides to speed up. When we don't have a technical problem, it is a social one.
>
> **Marketing:** Of course we put the system under pressure. If we didn't, it would take forever for R&D and manufacturing to get their act together.

FUNCTIONAL DIVERSITY

FUNCTION	UNIVERSALISM-PARTICULARISM	INDIVIDUALISM-COMMUNITARI-ANISM	NEUTRAL-AFFECTIVE	SPECIFIC-DIFFUSE	ACHIEVEMENT-ASCRIPTION	INTERNAL-EXTERNAL
Administration	64	32	72	75	80	49
Finance	76	51	62	76	63	62
HR	78	42	56	67	54	52
Legal	79	56	62	72	55	65
Manufacturing	63	52	54	78	72	59
Marketing	53	61	57	79	82	80
Public affairs	53	81	58	92	38	42
R&D	74	52	60	66	78	69

Manufacturing: Why don't we create cross-functional task forces? It is just a lack of communication. Often R&D and marketing have information we don't get.

R&D: In order to be innovative, we need to be left alone for a while. Too often we are asked to repair things on existing products. In order to be first in the market, we need to push our technology.

Most people will recognize these comments. The occurrence of these cross-functional tensions partly depends on the type of organization and the way it is structured. Our research shows that there might be deeper cultural reasons for miscommunication across functional teams. These tensions were examined within our US sample, in order to avoid influences by nationality. Further research, however, indicates that these tensions hold across nationalities. Consider the following table, which shows some significant differences.

Universalism-Particularism

The highest universalist scores are found among legal, financial, R&D, and HR managers. Following the rules is an obvious point of departure even for HR people. For them it looks like a countermeasure against too many particularist demands by the workforce.

On the other extreme, we see the significantly more particularistic public affairs, manufacturing, and marketing (including sales) scores. These areas are apparently more stimulated by the particular case than the universal rule coming from R&D, legal affairs, and finance. This reflects one of the main challenges that need to be reconciled in Western business. The universal truth of legal and R&D people needs to become the foundation for marketing and salespeople to adapt to the particular needs of the market.

Individualism-Communitarianism

We would expect a definite individualistic score for marketing and a group-oriented score for HR, manufacturing, and administrative job holders. This expectation is confirmed. The highest individualist score, however, is found among those in public affairs. Finance, R&D, and legal represent average scores.

Neutrality-Affectivity

Our data indicate that the most neutral of functional cultures are found in R&D and finance, and expressive employees are, as could be predicted, found in marketing (in particular, sales) and production functions. The most neutral people seem to be in the administrative functions. This is partly explained by the fact that the highest percentage of female participation is found in this job category. As discussed earlier, female administrative staff need to avoid falling into the male trap of believing that true professionals go for a heart attack rather than showing emotions.

Specificity-Diffuseness

On the specific side, the top scores are in marketing, manufacturing, and public affairs, while HR and R&D are patently diffuse in their approach. This is confirmed by the fact that the latter two seem to be at one with their clients (HR) and ideas (R&D). If you criticize them, it is seen as a personal confrontation that involves some loss of face. Marketing people tend to be much more open to brainstorming, during which they might tear your brain into pieces, but no problem: "next brain"!

Achievement-Ascription

In the orientation of status we see the highest achievers among marketing and production people, while status seems to be more connected to ascribed criteria (e.g., formal titles) and other personal background (e.g., age, gender) in legal, HR, and public affairs.

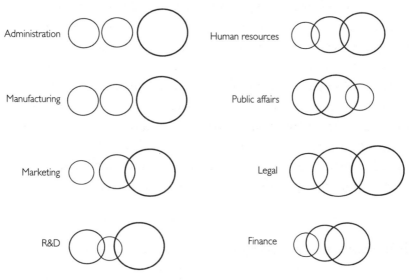

Figure 15.11. **Past, Present, and Future**

Internal-External Control

Although marketing scores have been very similar to those of salespeople, for internal versus external orientation we see marketing people at the extreme of internal control, while salespeople score at the extreme end of the external orientation (score 41). Marketing is joined by R&D on the inner-directed side, while administrative workers join sales and public affairs in other- or outer-directedness. Legal, finance, public affairs, and manufacturing scores are average. This makes sense if we view the essence of selling products as empathizing with clients' needs. Marketing, on the other hand, is more distant from the actual client and analyzes market segments, product/market combinations, and "grids" in preference to reality.

Time Orientation

The final dimension relates to time. Notable differences are unearthed here. We can see in Figure 15.11 that people from marketing share a predominant future orientation combined with a past that is best ignored. In R&D we see a fairly large future combined with a relatively small present and again a fairly large past. It seems that R&D is about re-creating the corporate future through the experiences and knowledge accumulation of the past. Public affairs staff has a relatively dominant present orientation with a relatively small future. Interesting to note is that administrative function and manufacturing seem to share a sequential approach, as is reflected in a low overlap between the circles they drew. Problems are perceived to be current and need to be solved now or, even better, yesterday. HR people seem to be the most balanced in terms of time orientation and combine this balance with a large overlap frequently expressing synchronicity.

Diversity in Industries

While ethnic groups and functions show significant differences, so do industrial groups (see the following table). As with the other cultural

Industry Diversity

INDUSTRY	UNIV.-PART.	IND.-COMM.	NEUT.-AFF.	SPEC.-DIFF.	ACH.-ASC.	INT.-EXT.	PAST	PRESENT	FUTURE
Academia	56	55	45	57	56	56	2.3	1.9	2.1
Aerospace	60	46	49	60	61	61	1.9	2.1	1.9
Automotive	41	29	45	54	75	75	1.9	1.8	2.1
Beverages	53	55	41	35	56	56	2.2	1.8	2.0
Chemicals	50	50	56	35	56	56	2.0	2.0	1.9
Computers	53	50	49	57	51	51	1.9	2.1	1.9
Construction	25	69	56	44	36	36	1.5	2.0	2.1
Detergents	36	29	37	36	41	41	1.7	2.1	2.0
Electronics	50	69	66	41	54	54	2.0	1.9	2.0
Financial Services	60	65	56	53	41	41	2.2	1.9	2.0
Food/Beverages	41	75	59	47	61	61	1.7	1.9	2.0
Government	36	37	75	57	25	25	2.0	2.0	1.8
Leisure	75	25	37	51	61	61	1.9	2.1	1.9
Metal	38	50	41	60	44	44	1.7	1.9	2.1
Mining	67	69	33	75	49	49	1.7	2.1	2.0
Oil	41	46	37	25	36	36	2.2	2.0	1.8
Pharmaceuticals	63	50	59	55	56	56	1.9	2.0	2.0
Telecom	44	46	63	25	41	41	2.2	2.0	1.8
Textiles	47	37	25	38	33	33	2.2	2.1	1.7

groups, these differences are the result of frequently recurring problems and dilemmas that are solved almost automatically. It is not puzzling that a group of banking people have a different time orientation from that of an employee of a high-tech firm. And would you expect a bank culture to nurture an ascribed status system more than a culture in the textile industry?

Some remarkable differences, though, are found in universalism-particularism. People in health (such as hospitals) and academia score on the very universalist side of the scale, while people in detergents, metal, and government seem to ride more on the particular wave. The most universalistic of cultures can be found in pharmaceuticals, financial services, and the leisure industry—would you like them to ignore the rules? Does it come as news that individualism tends to be high in academia, mining, financial services, and the construction industry, while government and automotive tend to be more oriented toward the group?

Individualism seems to be well developed in industries in which it might help obtain better products and services, such as in academia. The fact that oil companies, along with the motor, metals, and chemicals industries, are more communitarian in orientation is explained by the importance of shifts in their production facilities. Teamwork is the name of the game.

The leisure professions, textiles, and mining seem to be more expressive in emotions than their colleagues in the automotive, computer and electronics industries, and government. No comments are necessary here, since it seems self-explanatory.

Would you expect a government official who deals with your car taxes to be well informed about the planning of utilities in your neighborhood? If you are developing a microchip in the electronics industry, would you have as broad a scope as those who work in a refinery? Obviously you would expect different orientations. We observe diffuse orientations in aerospace, detergents, and the oil industry, while specificity seems popular among government and the electronics, telecommunications, and food industries.

In analyzing the way different industries accord status, we find high achievers in transportation equipment, aerospace, food, and government, while mining, textiles, and detergents seem to favor ascribed status.

Differences in loci of control are significant. Inner-directed cultures are, naturally enough, found in the food, computer, aerospace, and car industries, while other- or outer-directed cultures seem to be more successful in detergents (marketing driven), mining, and government.

Finally, we observe significantly different time orientations. Some are obvious. In interpreting the circles, we find very past-oriented financial services and textiles industries. The computer, aerospace, and telecommunications industries seem to be occupied by the present, which in view of their fast-changing environments can be an altogether reasonable orientation. The cultures that seem to need a future-oriented approach are detergents, oil, and the automotive industry: lower in technology but higher in the need to plan for the future.

General Conclusions

It must be emphasized that the data we have been discussing are averages of a variety of scores within a certain national group. We have found that ethnic differences within societies such as South Africa and, to a lesser degree, the US can be as big as international differences.

We have also analyzed other potential sources of major differences within national samples, such as gender, age, hierarchical level, and industrial and functional background. We can indeed conclude that national differences in value orientations are a major source of cultural diversity, but that other factors do account for a large portion of the diversity we find within a national culture.

Elsewhere in this book we stress that explanations regarding what is happening to cultures need a conceptual framework that is based on more than just a model of linear dimensions.

We believe that any researcher following a quest for a simple model that explains all the requisite variety of cultures is doomed to fail; it needs more than a simple linear model. The simple question of what the culture of country X is cannot be answered (and probably never could), without explaining or controlling for the context, religion, gender, generational differences, and other parameters, including whether we are discussing ideographic or nomothetic perspectives. These components, which contribute to the variance in our dimensions of culture, or any other linear model, can be determined only by sophisticated statistical analyses. As previously noted, we have found that the move to at least a two-dimensional model for each dimension has advanced the subject significantly.

Notes

1. See both Appendix A and our various research publications.
2. Although the raw data show considerable scatter, the trends lines are statistically significant at the 95 percent level especially when the raw data are controlled for job function and industry.
3. Also significant at the 95 percent level.
4. N. Broom, "I Work, Therefore I Am: The Ideographic-Nomothetic Dilemma" (thesis for the degree of doctor of business administration, Anglia Ruskin University, UK).
5. F. Trompenaars and P. Woolliams, *Marketing Across Cultures* (Capstone/Wiley, 2004).
6. K. Reich, "Exploring Age and Generational Differences in Culture" (thesis for the degree of doctor of business administration, Anglia Ruskin University, UK, 2006).
7. J. B. Rotter, "General Expectations for Internal Versus External Control of Reinforcement," Psychological Monograph 609 (1966): 1–28.
8. N. Adler, ed., *Competitive Frontiers* (Oxford: Basil Blackwell, 1994).

Summary and Conclusions

Sustainability: Securing the Long-Term Success of the Organization

We have traveled a long way since our early interest in cultural differences, during which time the world has evolved even further toward a global village. All organizations face difficult challenges during these difficult times; their initial approach to try to solve them is usually rooted in their culture and past behaviors. As we have said right from the beginning of this book, overadherence to any one established model, from "scientific management," to a "Theory Y" human-resource dimension basis, customer orientation, shareholder value, and corporate social responsibility, has been shown over time to be unduly restrictive when applied in isolation. A new embracing framework is required that meets the dynamics and competing demands of modern (global) business and that secures the business benefits of cultural differences.

When we reflect on the content, which extends from personal cultural orientations, to corporate culture, diversity and inclusion, major demographic and population changes, and, not the least, new technologies, we can conclude with justification that long-term success needs to be based on a reconciliation of the dilemmas created by the competing demands arising from the fundamental components described in classic general system theory—namely, those of internal business processes, employees, shareholders, society, and customers. New solutions are required that are grounded in a strategy that is aligned with the organization's values. *In other words, we need to link cultural differences more explicitly to the bottom line.*

"Organizational sustainability" is not limited to the fashionable environmental factors such as emissions control, green energy, savings of scarce resources, and corporate social responsibility. The future strength of an organization depends on the way leadership and management deal with the tensions among the five previously stated entities: business processes, people, clients, shareholders, and society. The manner in which these tensions are addressed and resolved determines the future strength and opportunities of an organization. The task for today is to connect and integrate these drivers in ways that are more than just compromise.

We have collected and analyzed some 8,000 of these tensions from our Web-based surveys from across the globe, which include the top Fortune 500 global companies and familiar household names, through to more local or specialist companies. From this we have identified the frequently recurring "10 Golden Dilemmas" that exist among these five components. (See Appendix B.)

Component	Sectional Interest
Business processes	Corporate effectiveness
Employees	Employee development and learning
Shareholders	Shareholder return, financial performance, and growth
Clients, customers, and suppliers	Satisfaction
Society at large	Contributions to society

These combinations of recurring dilemmas are listed in the following table with a relatively high level of abstraction. In practice we help clients restate them in terms of how they apply more specifically in their own organization.

On the One Hand	Golden Dilemma	On the Other Hand
(B: Employees)—We need to develop our people	1	**(A: Business Processes)**—We need to become more cost conscious and results oriented
(B: Employees)—We need to motivate and reward our people	2	**(C: Shareholders)**—We need to satisfy our shareholders
(A: Business Processes)—We need to focus on cash flow and working capital	3	**(E: Society)**—We need to serve the wider community in a sustainable and responsible way
(E: Society)—We need to supply products and services that enhance our reputation in the wider community	4	**(D: Clients/Customers/Suppliers)**—We need to supply products that our clients and customers specifically want
(A: Business Processes)—We need to supply global (or standardized) products/services	5	**(D: Clients/Customers/Suppliers)**—We need to supply products/services that respond to local tastes and needs
(B: Employees)—We need to educate customers with new solutions we can offer	6	**(D: Clients/Customers/Suppliers)**—We need to keep the customer in focus ahead of our own personal preference
(B: Employees)—We need to retain equal opportunities for all existing staff	7	**(E: Society)**—We need to apply some positive discrimination in areas of recruitment

(C: Shareholders)— We need to cut costs wherever we can for the sake of our shareholders' return	8	**(A: Business Processes)**— We need to invest for long-term sustainability
(C: Shareholders)— We need to maximize shareholder return from our existing business	9	**(E: Society)**—We need to adapt to the future as society evolves
(D: Clients/Customers/ Suppliers)—We need to satisfy our clients'/ customers' needs at all costs	10	**(C: Shareholders)**— We need to satisfy our shareholders

The Challenges for Securing Long-Term Success

Every organization seems to have different priorities when focusing on these dilemmas that need to be reconciled in order to achieve long-term success. It is not a matter of choosing one extreme, or side, of the dilemma, nor adopting a compromise (that will always be lose-lose). There would be nonstop culture clashes, and by "culture" we mean not simply the cultures of different nations but also those of different disciplines, functions, genders, classes, and so on.

Assessing Corporate Performance

We described our OVP (Organization Values Profiler) in Chapter 14. When the OVP is applied to assessing corporate performance in the arena of the golden dilemmas, we use combinations of questions that capture *both* sides of the dilemma. For example: "We are able to meet short-term demands without compromising our long-term vision" and "We integrate the products/services we develop with the evolving needs of the client/customer in mind."

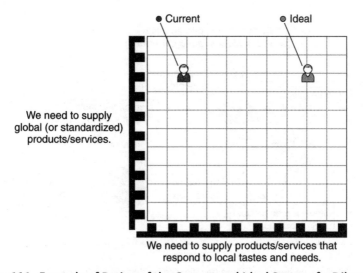

Figure 16.1. **Example of Rating of the Current and Ideal Status of a Dilemma on an x-y Grid**

We also invite respondents to place their organization on two-dimensional grids to obtain the current-versus-ideal state of each dilemma. (See Figure 16.1.)

As expected, such measurements are culturally determined. A US corporate giant is likely to be currently more focused on exporting its standard product worldwide, whereas a Taiwanese exporter may be more concerned with supplying a multiplicity of products to meet local needs through high-tech manufacturing, which can lower costs of small production runs.

We also assess the current status of the dilemma against an ideal state that would result when the business benefits have been realized. We are then in a position to evaluate the business benefits against the costs, time scales to realize the benefits, and the degree to which the dilemma solutions are located in one profit center or involve cooperation across multiple business units. (See Figure 16.2.)

This type of analysis provides an objective evaluation of where the highest return on investment can be achieved in resolving cultural conflicts and thus secures the best benefits to the business.

In this particular example, the most important cultural dilemma to be addressed was the need for technology push (what the company

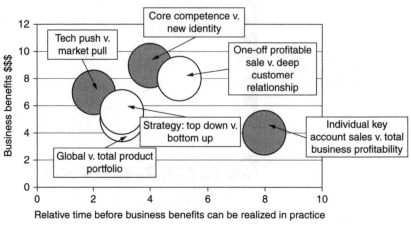

Figure 16.2. **Dilemma Portfolio Analysis**

can make from its own intellectual capital) versus what the different markets want (what the organization could sell).

When applied to major decisions such as these, involving high levels of funding and human capital, such analytical approaches help leaders to validate their tacit insights by making them explicit and open to debate.

Linking Culture to Business Performance

Many of the conceptual frameworks for explicating culture are based on describing how different cultures give different meanings to relationships with people, their interaction with the environment, their orientation to time, and similar cultural dimensions. Likewise, much attention has been given to the recognition and respect for cultural differences. However, if we limit ourselves to only these first two stages, we run the risk of supporting only stereotypical views on cultures.

So our agenda follows the logic that in order for an organization to secure long-term success, the cultural dilemmas between the various stakeholders need to be reconciled. In so far as innovation could be defined essentially as combining values that are not easily joined, this process is created by and leads to innovation. It is innovative capability—from process to product, from R&D to HR—that will make an organization sustainable. And that is far more than just corporate social responsibility.

APPENDIX A

Assessing Cultural Competence

W<small>E HAVE</small> emphasized from the start that we have not followed the "blind leading the blind" researchers who continue to try to describe and measure culture on linear scales. As we have repeatedly shown, approaches of that type are thwarted by difficulties in trying to make them free of cultural bias. These linear scales might be of interest to anthropologists in exploring historical acculturations, but they do not help business leaders and managers overcome cultural differences or derive business benefits from joining different cultural values. Although we continue to use our original linear dimensions of culture in the early stages of any training or development to explain the underlying constructs, we seek to progress quickly to more comprehensive approaches. We summarize here how we assess cultural competence as a precursor to development.

Even without the complexity of the cultural context, confusion arises over the use of the term *competence* in different cultures. It is applied variously to denote the capacity of an individual but also as an element of a job role. Popularity of the term has its origins in the research of the McBer Consultancy in the late 1970s in the US as part of an initiative by the American Management Association to identify the characteristics that distinguish superior from average managerial performance. The work was encapsulated in the seminal book *The Competent Manager* (Boyatzis 1982). Thus was spawned a mass of literature and initiatives in organizational attempts to identify and construct the "competent" manager.

However, the term and its related concepts have become problematic as they have been appropriated and adapted to different environments. Some practitioners prefer to define the term as "an underlying characteristic of a person." It could be a motive, a trait, a skill, an aspect of a person's self-image or social role, or a body of knowledge that a person uses. Others would use the variant *competency* and define it as "a set of behavior patterns that the incumbent needs to bring to a position in order to perform its tasks and functions with competence." Furthermore, the terms *skill* and *competence* are often used interchangeably. In discussions of management training needs-analysis or organizational review and development, most authors fail to clarify which of these meanings they are ascribing to *competence*. Such differences amount to more than just American versus European usage. (See the following table.)

EXTREME DEFINITIONS

SINGULAR	PLURAL	DEFINITION
competency	competencies	The skills and knowledge that employees must have, or must acquire, to *input* into a situation in order to achieve high levels of performance (*what you know*—skills and knowledge) [Definition more commonly used in the US]
competence	competences	A system of minimum standards and effective behaviors demonstrated by performance and *outputs* (*what you do*—how you apply your knowledge in practice) [Definition more commonly used in Europe]

The recruitment and selection of employees for assignments over many years has left many organizations staffed by people comfortable with the old ways of working, or old paradigms. The greater the need for global change, the greater the likelihood that new blood will be required, not simply to replace losses due to depletion and retirement but also to bring in new key skills. Selecting the right person for a post is a fundamental decision for HR, and various tools and systems have been developed to support the decision-making process. There is considerable pressure on HR to make sound decisions in recruitment: on the one hand to hire the right person, on the other to avoid discrimination; on the one hand so the appointee can do the current job well, on the other to grow the job in the future. HR faces a series of such dilemmas.

We have been surprised to find in our many interactions with the HR community and HR professionals that there are few or no conceptual frameworks and corresponding instruments that serve these needs. Instead, we have frequently observed the continued use of established models such as MBTI, 16PF, or DISC without any adaptation or regard to cultural factors—within the instrument itself or even in the interpretation or application of any data generated. We have also observed the use of poorly constructed tools—often (literally) made up—that had not been subjected to any critical development or evaluation, purely because the practitioner was desperate for something to help. In many cases the latter were the worst possible (because they do not measure competence or predictors of performance) and were often based on questions about "dos and don'ts" in specific cultural situations. For instance: (a) When in Dubai, should you give your business card at the start or end of a meeting? (b) When making a list of delegates to a multicultural meeting, should you sort and print their names by surname or given name—remembering that some cultures (e.g., China) normally use their family name followed by a given name?

Toward Cultural Competence

With this situation in mind, we recently assembled our Cultural Competence Profiler and an associated research database to explore differences across cultures. We describe this new conceptual idea and its origins, not simply to promote this particular instrument, but to provide a forum so that other practitioners and researchers may develop and/or adapt these ideas for their own situations and circumstances. We have not found parallel or competitive models with which we could have made comparisons and certainly not any that have been published to lay their frameworks open to such critique.

Our model is an attempt to describe and measure certain modes of thought, sensitivities, intellectual skills, and explanatory capacities that might contribute to the formation of hypercultural competence. Our research reveals the need to embrace several paradigms.

The evidence from our formal academic research (by our cohorts of Ph.D. candidates) combined with our practitioner-led, client-based consulting suggests that we should differentiate between and include different layers. The following table illustrates how we would thus separate and define the components of hypercultural competence (hypercultural competence being the total of all subunits).

We therefore sought to extend our models to allow for the integration of cultural differences—that is, the process of reconciliation.

Extending the Seven Dimensions of Culture Model: Response to Dilemmas

We experimented with several alternatives to overcome the known limitations. One of our first new questionnaires featured multiple-choice questions describing alternate courses of action to respond to dilemmas. The different combinations of answers that can be selected are intended to probe whether the respondent does the following:

- Maintains his or her own standpoint and rejects reconciliation (win-lose)
- Tends to abandon his or her own values and reject reconciliation—"When in Rome . . ." (lose-win)
- Seeks a compromise position (lose-lose)
- Seeks to reconcile the seemingly opposing orientations (win-win)

The value systems underlying each dilemma that is posed originate in one of the seven dimensions of culture within our model. This means

SUBLEVELS OF HYPERCULTURAL COMPETENCE

			OUTCOME
CULTURAL COMPETENCE	Cross-cultural competence	The capability to function according to the cultural rules of more than one cultural system; the ability to respond in culturally sensitive and appropriate ways according to the cultural demands of a given situation	Avoid blunders Avoid embarrassment Avoid exhibiting ethnocentricity
	Intercultural competence	The capability to communicate successfully and collaborate effectively with people of other cultures through recognition of differences and respect for other points of view	Communicate and work with other cultures
	Transcultural competence	The capability to connect different points of view through the elicitation of dilemmas and their reconciliation	Reconcile differences
		The capability to deliver the business benefits of cultural reconciliation through servant leadership	Leverage business benefits
	Intracultural competence (aka servant leadership)	The capability to leverage cultural and/or ethnic diversity and differences within teams	Manage and leverage business benefits of diverse teams and employees

that the question can be used to simultaneously identify the respondent's value orientation (e.g., preferences for rule or exceptions, individualism or communitarianism) *and* his or her propensity to reconcile.

Where appropriate, respondents were also asked to indicate how they believe others in their organization might answer.

Example question: Dilemma based on extending the car accident question in Chapter 4.

EXTENDED QUESTION: THE CAR AND THE PEDESTRIAN

You are riding in a car driven by a close friend. He hits a pedestrian. You know he was going at least 35 miles per hour in an area of the city where the maximum allowed speed is 20 miles per hour. There are no other witnesses. His lawyer says that if you testify under oath that he was driving only 20 miles per hour, it may save him from serious consequences.

How would you act in this case?

- **A.** There is a general obligation to tell the truth as a witness. I will not perjure myself before the court. Nor should any real friend expect this from me.
- **B.** There is a general obligation to tell the truth in court, and I will do so, but I owe my friend an explanation and all the social and financial support I can organize.
- **C.** My friend in trouble always comes first. I am not going to desert him before a court of strangers based on some abstract principle.
- **D.** My friend in trouble gets my support, whatever his testimony, yet I would urge him to find in our friendship the strength that allows us both to tell the truth.
- **E.** I will testify that my friend was going a little faster than the allowed speed and say that it was difficult to read the speedometer.

Here we have overcome the limitations of the linear model, which would otherwise assume that if you are more universalistic, then you can't be simultaneously particularistic.

We converted each of the original questions discussed throughout this book to this dilemma format.

Deriving Scales from the Responses

For these dilemma-type questions, we can extract an assessment from a single response on two separate scales.

First, we can categorize answers on the basis of the respondents' cultural orientation in reference to the seven-dimensions model.

Thus, *irrespective of whether they are selecting an option that involves or rejects reconciliation,* we can note which extreme cultural orientation they are exhibiting. In the car scenario either of the following options indicates a universalistic orientation (adherence to universal rules):

A. There is a general obligation to tell the truth as a witness. I will not perjure myself before the court. Nor should any real friend expect this from me.

B. There is a general obligation to tell the truth in court, and I will do so, but I owe my friend an explanation and all the social and financial support I can organize.

In contrast, the following options indicate a particularistic orientation—the need to account for the particular circumstances (the relationship with the friend is more important than any abstract universal truth):

C. My friend in trouble always comes first. I am not going to desert him before a court of strangers based on some abstract principle.

D. My friend in trouble gets my support, whatever his testimony, yet I would urge him to find in our friendship the strength that allows us both to tell the truth.

By combining responses from the dilemma-based questions that relate to each dimension, we can assign a score to the respondent's cultural orientation.

The answers are then reexamined for the propensity to reconcile. In fact, there are further subtle differences to examine. Let us assume that a respondent answers from a cross-cultural perspective and is more universalistic than particularistic.

The possible responses are detailed in the following columns.

Answer Selected	Interpretation	Reconciliation Score
A. There is a general obligation to tell the truth as a witness. I will not perjure myself before the court. Nor should any real friend expect this from me.	As a universalist, the respondent is rejecting reconciliation. This is a "do it our way" syndrome.	None
B. There is a general obligation to tell the truth in court, and I will do so, but I owe my friend an explanation and all the social and financial support I can organize.	As a universalist, the respondent is starting from his or her own orientation but encompassing the other extreme orientation. The person is trying to reconcile the differences by integration.	High (counterclockwise spiral)
C. My friend in trouble always comes first. I am not going to desert him before a court of strangers based on some abstract principle.	The respondent is unlikely to select this answer. This is a committed particularistic approach, rejecting reconciliation.	None
D. My friend in trouble gets my support, whatever his testimony, yet I would urge him to find in our friendship the strength that allows us both to tell the truth.	This answer indicates the attempt to reconcile the differences. However, in this case the respondent is starting from the other orientation but then accommodating his or her own orientation.	High (clockwise spiral)

| E. I will testify that my friend was going a little faster than the allowed speed and say that it was difficult to read the speedometer. | This is an attempt to avoid the dilemma—a compromise solution that fails. | None (still a lose-lose outcome) |

The total spectrum of dilemma questions provides data in different combinations to a series of scales:

- Scores on each cross-cultural dimension (i.e., a full cross-cultural profile); and for each dimension, scores on the following propensities:
- Compromise
  Reject reconciliation
  Seek reconciliation from *one's own cultural orientation first* and *then* accommodate the alternate
  Seek reconciliation from the *alternate cultural orientation first* and *then* accommodate one's own

We thereby attain the following:

- A total reconciliation score per dimension

And—in summary—

- A set of total scores for reconciliation across all cultural dimensions (clockwise and counterclockwise spirals), rejection, and compromise

As a result, based on the linear model from the original questionnaire, a respondent might score 40 percent universalism and 60 percent particularism. His or her profile would include a dimension bar, as in Figure A.1.

But based on the extended model, a more insightful score can be shown, as in Figure A.2.

Figure A.1. **Universalism-Particularism Assessed on Classical Linear Scale**

Figure A.2. **Universalism-Particularism Scored on Two-Dimensional Scale**

Here the respondent has also scored 60 percent on particularism. In addition, however, we see the extent to which the respondent has reconciled the various dilemmas that constitute the total scale. In this case the spiral is "filled in" by 75 percent.

In summary, the respondent has "scored" 60 percent on particularism and 75 percent on reconciliation.

This finding yields the opportunity to provide personalized feedback to develop the propensity to reconcile.

In contrast, a second respondent (see Figure A.3) is much more universalistic (90 percent) but with a similar capacity to reconcile (75 percent).

The type of feedback that we might offer a respondent with this profile on this dimension is exemplified in the following section.

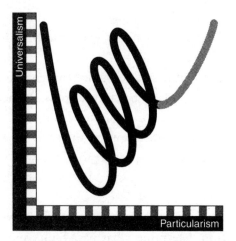

Figure A.3. Universalism-Particularism Scored on Two-Dimensional Scale for Respondent of the Opposite Orientation to Figure A.2

HOW YOU RECONCILE ON THIS DIMENSION

You have consistently chosen the universalistic response in the way that you approach dilemmas. In most cases you have been successful in reconciling one extreme with the opposite orientation, and this signifies a high level of transcultural competence on this dimension. Remember that if you have selected a compromise option, this is not a win-win solution and does not lead to reconciliation. Your approach suggests that you start from a universalistic orientation and usually are able to recognize, accommodate, and reconcile with the alternate, particularistic extreme. Knowing the orientation from which you start can help you understand your approach to reconciling dilemmas.

DEVELOPING YOUR INTERCULTURAL LEADERSHIP COMPETENCE

You are achieving a high level of reconciliation. To help you maintain this level, we encourage you to increase the value of the particular by testing it with and acknowledging universal instances and also try to increase the value of the universal by testing it with and acknowledging particular instances. For example, you might learn from the difficulties arising in particular projects, which will enable you to rewrite your standard contract terms, rules, or procedures. Similarly, test the resilience of your standard systems and procedures in a wider range of applications and situations.

The focus now shifts from simply the single dimension score to the approach adopted by the respondent when faced with the dilemmas posed in the questions.

So while different cultures *all* recognize the tensions inherent in the dilemmas, what distinguishes one culture from another is the *starting point* in approaching the dilemmas. On this dimension, an American might be expected to start from a universalistic perspective but embrace the particularistic perspective; someone who is French might start from a particularistic perspective but embrace the universalistic perspective.

In trying to develop our new integrative framework, we used a range of methods to determine what paradigms and components of competence this new model should comprise. Here are the major ones we identified:

- A critical review of extant knowledge of competence frameworks
- Observations of best practices of high-performing leaders (see Trompenaars et al., *21 Leaders for the 21st Century* [New York: McGrawHill, 2001])
- Inductive analysis of our own cultural and competence databases
- Job analysis of global leaders and senior managers that shows how they have to deal with dilemmas
- Our own Academy (including some 15 Ph.D. student completions)
- Best practices from our client organizations that face the challenges of multiple cultures and/or diversity

Our multifunctional instrument enables participants to assess their current cultural competence in a form that embraces the more important components of hyperculture. Unlike the case with other competence tools, it does not focus on a single basic area of cultural knowledge or behavior. It addresses the complete spectrum from cross-cultural awareness through to the business benefits deriving from effective action in multicultural situations. We developed it by combining our earlier frameworks based on our extensive research and intellectual property that originally addressed each area separately. Each component has been subjected to rigorous research and testing with many Ph.D. projects, together with extensive application in many client situations across the world. We have also confirmed the reliability of the combined integrated instrument with many samples, which included M.B.A. students as well as senior managers and business leaders from our client base, and triangulated with our own databases of separate components.[1]

Extensive feedback, extended interpretations, and theoretical background to the model are available in a series of interactive pages from the Web-based support center. Participants can explore their own profiles through online tutorials that offer further insights, coaching advice, and suggestions for competence development. See Figure A.4.

Rather than follow the incremental levels of the previous table, we approached the problem of cultural competence holistically and concluded by distinguishing 12 components in four clusters:

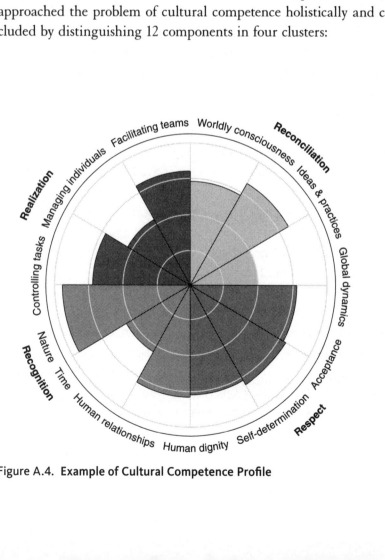

Figure A.4. **Example of Cultural Competence Profile**

1. **Recognition:** How competent is the person to recognize cultural differences around him or her?
2. **Respect:** How respectful is the person about those differences?
3. **Reconciliation:** How competent is the person to reconcile cultural differences?
4. **Realization:** How competent is the person to realize the necessary actions to implement the reconciliation of cultural differences?

The four clusters help to ensure we are building an approach that is free of cultural bias and that follows the logic we have described throughout this book. Based on those clusters, the full instrument comprises some 100 questions that are used in different combinations to contribute to the total profile. Ratings are not simply added and averaged for the different scales. In many cases the sectors are computed from the Root Mean Square (RMS) quadrature of competing questions to assess their mutual interaction.[2] This is especially important for assessing the competence to reconcile in cluster 3.

To accommodate different client/participant needs, we have developed several versions. For example, in the 360° version, a participant's own self-assessment scores can be triangulated with peer feedback.

Further information about our tools is available at www.ridingthe wavesofculture.com.

More about our approach to competence can be found in Trompenaars and Woolliams, "Towards a General Framework of Competence for Today's Global Village," chapter 26 in *The Sage Handbook of Intercultural Competence*, ed. Deardorff D., Sage, 2009.

Notes

1. Reliability was confirmed based on Cronbach alpha studies of component scales.
2. For example: a contributing component score might be the square root (Question A score × Question B score), emphasizing that both extremes of a dilemma need to be included.

APPENDIX B

The Trompenaars Databases

Peter Woolliams, Professor Emeritus,
Anglia Ruskin University, UK,
and partner in Trompenaars Hampden-Turner Consulting

T HIS APPENDIX summarizes aspects of the development and analysis of the research databases assembled by the researchers that underpin the main text. The original single database has been extended and also expanded to several databases, and all derive from responses to various cross-cultural instruments. The principal interest here is to review the data from the perspective of the level of national cultures, although extensive analysis of individual variations or variations through management function, industry sector, religion, and gender are also available. For a comprehensive review and detailed data and statistical analysis, research monographs are available. The additional databases encompass our more recent work, including the reconciliation database and text and keyword analysis.

The primary purpose of the core cross-cultural database is to help managers structure their cross-cultural experiences in order to develop their competence for doing business and managing across cultures. To enhance the estimates of the average characteristics of managers in a given national culture, considerable efforts have been made to extend the size of the samples, reduce measurement errors, and maintain homogeneity. The fundamental raw data set comprises some 80,000 cases from more than 100 countries, with an additional 20,000-plus responses to several selected questions, such as the car accident scenario. Analysis of the variety reveals functionally equivalent sets, since nearly all the selected managers were pursuing similar ends. It should be noted that the whole approach was not to seek an orthogonal data set typified by classical market research. In the latter, a sample is targeted with the minimum number of cases to cover each attribute (country, gender, age, etc.). This presumes we know what attributes to measure in advance and also has practical difficulties; for example, where does one find a young female Arab senior manager working in a Gulf country? We have, therefore, adopted the approach of collecting a larger data set with extensive internal variety that enables a deductive analysis through data mining to be performed. These are complemented by additional data on key issues such as diversity.

Work was also undertaken on improving the language of the questionnaires to make them more transparent across cultures and more acceptable where value systems and integrity are challenged. Cluster analysis was used to examine whether highly correlated items do in fact cluster around the concepts being tested. Validating interviews and cognitive mapping were also applied. Exhaustive quantitative analysis was applied to assess the validity of alternate questions and combinations of questions at both the "world level" and ecological (country) level.

Each dimension is a scale based on a combination of finite alternatives to each of a series of finite alternatives, which therefore generates a combinatorial (binomial) rather than normal distribution. However, the central limit theorem suggests that parametric methods may be applied to this nonparametric data in view of the large sample sizes. While this approach was accepted for convenience, analysis was also performed on a strict exact tests basis as a precaution. In fact, the latter shows the distributions to be leptokurtic (even more closely clustered than for a normal distribution).

Some authors have misinterpreted the origin of Trompenaars's rationale for these scales and derived incorrect conclusions.[1] A case in point: in an early comment, Hofstede used only a subset of the data from individual questions or averages rather than the weighted combination of these questions that provide scale values for each of the seven dimensions.[2] Saying that 65 percent of US managers chose the universalistic option when answering a question is not what the authors mean when they assert that the typical US managers can be placed 65 percent along the universalistic-particularistic scale. Trompenaars combines responses from different questions to give a scale along each dimension, not a polarized bimodal measure at each end. These combinations are chosen and have constantly been redefined so as to maximize the discrimination between countries along each scale. The individual questions show not only high validity but also high reliability. Responses to component questions are, by design, not perfectly correlated within the scales. If they were, only one question would be required for each dimension! And as explained later, such results are validated by both earlier and more recent additional triangulation studies.

Cronbach's alpha test of reliability was applied to questions and combinations of questions. In some cases, and especially for corporate culture, questions were successively modified or removed where such change produced an increase in alpha. For each scale, alpha was maximized, and the final design of the core cultural database has the performance shown in the following table.

PERFORMANCE

	SCALE VARIETY	ALPHA
Universalism-particularism	216	0.71
Individualism-communitarianism	64	0.73
Specific-diffuse	25	0.63
Neutral-affective	243	0.75
Achievement-ascription	1024	0.64
Internal-external	1024	0.71
Time		0.74

The scale for the time dimension that is based on the circles test required different treatment. With the wide diversity of diagrams, the aim was to identify common factors, underlying themes, or cultural concepts that the respondents were trying to express. The search was to find an algorithmic relationship with the coordinate system of their drawings and quantitative scales that could serve as the basis of cross-cultural discrimination.

In respect to time, as a result of extensive trials, it was concluded that three factors could be discerned that owed their origin to the degree to which the circles overlapped, touched, or were separate and to the relative sizes of the circles. Earlier hand drawings were assessed visually, but with Internet-based responses, in which the circles are drawn by the respondent directly on a computer screen, the scales were derived directly from the coordinates by integrating the area subtended at the base and the relative position of the center of gravity. A scale from 100 (maximum overlap = synchronic culture) through to 0 (no overlap = sequential culture) was then derived. A second scale assessed the relative component of past, present, and future orientation. A third scale could also be derived that measures a "time horizon" (short-term thinking and planning versus longer-term thinking and planning). In many ways, these scales suffered fewer problems than the dimensions based on forced text questions.

The scales for corporate culture were examined, reviewed, and treated to the same degree of rigor to derive components with the reliabilities shown in the following table.

CRONBACH'S ALPHA

Role culture	0.79
Task culture	0.75
Person culture	0.63
Power culture	0.74

In some situations, the set of scores on each dimension scale was subjected to a parabolic transform function to account for skew and kurtosis. This step has the effect of maintaining the sequence and relationships between country scores (i.e., rank order) but making the distribution more symmetrical for the purposes of presentation.

In addition to applying statistical tests of validity and reliability and reporting orientations along each cultural dimension, other types of analysis were performed to support the postulates and frameworks on which this book is based.

In particular, nonparametric data mining was used to investigate the variety within the data as well as investigating dimension reduction with factor analysis. This approach sought to answer two key questions:

1. What is the relative importance of each attribute (age, gender, religion, country, job function)?
2. How many dimensions of culture are required to explain the variety in the data?

Relative Importance of Attributes

For this discussion, the model can be considered in the following form (for each dimension):

dimension score =

$c1 \times country + c2 \times age + c3 \times religion + c4 \times gender + c5 \ldots etc.$

It is tempting to "throw" established statistical techniques at the data to identify possible coefficients (c1, c2, c3, etc.) using correlation and partial-correlation analysis or factor analysis. Some other authors have often done just that with their own more limited data sets or with incomplete or extracted sets of the earlier data that were previously published. This has been especially true of researchers with primarily a statistical mind-set rather than open-minded inquirers or students with a genuine interest in contributing to the debate and frameworks of cross-cultural analysis.

On examination of the data, it should be noted that these parametric methods are not strictly appropriate. Many of the data items are simply categories (nominal data) such as gender, religion, or management function. Classical statistical nonparametric methods are not readily available for this particular problem, and certainly none is included in industry-standard statistical software. While analysis of variance and conjoint (categories) analysis can help with questionnaire design and testing, it cannot produce the analysis required here.

In order to explore the data set, it is therefore appropriate to apply a different body of mathematics, one that is suitable for this cause. Recent developments in relational database technology, database mining methods, and knowledge elicitation (expert systems) come to the rescue.

Because the database is large and contains categorical as well as scale values over an extended period, it merits an extensive analysis over and above "simple statistics" to explore more than just average country scores.

The basic principle is to find the relative importance of the various attributes in determining the goal attribute. The first step is to normalize (arrange) the data to the so-called third normal form in separate tables (as would be required for representation in a relational database).

For the full database, the amount of entropy for each attribute can be computed. This computation gives a measure of the uncertainty of classification of the goal by each attribute. As the entropy increases, the amount of uncertainty gained by adding each attribute increases. However, the quest is to find how much information there is, given the value(s) of any particular attribute. The answer can be found simply by weighting occurrences.

To explain the total variety, it would be necessary to use the same variety as there are cases. This is the same as saying that 30,000 respondents are all individuals, and 30,000 attributes are required to describe them. Alternatively, one could use one attribute with 30,000 values (such as name!) to identify them uniquely. In the preceding parlance, "name" has the highest information content and lowest entropy. However, this is not the aim. Recall that the authors are seeking to develop a model based on a number of dimensions (attributes) that help structure managers' experiences. The analysis attempted here is intended to support this aim by exploring the relative importance of different attributes rather than containing the total variety within the data set, as an ideological statistician may prefer.

"Country" is confirmed to have the lowest entropy of classification, and thus this corresponds to the least uncertainty. In other words, country has the highest information content, so country is the major contributor in explaining the cultural orientation on the dimensions. A manager's function, for example, has a smaller contribution. These computations support and justify the emphasis throughout this book on analysis at the ecological (country) level rather than that of individual respondent. The results of this analysis are further discussed in Chapter 15.

How Many Cultural Dimensions?

The question of how many cultural dimensions to use is more difficult to answer, because it partly depends on why the question is being posed. A fundamental issue to consider is whether all the seven dimensions of the model are required and whether each is measuring a different aspect of culture. Culture is a construct that is derived from these individual dimensions, but are these dimensions themselves orthogonal (individual)?

Perhaps there are alternative and simpler models of culture. For example:

culture = c_1 × *(inherited characteristics)*

c_2 × *(acquired characteristics)* ....*equation i)*

Or:

culture = c_1 × *(relationships between people)*

c_2 × *(relationship with nature)*

c_3 × *(relationship or orientation to time)* ....*equation ii)*

In the former case one would need to have only two dimensions (and to determine the coefficients c_1, c_2), while three dimensions would suffice for the latter model. Thus, possible interrelationships between the dimensions need to be explored.

The following table shows the correlation between the dimensions. One can start the analysis with the use of parametric models by invoking the central limit theorem. If the correlations between the dimensions are zero, then they are individually and uniquely measuring a different aspect of culture. Using the average country scores from the database shows values that are not zero but are all less than 0.5. Bartlett's sphericity test can be used to consider the hypothesis that the correlation matrix is an identity matrix (i.e., the diagonals are 1 and the off-diagonal elements are 0). Thus, the chi-square of the transformation of the determinant of the correlation matrix is computed. This value is not low, and therefore, the hypothesis that the correlation matrix is an identity matrix should not be rejected.

CORRELATIONS BETWEEN DIMENSIONS

	UNPA	INDCOM	SPDI	NEAF	ACHASC	INTEXT
unpa	1.0000	0.1269	0.4669	0.1209	0.4223	0.4013
indcom	0.1269	1.0000	0.4236	0.0697	0.4397	0.2753
spdi	0.4669	0.4236	1.0000	-0.0239	0.4006	0.04678
neaf	0.1209	0.0697	-0.0239	1.0000	0.2177	-0.0444
achasc	0.4223	0.4397	0.4006	0.2177	1.0000	0.4976
intext	0.4013	0.2753	0.4678	-0.0444	0.4976	1.0000

Further probing is required to investigate whether there is any significance in the small off-diagonal correlation coefficients. However, Bartlett's test is strictly valid only for ratio data from a multivariate normal population, and the Trompenaars data are intended to indicate only ordinal/ranked measurements of cultural components. In addition, country averages are being discussed, not individual responses. If individual cases are taken, much lower cross-correlations are found. This in itself may be sufficient to explain the small off-diagonal correlations here.

The partial correlation coefficients are a further indicator. If the dimensions share common factors, then again the off-diagonal correlation coefficients should be small when the linear effects of the other dimensions are controlled. The following table shows that the off-diagonal partial correlation coefficients are again small, but not zero.

PARTIAL CORRELATIONS

	UNPA	INDCOM	SPDI	NEAF	ACHASC	INTEXT
unpa	-1.00000	-0.33034	0.28868	0.04792	0.45555	0.05059
indcom	-0.33034	-1.00000	0.55267	0.08339	0.22835	-0.03604
spdi	0.28868	0.55267	-1.00000	-0.18283	0.18540	0.15654
neaf	0.04792	0.08339	-0.18283	-1.00000	0.26277	-0.16338
achasc	0.45555	0.22835	0.18540	0.26277	-1.00000	0.34040
intext	0.05059	-0.03604	0.15654	-0.16338	0.34040	-1.00000

A better insight into the source of these small effects can be gained from computing the Kaiser-Meyer-Olkin (KMO) index.[3] This statistic compares the observed correlation coefficients with the partial correlation coefficients. If the sum of the squares of the partial coefficients between all dimensions is small compared with the sum of the squared total correlations, then the KMO will be close to 1. The small value of KMO indicates that correlation between the dimensions cannot be explained by the other variables. This is further evidence to support the need for all of the cultural dimensions.

The foregoing statistics can be regenerated from the core of the original database. However, slightly different correlations can be produced by taking different "cuts" of the data. As explained in Chapter 15, there are changes over time that are easily subject to misinterpretation. If different data sets are "thrown" at a correlation matrix, then the inter-item correlations can vary considerably. These changes are reduced if the data analysis is controlled for age, years worked abroad, and so forth, and in this way basic reliability of the conceptual model is restored.

Using different cuts, we can demonstrate that the new generation of middle and senior manager, who is well traveled and has more experience working abroad, tends to retain an ideographic country profile but shows convergence to regional or global norms in terms of the manager's nomothetic orientation for the given industry or corporate sector. Far from diluting the reliability of the database, these smaller effects, which are only now discernible with our much longer and longitudinal data sets, simply mean that multivariate analysis is required to explain variety. This would also suggest that other research, seeking single and simple linear measures to provide a complete picture for country culture, is insufficient.

One can also use factor analysis to seek a smaller number of factors that can be used to represent the relationship between the dimensions of culture. The goal is to represent culture parsimoniously—that is, with as few indicators (factors) as possible. If one can reduce the number, then not only is simplification achieved, but also new insights may arise. Ideally, the new factors should be interpretable, because it would then be possible to derive the model of interest based on the constructs sought, rather than simply those that can be measured (the raw dimensions). Thus:

1. Can the aspects of culture that are not so directly measurable be extracted from the observable dimensions?
2. Can original data be explained by a model similar to equation i) or equation ii), presented earlier?
3. Are the observed correlations due to the sharing of common factors?

The KMO index, as previously discussed, indicates that factor analysis is likely to be unsuccessful. Further, factor analysis is not simply multiple regression. The aim is not to express culture as a combination of dimensions; it is to combine dimensions into higher-order factors that are not known in advance. However, the objective of factor analysis is to reduce the number of dimensions required to explain the data. Obtaining fewer factors by factor analysis does not mean that the seven-dimensional culture model is invalid or that the number of dimensions should be reduced. If the correlation coefficients had been higher, one might have expected to be able to extract valid factors because the interrelationships between the dimensions would have been due to the presence of these factors.

For the sake of completeness, principal components analysis can also be considered. Linear combinations of the observed dimensions are taken to estimate possible factors. The first component is the combination that accounts for the largest amount of the variance in the database. Successive components explain progressively smaller portions.

The following table shows the eigenvalues for each factor. Having attempted to represent culture with two factors, similar to equation i), we find that we can explain only some 50 percent of the variance, and either seven replacement factors or all the original dimensions are required to account for the variance (cultural diversity). A scree plot (i.e., cumulative curve) of the data also reveals this. This result is not surprising, since both Bartlett's test and the KMO index indicated that there were unlikely to be underlying simpler factors.[4]

EIGENVALUES

achasc	41.3% (cumulative)
indcom	52.5%
intext	76.6%
time	85.7%
neaf	92.7%
spdi	97.3%
unpa	100.0%

Factor Matrix and Rotations

Again, little or no benefit from factor matrix and rotations is revealed, nor is there any underlying model that justifies using these new factors rather than the original dimensions. If the rotation had achieved a simple structure, clusters of the dimensions would occur either near the ends of each axis or at their intersection. As expected, it is found that the original dimensions are widely scattered in the factor space.

Therefore, it cannot be concluded from the preceding discussion that fewer cultural dimensions can usefully explain the variance in the data. This could have been expected simply on the basis of the low correlations given. However, further probing was undertaken with an open mind to contribute to the debate. In addition, the question set is not ipsative (independent), because some questions are used for more than one scale, and factor analysis does not correct for this in-built correlation.

One might also wish to reject the preceding discussion on the basis that the data collected are not genuine multivariate (ratio) normal data. If the data are ordinal or nonparametric, then one should really use nonmetric MDS (multidimensional scaling) rather than factor analysis to probe variety reduction. Here the original data have to be transformed into a matrix of cultural differences. It is therefore necessary to compute (for each country, for each dimension) the difference between each case and all other cases. Normally this is obtained by computing the Euclidean distance (square of the differences) to obtain a measure of dissimilarity. In the MDS model, each country is represented in multidimensional space and arranged so that the distances between all pairs of cases (countries) are based on these differences—countries that score similarly on universalism-particularism will be closer together, and so on. As with factor analysis, if the aim is to reduce the number of dimensions, it may be possible to take combinations of cultural dimensions that cluster together, which means they are measuring the same thing. It is necessary to assume that the data are always symmetric (e.g., the difference between the US and Japan is the same as the cultural difference between Japan and the US), and the analysis must be repeated for each dimension. Thus, a full RMDS (replicated nonmetric multidimensional scaling) algorithm (after McGee) is required, which applies the analysis of dissimilarity to each (cultural) dimension simultaneously.[5] The plot of the RMDS stimulus coordinates produces a scatter plot with the dimensions spread between the axes. If the cultural dimensions were components of common factors, then the RMDS plots would show the dimensions more significantly clustered. Here the same conclusion is reached by applying this nonparametric assessment, namely that the model of culture cannot simply be reduced to one or two new dimensions.

Finally, agglomerative hierarchical clustering should also be reviewed. Here the aim would be to try to form groups of countries with similar cultural orientations. However, it should be remembered that cluster analysis is a subjective rather than analytic technique. When group (cluster) membership is known, discriminant analysis can be applied. Here group (cluster) membership is not known, so again Euclidean distance is resorted to. Classically, the countries that are most similar would be clustered, then the next, and so on. By transposition, attempts are made to cluster the cultural dimensions rather than the cases.

Only very weak clustering can be found. Again, this fact derives from the very weak correlation coefficients previously discussed. The sequence of clustering shows a possible and interesting aspect, namely that there is more variety in achievement-ascription than in the other dimensions. This finding has some face validity too. When two people first meet, the initial greeting takes one of the following basic forms: "Hi! I'm Mr. US, and I'm a lawyer" or "I'm Sheik Haasam, and I'm the brother of El Refaie." Does this confirm that on meeting someone, we run our built-in survival program (shall we flee or fight?) and that who the person is or what the person does is the first thing we need to know about our assailant? As discussed elsewhere, in business applications other dimensions may have a higher priority in establishing the first point of cross-cultural communication.

In his comment on the Dutch author's earlier work, Hofstede's exclusive use of parametric analysis (as pointed out at the beginning of this appendix) is surprising. He should have used nonparametric methods such as correspondence analysis or homogeneity analysis for performing optimal scaling. However, all of these procedures are designed to achieve dimension reduction rather than to identify the number of dimensions required to explain the variety in the original data. Saying that the data can be summarized as two or three statistical derived factors is not the same as claiming that Trompenaars's seven-dimensional model is not supported by his data or that fewer than seven dimensions are required. In particular there is the case of "outliers." Although, as Hofstede claims, responses to some of Trompenaars's questions may correlate for many countries and, therefore, these dimensions might be combined, the separate dimensions are required for many specific cases. An example is the Gulf countries, ignored by Hofstede; for these countries they do not correlate. Thus, for G7 countries compared with GCC (Gulf countries), different dimensions are required to explain these intercountry differences compared with the intra-G7 country differences.

In summary, we may conclude that, although fewer dimensions may be used to explain some of the data, in practice they are all needed to explain the full diversity across the globe. In different practical situations (e.g., making comparisons between any two particular cultures), we can select those dimensions that best discriminate the two cultures. And let's remember that in the same way that gender correlates with height, saying that two dimensions correlate is not equivalent to saying that they are measuring the same construct.

External Validation Studies

We have sought to triangulate our core cultural database with other data sources as a means to strengthen our claims of reliability and validity.

For example, the Dutch author often suggests in his conference presentations that universalistic cultures such as the US tend to have more lawyers to codify and/or to expose different interpretations of written laws. Given this premise, we tried to correlate the number of lawyers per capita in several countries, based on the number of practicing lawyers, against our own scale of universalism. Such ideas are subject to all sorts of practical difficulties, notwithstanding the problem of accessing the external data. Also, what is the definition of a lawyer to include in the sample when in other countries we have a multiplicity of solicitors, procurators, and notaries? In fact, only in universalistic cultures might we have more precise (universal!) definitions of what a lawyer is in the first place.

We also started from the opposite perspective, asking what data did exist that we could access, and sought connections between such statistics and our own measures. The CIA database, for one, has extensive data on the dwelling unit—that is, the number of people living together in a household unit. Do people live only in a nuclear family, or do they live with their grandparents and other elders? We did find that this parameter correlated highly with our individualism-communitarianism dimension, for example. At least it did for major developed countries where other effects such as GDP might interfere with this measure. But generally, apart from face validity of such comparisons, there was insufficient evidence to justify the supportive correlations we obtained.

More successful was to use surveys published by other reliable sources where there were isolated areas of direct comparability. However, most of these are surveys carried out at a particular time, so we need to compare their results with ours from the same period.

In the "Going Global Survey" for *Time* by the market research company (MORI), results were based on 1,225 face-to-face interviews conducted during February and March 2001. The researchers surveyed 21- to 35-year-olds in Britain, France, Germany, and Italy about their hopes, habits, and hang-ups. The results depict a generation in transition, propelled by globalization into ever closer political and economic union but still firmly rooted in national and local identities. Though young Europeans share some of the same worries about biotechnology and the environment, what really binds them together is an avid embrace of change. Most young Europeans consider themselves to be primarily British, French, German, or Italian rather than European. Yet almost one-third now regard themselves more as Europeans than as nationals of their home country. The Italians see themselves as more European than the other nationalities surveyed, with two in five regarding themselves as more European than Italian. The Italians also have the greatest enthusiasm for integration. The results of this survey correlate highly with our own ideographic-nomothetic analysis and support this divergence.

Around the same period, the *Wall Street Journal* published comparisons on issues faced by women versus men in the workplace in the US and five European countries. The data correlate highly with tensions deriving from our achievement-ascription dimension in our reconciliation database.

The Global Surveys (especially the Millennium survey) published by the well-respected and well-known Gallup (polling) organization show similar high cross-validation in many areas.

Finally, the large socioeconomic database of the ongoing World Values Survey also included a number of key questions with very close meaning to that of our original cross-cultural questionnaire. As an example, question V46 in the survey, shown in Figure B.1, is very similar to our internal-external dimension question.

Some people feel they have completely free choice and control over their lives, while others feel that what they do has no real effect on what happens to them. Please use this scale where 1 means "no choice at all" and 10 means "a great deal of choice" to indicate how much freedom of choice and control you feel you have over the way your life turns out (*code one number*):

No choice at all							A great deal of choice		
1	2	3	4	5	6	7	8	9	10

Figure B.1. **Similarity Between Trompenaars and World Values Survey Qustion**

And from our questionnaire:

Of the following two statements, which do you believe to be more in line with your reality?   Your Answer

When I make plans, I am almost certain that I can make them work.

It is not always wise to plan too far ahead, because many things turn out to be a matter of good or bad fortune anyhow.

By one's taking comparable samples, again high degrees of correlation are found. The World Surveys Group does not derive inferences from its findings or offer comments but rather seeks to collect reliable data for other researchers to explore.

Dilemma Database

As summarized in Chapter 15, we have collected more than 10,000 examples of specific dilemmas from our research and consulting, which include around 2,000 related to mergers and acquisitions. We observe that these dilemmas can be categorized or clustered as 10 frequently recurring dilemmas in the minds of leaders and senior managers. We describe these as the 10 Golden Dilemmas. Every partner organization seems to have different priorities when focusing on these golden dilemmas, which need to be reconciled in order for the organization to achieve future success and sustainability; they are also referred to in Chapter 16.

We have sought to categorize these dilemmas and then correlate them against corporate and national culture characteristics. We have used KWIC (keyword in context) analysis and linguistic methods to semiautomate this mining. We have constructed "dictionaries" of frequently recurring keywords that correlate highly with the corresponding corporate culture stereotypes. This type of analysis is indicative of the Sapir-Whorf hypothesis in that the semantic structure of a language shapes or limits the ways in which a speaker forms conceptions of the world, although we might argue the reverse is also true.

The principal finding is again to confirm that there are frequently recurring dilemmas faced by all cultures but that it is how these dilemmas are interpreted and how they are approached that is culturally determined.

We continue to accumulate responses and build supplementary databases. These databases include intercultural competence, team effectiveness and remote teams (especially the dilemmas of working in multicultural teams), leadership (especially servant leadership), and, more recently, innovation (especially the dilemma between invention and adaptation).

Further Research

The suite of Trompenaars cross-cultural databases is one of the largest and richest sources of social constructs. Research is continuing to refine the instruments (particularly to avoid polarized dilemma options), to extend the number and variety of subcases, and to apply further methods of analysis, such as neural networks. Access to the data is offered to bona fide researchers and to client companies with

particular interests or needs. Again, the reader is referred to www
.ridingthewavesofculture.com for more comprehensive treatment of
the summary presented here.

Notes

1. G. Hofstede, "Riding the Waves of Commerce," *International
   Journal of Intercultural Relations* 20, no. 2 (1996): 189–98; C.
   Hampden-Turner and F. Trompenaars, "A Response to Hofstede," *International Journal of Intercultural Relations* 22, no. 4
   (1997): 189–98.
2. P. B. Smith, Appendix to *Riding the Waves of Culture*, 1st ed.
   (Boston: Nicholas Brealey Publishing, 1993); P. B. Smith et al.,
   "National Cultures and Values of Organisational Employees,"
   Journal of Cross Cultural Psychology 27, no. 22 (March 1996).
3. H. Kaiser, "Factor Analysis," *Psychometrika* 30 (1965): 1–14.
4. Ibid.
5. V. E. McGee, "Multi-Dimensional Scaling," *Multi-Variate Behav-
   ioural Research* 3 (1968): 233–48.

Index

About the Authors

Fons Trompenaars is known all over the world for his work as consultant, trainer, motivational speaker, and author of many books on the subject of culture and business. He has spent more than 25 years helping Fortune 500 leaders and professionals manage and solve their business and cultural dilemmas to increase global effectiveness and performance, particularly in the areas of globalization, mergers and acquisitions, HR and leadership development.

Fons was voted one of the top 20 HR Most Influential International Thinkers 2011 by *HR Magazine*. In November 2011 he was also shortlisted in the Thinkers50 as making substantial strides in contributing to the understanding of globalization and the new frontiers established by emerging markets.

In 1989 he founded the Centre for International Business Studies, a consulting and training organization for international management. In 1998, they changed the name to Trompenaars Hampden-Turner. Fons has worked as a consultant for Shell, BP, ICI, Philips, Heineken, TRW, Mars, Motorola, General Motors, Nike, Cable and Wireless, CSM, and Merrill Lynch.

Fons Trompenaars studied Economics at the Free University of Amsterdam and later earned a PhD from Wharton School, University of Pennsylvania, with a dissertation on differences in conceptions of organizational structure in various cultures. He experienced cultural differences first hand at home, where he grew up speaking both French and Dutch.

Charles Hampden-Turner is the Director of Research and Development for Trompenaars Hampden-Turner. He is also a Senior Research Associate at the Judge Institute of Management Studies at Cambridge University and a Fellow of the Cybernetics Society.

Charles's corporate work began in 1985, when he was appointed Royal Dutch Shell Senior Research Fellow at the London Business School, moving to the Cambridge University Judge Institute in 1992. He has consulted to, among others: Royal Dutch Shell, Rockwell Automation, Motorola, Advanced Micro Devices, Applied Materials, BZW, KMPG, AT Kearney, McKinsey, The British Council, Scottish Enterprise and British Airways.

Charles Hampden-Turner graduated from Cambridge University and received his master's and doctorate degrees from Harvard University. He has taught at Harvard University, Brandeis University and the University of Toronto. A recipient of Guggenheim, Rockefeller and Ford Foundation Fellowships he is also a past winner of the Douglas McGregor Memorial Award and most recently has been appointed Goh Tjoei Kok Distinguished Visiting Professor at Nanyang Business School, Singapore. He has taught at the University of California and the Wright Institute.